THE ELIJAH TASK

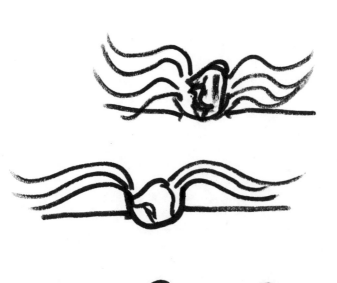

THE ELIJAH TASK

JOHN AND PAULA
SANDFORD

VICTORY HOUSE, INC.
Tulsa, OK

Table of Contents

Foreword

This book is magnificent! It illumines the Bible like a searchlight, pointing out the mysteries of God. It explains the deep working of the Creator within the spirit of man and the ordering of man's life by the Spirit of God.

Beginners may find this book difficult. Those who have never experienced God's healing and illuminating power would benefit from first reading simpler books on prayer and healing. But after basking in the pleasant pastures of faith, this book is as exciting as a high wind over the mountaintops or a storm at sea!

There are people who have waited all their lives for a book like this, illuminating as it does the high mind of God and the deep mind of man.

Agnes Sanford

Preface

This is not a book for beginners. Whoever presents new truth has the dual fear that if what he says is true, it may be hard to live with and thus be rejected, or worse, that it may be rejected because it ought to be. In publishing, we are acting on faith that God will overcome His servants' errors and make whatever use He intends.

It is not popular now to speak of special offices, talents, and gifts. This is an age of brotherhood. But just as we must never let democracy and equality snuff out leadership, so that same leveling tendency must not be permitted in spiritual matters. True unity will never cancel authentic distinctions. The jealous sons of Jacob sold Joseph into slavery, but the Lord raised him to authority and thus restored the unity of the brotherhood.

We cannot advance into the seemingly uncharted without error. Only after the new age had come could the early disciples look back to see that the way had been clearly charted within the Scriptures all along. Though the Word is utterly true, there shall be no guarantee that we shall walk into its depths without making a lot of mistakes. In fact, the guarantee of apostolic example is that we shall stumble into the kingdom, every one of us. The Holy Spirit guarantees only the finished product, not our dignity along the way. We write, therefore, to the flexible, not the uptight. The prophet often knows the end of a scene, only to find that he knows nothing in between, and life may not go as he has seen it at all. Whoever then is willing to be humbled and humiliated should read on with delight—he may find his history already here.

Since Paula and I have conceived this book as a dual effort, I often use the words "us" and "we." I write, Paula edits and challenges, and types the final copy. We hope the pronouns do not confuse the reader, for we do regard the writing as a team ministry.

Chapter One
THE SUMMONS

The office of the Christian prophet is not to be confused with the gift of prophecy. The gift of prophecy is an immediate word from the Lord to the church in meetings, for its direction, exhortation, rebuke, or consolation. The Holy Spirit may speak thus through any person. However, such speaking does not commission the prophet of the moment to the standing office.

A Christian prophet is a watchman. His task upon the walls of the city of God claims him entirely. God acts in and through all that we are. In everything a prophet is, the Spirit of God lives and moves and acts. We shall see this also means that the Christian prophet's very life and breath is intercession within the church.

The office of the prophet, alone among the offices of the New Testament, is fully developed in the Old. For example, the office of apostle seems entirely new. Teachers existed before, though we hear little of them. Healers were known, though often the healer was also the prophet. The gift of tongues was spoken of in Isaiah 28:11, but whether the gift was exercised or merely prophesied has been questioned. For instance, Saul's prophesying—was it tongues or interpretation? If not that, what was it? (1 Sam. 10:8-13.) Pastors or shepherds are spoken of, as in

1

Jeremiah 23, but again who were they then—priests? prophets? or both? Prophecy, and the office of prophecy, however, were not only fully developed, but central to the Lord's plan. In and through His prophets He warned, scolded, blessed and healed, taught, foretold, called Israel to repentance, subdued froward kings, laid down revelation for doctrine, chastised and rescued. Every book from Isaiah to Malachi is written by or about a prophet.

God did not do away with prophets and prophecy when Jesus came and the church was born. Instead He expanded their function and power by virtue of the cross and resurrection. So the prophet ceased to be a lonely watchman who was often put to death by his own people, and became an integral part of the church which, by the guidance of the Holy Spirit, learns to protect and cherish its prophets. And, even though the flesh may deafen the church's ear to its prophets, they no longer seem to be in imminent peril of their lives as were their Old Testament counterparts.

The Christian prophet, like all Christians, has absolutely no power in himself. All that he accomplishes must be done by the Holy Spirit's power. To the extent that he neglects this fact, he will fail.

God the Father is a God of order, not of confusion (1 Cor. 14:33—we substitute the word "order" for "peace"). His first acts of creating and dividing brought order out of chaos. Therefore we must discard the notion of wild-eyed, scatter-brained prophets. Samuel is distinguished (1 Sam. 9:6,9) from the ecstatic, among whom Saul is categorized in 1 Samuel 10. The prophets of the Old Testament sometimes indeed did weird things, like going naked and barefoot (Isa. 20), or marrying prostitutes (Hos.), or wearing ox yokes (Jer. 27 and 28), but these were by command of the Lord in order to startle the conscience of the people. Old Testament prophets were men of discipline, wisdom, counsel and insight, not of wild ecstasy.

In the Old Testament God did not act unless He first informed His prophets (Amos 3:7). Under the new covenant the body of Christ needs prophets more than ever, for the Father will not act without the seeing cry of the watchmen summoning the body to give Him no rest in ceaseless prayer until He establishes Jerusalem (the church) and makes it a praise in the earth (Isa. 62:6,7).

It will not suffice to say, "We have the Scriptures; prophets are no longer needed." That would be the same as saying to a general in battle, "We need not respond to your couriers; we have the original battle plans, drawn up before the war began!" Present interpretation and fresh revelation are always needed for life with a living God.

A tremor of anticipation has raced through the church these days as the Holy Spirit has prompted teacher after teacher to speak on unity, authority and discipleship. The least perceptive can see that the Lord is making His church ready for the final chapter of history. We all need to be under authority. Thus we need apostles. We need prophets. God has provided groundwork for such leaders throughout the New Testament (Luke 11:49, Acts 15:1-6, 22, 23, 1 Cor. 12:28, 15:7-9, Eph. 2:20, 3:5, 4:11, 1 Thess. 2:6, Rev. 18:20). The church is presently, now, not merely in the first century, "built upon the foundation of the apostles and prophets, Jesus Christ himself being the chief cornerstone" (Eph. 2:20).

It is not that the Lord will return from heaven to take up His authority, but that the authority which He already has been expressing through His church on earth will be culminated and climaxed by His return. That authority is now being worked out, recognized and developed within His body. The church will be fully prepared to receive its king, joyously casting their crowns before Him when He comes. Thus we see a conquering and presently reigning Lord ever more openly victorious in the midst of tribulation until the sorrow of the night breaks forth into the joy of the dawn of the new age.

The prophets of the end time must know that the Word of God is utterly true and cannot be broken, for it teaches that from the ashes of tribulation the Lord of heaven and earth shall bring forth a new

3

age of glory. As Jesus seeing *"the joy that was set before him* endured the cross, despising the shame, and is seated at the right hand of the throne of God,"* (Heb. 12:2) so His church, seeing the victory of our Lord set before it, must endure the suffering to be resurrected into the fulness of the new age.

What is a prophet? A prophet is one whose mouth has been touched to speak for God (Isa. 6:7 and Jer. 1:9). Since the Lord sometimes speaks of the future, and such revelation carries a certain mystic drama, we have sometimes tended to limit, falsely, our view of prophecy to this solitary aspect. Writers often, speaking of biblical prophecy, limit their quotes and comments to those prophecies which either have found their fulfillment in the life of nations and of our Lord, or will yet. This, however important, is only one small detail of the prophet's task. He admonishes, warns, directs, intercedes, teaches, and counsels. Far more importantly, he stands at the walls to see what the Lord is doing that he may call the body to respond appropriately (Ezek. 33:7).

Dreams and visions and the word of power in prayer are not mere figments of an impractical bent of mind. Consider the house in which you are sitting. How did the mortar and glass, wood and other materials come together into the shape that now warms and comforts your physical body? Did "practical" workmen merely get together and start slopping pieces like patchwork onto one another? Or did they follow a plan? Where did that blueprint come from? Someone had a dream. Someone had a vision. Someone saw the picture of what the house was to become and set it into lines of measure and structure. Right there stands the prophet between God and His creation. "By faith we understand that the world was created by the Word of God, so that what is seen was made out of things which do not appear" (Heb. 11:3 RSV). What does not appear is the idea, the vision in the mind of God. The prophet sees that vision and is moved to speak or to pray. "Jesus said to them, 'Truly, truly, I say to you, the Son can do nothing of his own accord, but only what he sees the Father doing; for whatever he does, that the Son does likewise" (John 5:19). So stands the Christian prophet.

Consider the call of Jeremiah. "Then the Lord put forth his hand and touched my mouth. And the Lord said unto me, Behold, I have put my words in thy mouth. See, I have this day set thee over the nations and over the kingdoms, to root out, and to pull down, and to destroy, and to throw down, to build and to plant" (Jer. 1:9,10).

The prophet stands at the water tap of Lordly favor. At the Father's command the prophet turns on or off the spigot of life. The supply of the rivers of grace is at his hand. If he turns off the power at the Lord's command, the land dries up and withers. If he opens in response to the hand of God, the land flourishes. This stands for nations as well as individuals. What a position! You think this is Old Testament only? See then James 5:16-18: "The effectual fervent prayer of a righteous man availeth much. Elias was a man subject to like passions as we are, and he prayed earnestly that it might not rain: and it rained not on the earth by the space of three years and six months. And he prayed again, and the heavens gave rain, and the earth brought forth her fruit." James here indicates what power the Christian also ought to have. We are to turn the very desert into streams of living water (Isa. 35 and Rom. 8).

Such was the power and the glory of the prophet during the fading dispensation of death. How much greater the dispensation of the Spirit (2 Cor. 3:7-11). The whole body awaits the prophet's summons—"Here, children of God, turn the hose of prayer upon this troubled spot; wash it clean." "Your president is in trouble; repent and pray." "God would heal your land; repent." "The Father would prevent natural disasters and keep His land secure;

hear O Israel, and seek His face in prayer." "The Father has a job for John Jones who is out of work; let the local body now pray and He will provide." "The Lord warns that Mary is about to have a miscarriage; let the church pray and He will save the child." "The Spirit alerts us, an accident looms; pray protection."

His will shall be done. Jesus Christ *is* Lord, Lord of heaven and earth. Every detraction, every sin, every work of Satan He came not only to destroy (Heb. 2:14,15) but to transform into glory (Rom. 8:28) "for which cause we faint not; but though our outward man perish, yet the inward man is renewed day by day. For our light affliction which is but for a moment, worketh for us a far more exceeding and eternal weight of glory; while we look not at the things which are seen, but at the things which are not seen: for the things which are seen are temporal; but the things which are not seen are eternal" (2 Cor. 4:16-18). Ours is but to listen and to obey. If we fail to obey, He will raise up others who will.

What discipline, training, and chastisement is required! The prophet, more than all others, save the apostle, must die to self daily. His word *must* not be his own. What dire warnings Jeremiah 23 and Ezekiel 13 heap upon the soulish prophet who speaks not out of God's Spirit but from the contrary winds of his own soul. No beginner can be that pure. God teaches in the rude world of trial and error. Therefore the budding prophet will be thrashed, beaten, humiliated, scorned, laughed at and rejected, will fall into error and arise—only to fall again, until, in every part of him, like Nebuchadnezzar, he knows—with grass in his mouth—that the ". . . Most High rules the kingdom of men and gives it to whom he will" (Dan. 4:32).

Only if the prophet stands as the point of a sword glistening in the hand of Him who wields it, shall the church cleave the earth "to the division of soul and spirit, of joints and marrow, and discerning the thoughts and intentions of the heart" (Heb. 4:12).

Chapter Two

IN THE SPIRIT AND POWER OF ELIJAH

God's children, in whom He has done mighty things, have come from checkered careers. Moses was a murderer. Look what Jacob did with Esau and Laban. Abraham tricked King Abimelech. David committed adultery with Bathsheba and had Uriah killed. Peter denied Jesus three times. John and James fought to be the highest. Paul went to Damascus breathing murder and threats. Our checkered careers, our utter sinfulness and degradation, our falling into all manner of vain seeking, become by the grace of God on the cross and in the resurrection the inevitable writing of wisdom on our hearts. Our hurts and sins have become our schooling and preparation. Would that we could learn purity the easy way. Praise God that His mercy is such that He turns the depth of our sin into the strength of ministry. We are not proud of our wrongdoing, but the sweet grace of God is such that in the end we thank Him for it. Our sins have rather become our training for high calling than our disqualification.

Accordingly we say to all those who have thought, "I am Elijah," or heard some such crazy words purporting to be from the Holy Spirit, perhaps you are! Perhaps you did hear rightly. You shook your head as though to clear the fog that day. You wondered

7

if you had become drunk in the Spirit. Maybe you embarrassed yourself by telling your minister or some other friends, who told you to forget it. But it nagged at you, until you thought you were insane, or perhaps you felt called without any of this emotional pressure. And sometimes it happens that the church will even suggest to one of its members that they may have a call.

If that is or is not happening to you now, neither is final. The Holy Spirit will confirm His calling by sure signs. If He doesn't, you weren't really called, but give Him plenty of time. If you feel nothing now and never have, He may not yet have given you the calling. We do not proceed on the basis of feelings, but according to His sure Word and the surety of His confirmation within the body of Christ. "This is the third time I am coming to you. In the mouth of two or three witnesses shall every word be established" (2 Cor. 13:1). Neither sins nor hunches and senses of calling equip or disequip you for the summons to stand in the spirit and power of Elijah. It is God who calls. Who can stand before Him? (Mal. 3:2). Rest easy. He will call whom He wills, and He is big enough to get through to those He truly wants.

What then, is the Elijah task? It is wisest always to begin with what our Lord himself says.

As they went away, Jesus began to speak to the crowds concerning John: "What did you go out into the wilderness to behold? A reed shaken by the wind? Why then did you go out? To see a man clothed in soft raiment? Behold, those who wear soft raiment are in kings' houses. Why then did you go out? To see a prophet? Yes, I tell you, and more than a prophet. This is he of whom it is written, 'Behold, I send my messenger before thy face, who shall prepare thy way before thee.' Truly I say to you, among those born of women there has risen no one greater than John the Baptist; yet he who is least in the kingdom of heaven is greater than he. From the days of John the Baptist until now the kingdom of heaven has suffered violence, and men of violence take it by force. For all the prophets and the law prophesied until John; and if you are willing to accept it, he is Elijah who is to come. He who has ears to hear, let him hear."

Matthew 11:7-15

John the Baptist preached by the shores of Jordan. In that region were beautiful reeds. In the morning these reeds stood tall in the mist and rays of sunlight; during the heat of the day they sank down. In the cool of the evening they rose again, shaking gently in the touch of the breeze. Tourists came for miles solely to sit and watch the beauty of the rising and shaking of the reeds. Jesus therefore could have been saying many things to His hearers: "Did you really hear what John the Baptist was saying, or did you get distracted by watching the reeds?"* This would be the same as he may say to some at judgment day, "I said to you this or that needful thing in church on a certain day through my preacher, Rev. Brown (or Jones or Kowalski); were you looking out the window that day?" The people very well could have become distracted, just as we do in our pews today. Or, He may also have meant, "Did you go out there expecting John the Baptist to be like others, shaken and tossed about (by every wind of doctrine and the cunning of men, Eph. 4:14)? Did you expect him, like so many others, to be beaten down by opposition, only to arise, shaking, when the comforting breezes of a safe evening have come? Is that why you did not hear him?" Whatever meaning we prefer, he was clearly contrasting the weakness of the reeds to the strength found in John.

John wore a camel's-hair shirt, with the soft side turned out, the bristles turned in. Ouch! Anyone who has rubbed his young face against his father's unshaved morning bristle has a hint. Anyone who has scraped a bare foot on the bristle of a welcome mat has a touch. Whoever has tried rubbing sandpaper on his arm or chest has even a better idea. John was a flagellant. A flagellant is one

---

* This information on the reeds and in the next paragraph concerning John's camel's-hair shirt comes from notes taken while listening to Bishop K.C. Pillai of India teaching about the culture behind the Bible.

who punishes himself for his own mortification and for repentance on behalf of others. The pain of camel's hair turned inward was a constant call to repentance for the grating of our sins, like camel's bristle, against the righteous nature of God.

The people knew the symbolic nature of clothing. Was Jesus therefore saying to them, "Your mental clothing, the way you think, your habits and traditions, are too comfortable for your spirit. Have you wrapped about you the easy ways of living which are the wide road to destruction?" John wears not merely the exterior chafe of a camel's bristle; his inner clothing stabbed him sharply to continual repentance and change.

Whoever would stand in the spirit and power of Elijah must be willing to wear the inner camel's bristle. He may never take it off. For the spirit of Elijah is the spirit of repentance. Repentance is not sadness. Repentance is change. Change is joy. The prophet's nature must never become fixed, stationary, and unbending. He wears an inward bristle.

Like a spoiled vase upon the potter's wheel, which is constantly being reworked (Jer. 18), so is the Elijah spirit. The soul, which is, among other things, our character and personality, is the clothing of our spirit. This is one meaning of the fig leaves. Adam and Eve developed personalities full of guile, hiding the true attitudes of the spirit from the sight of God (as though He did not already know). This is why Psalm 32 says "*in whose spirit* there is no guile" (v. 2). John's inner garment is the garment of continuous piercing, pricking of the conscience, exposing every deception. We build the sort of self-congratulatory walls of pride and self-righteousness which John the Baptist opposed, and which God would hew down, for "all our righteousnesses are as filthy rags" (Isa. 64:6).

Let us pass for a moment the next verses and ask why the statement, ". . . yet he who is least in the kingdom of heaven is greater than he. From the days of John the Baptist until now, the kingdom of heaven has suffered violence, and men of violence take it by force" (Matt. 11:11b-12, RSV). What is wrong with

John? Why is he the greatest of the old but the least of the new? What does our Lord mean that *"From the days of John the Baptist until now,* the kingdom of heaven suffereth violence, and the violent take it by force?"* With the coming of John the Baptist, a change came in the approach to heaven. Jesus was speaking of a very brief period of history. How long did John preach before Jesus began His ministry? Probably fewer than ten years. In that short span of time he introduced a radically new approach to God. Jesus took note of the change when He said, "From the days of John the Baptist *until now"* and "All the prophets and the law prophesied *until John."* Something more than prophecy was at work in John; therefore the kingdom of heaven suffered violence as never before, and violent men took it by force. How? What violence? What had changed?

The answer is profoundly simple. Man inevitably attempts to live heaven's way by striving to be good, good enough to be worthy of heaven. In the Old Testament repentance was preached by all the prophets, but until John, repentance never became a thing in itself, never itself the means to heaven. Repentance was the antidote to falling short of the glory of God. It was a returning to the established path of righteousness. Living in righteousness, obeying the statutes of God, was the sole way of heaven preached among men. Repentance only summoned a return to that way.

In John, however, repentance became something completely radical. In him the axe was to be laid to the root of the trees. Men came to John thinking it would be enough to repent as before, by returning to the established ways. John rejected such thought and demanded fruits befitting a new form of repentance. John had despaired of man's capacity for righteousness of any kind. He called men not merely to return to an outward show of righteousness by doing good deeds but to entire death of self. He said, yes, to do good deeds, but no longer could that be thought of as enough. The axe must go to the root. John's way is the way of death. There is *nothing* good in man that by repenting he can return

11

to. The whole structure must disintegrate and man must stand naked before God.

This understanding became the crucial message of Pauline theology. John's message was vindicated. Man *is* utterly sinful. There is nothing worth saving. Death and rebirth are God's only answer for sin.

What therefore was wrong? Why was John's way spoken of as violent? The question is, "*Who* was doing this thing?" John was—and so is the person who follows John's way instead of accepting grace as a gift. The previous way was the way of earning heaven by dint of righteous deeds done by men. This was as exterior as our "social action" of today, done by men who think to change man by changing his conditions. John saw that by itself the doing of good deeds, no matter how often or how many, could never change the heart, which is the only change that really matters. Therefore he set about to remake man inwardly. But historically John's way came before the cross and the resurrection. His way was no less an earning of heaven than the previous way of doing good deeds! No way could he know the free gift of salvation, which had not yet been revealed. He would therefore earn his way to heaven by negative means, by tearing down what is evil. The kingdom (all men who try his way) therefore suffered violence.*

John's way was a preparation for the coming of the Lord, the lowering of inner mountains and the raising of inner valleys. This work is still as true and needed now as then. Men's inner citadels, those rigid ways of thinking, those unquestioned biases and prejudices, those unchecked automatic responses, unseen false motives, hidden sins of the spirit, all the quirks and complexes that run unchecked behind the do-gooder, must be laid open to the surgical sword of the Spirit, or the cross cannot penetrate to the

---

* One translation reads, "The kingdom of heaven *is coming violently*," which of course happened in Jesus' death. But it still says that all men enter the kingdom violently or by violence. Many scholars understand this to mean the violence of death to our own self, which is the meaning we embrace here, for there is no way that anyone could do violence to the Father's perfect kingdom.

core of man. The Elijah task always precedes the redemptive work of the cross. Every preacher is aware of that as he pours forth the dual message that first reveals sin and then applies the balm of the gospel.

Let's say it another way. When John began to preach this radical repentance, which blasted every pillar of the human mind, men were shown a new way of obtaining the kingdom. This was no longer the positive way of building goodness into the inner character system, but the violent way of destroying the false. The axe is by nature violent. It cuts. It hews. It undercuts. You do not rest on the blade of an axe! Once the swinging of John's mental axe begins, it never stops. It gets out of hand and has an unstoppable life of its own. It becomes something like the horror of Edgar Allan Poe's *The Pit and the Pendulum*. Whatever bit of self-confidence you find to stand on, the swing of the axe of truth finds your hidden motives, and you slip another step into the pit of despair. There is no escape. Since sin has infiltrated absolutely every good thing we have ever done, the swish of the axe, once started, sooner or later cuts the root. Depression and self-death await us.

Many, unsure of trust and grace in Jesus, have fallen into the pit of despair. Invariably in counsel with the depressed we have seen the swing of John's axe behind the depression. In ever-widening circles it cuts all ground of good feeling from under its victims, until despair overcomes them. Depression is often the result, where freedom in the Holy Spirit ought to be.

Imagine the play of this axe before the mercy of the cross and before the coming of the Holy Spirit to the multitudes! Only when pride and self-confidence were shattered could the good news of the cross be heard. John's work was necessary and is today. But it mustn't stand by itself. The negative is only to clear the way for the positive.

Those who come today in the spirit and power of Elijah must come in the rejoicing, celebrating power of the feast of God. Else, like John, they will bring death to the happy festival of the kingdom. Not "either-or" but "both-and" is to be their hallmark. They call for inner death. They were the inverted vest of pain, but only to pierce the deceptions which mar the joy of the party. More importantly, the scouring of the inner man is not their task, but that of the Holy Spirit, for whom they prepare the way. Our Lord *has* come. This is a new day!

Our gracious, loving heavenly Father would happily *give* us the kingdom. Unfortunately, even He can't pour new wine into old wineskins. If we could but shuck the skin of our old carnal nature merrily and quickly, all would be fun and games in the joy of the new age. But we're stubborn. We tenaciously cling to the old ways. Worse, we are unconscious, unaware of most of our sinful nature and of its practices within us—we have hidden from our own flesh (Isa. 58:7). Therefore John must come. The old must be taken down and utterly destroyed before the new can arise. "Behold, I make *all* things new" (Rev. 21:5). Now He undergirds us with the new, filling us with the blessedness of His Holy Spirit before He works the mystery of sanctification in us.

We need to abide firmly in the good news, for whoever enters the process of dying to self and falls back from Jesus to John gets beheaded! Once the mind and conscience are moved to set in motion the axe of self-perception, they never stop. They continue to work, even subliminally, seeking weaknesses and guilts which, without faith, destroy us through tension and anxiety. Some have been driven to suicide. Countless children of God, unable to stop their accusing and excusing thoughts, have been driven to drink, drugs, lasciviousness, anything to escape the tensions of guilt. The mind overladen with guilt, incapable of arresting the cutting work of conscience, finally burns itself out. The person can become depressed, manic, catatonic, flipped out in drink or dope, or beheaded by the axe of thought. But this need never be if the person has opened his heart sufficiently to the gentle forgiveness and healing love of our Lord Jesus Christ.

The violence then is to the self and to all around us. Radical repentance was a new way begun in John, which was blessedly short in history. So should it be with us. Where the axe of John works, the cross and resurrection should follow immediately. The kingdom *comes* violently, and *remains* in peace.

Many, however, work the reverse and hide from themselves behind the seeming shelter of the cross. Claiming with their lips to honor the Lord, they won't let the slice of the axe touch their hearts when it should. They regard the cross a cheap grace which avoids the pain of the blade stripping us bare before God. Whenever the preacher touches home, he has "quit preachin' and gone to meddlin'." For them the facing of the sinful nature ceased when they accepted Jesus as Savior. Millions of Christians are hiding from God and from their own flesh in the very sanctuary of the Lord!

But, if he would grow in our Lord, there is no escape from the sword of truth. We're lazy spiritually. Like those to whom Jesus spoke, we see soft raiment in all that is said to us. "Speak unto us easy things, not hard things." This is why prophets of the Lord must rise and stand in the spirit of Elijah. Wearing their own inner camel's-hair shirt, taking first the logs out of their own eyes, they must follow John's way and perform the Elijah task, to turn the *hearts* of men to their children, and the *hearts* of children to their fathers (Mal. 4:5,6). Their task is to cut to the innermost being.

If only the church were responsive, like a hart bounding joyfully over the mountain, leaping the walls of self-deception, this much of the Elijah task would be unnecessary. But we are dull of mind and spirit and evermore shall be. And so the Lord must raise anew for every age, and for every person, His Elijahs who hack through our encrusted thorns of thought, that the Prince of Peace may call us forth from death to life.

So far we have spoken only of the *spirit* of Elijah, that of repentance. Elijah comes in power as well. "But what went ye out for to see? A prophet? yea, I say unto you, and more than a prophet"

(Matt. 11:9).

John was more than any prophet of the Old Testament. He would "prepare thy way before thee." John's commission was more than that of any other prophet. Jeremiah uprooted and toppled kingdoms (Jer. 1:10). Isaiah turned the clock back ten degrees (Isa. 38:8). Moses led Israel out of captivity, received the ten commandments, worked miracles, and spoke with God face to face (Num. 12:8). Elisha multiplied oil, raised the dead and caused iron to swim in water (2 Kings 4:1-16). Elijah deposed King Ahab and Jezebel, slew 850 prophets of Baal, purged all Israel, anointed Jehu king, called down fire from heaven upon a bullock covered with water, kept back the rains for three and a half years, then gave rain, called down fire from heaven and burned up a captain and his fifty and then another, and was finally translated to heaven in a fiery chariot! Yet Jesus tells us that among men born of women none was ever greater than John!

Here lies a mystery. We are told of no miracles performed by John. He toppled no kingdoms, and was beheaded instead by a king inspired by a dancing girl. As to preparing the way for Jesus, on the face of it one could wonder just what John accomplished. The way was supposed to be smoothed and the crooked made straight, mountains leveled and valleys exalted. Yet Jesus was seized to be cast headlong over a precipice (Luke 4:29), was in danger of being stoned to death (John 10:31-34), was deserted, betrayed, and finally crucified. What was smooth and level about that? What power did John exercise? Wherein was he great? How did he prepare the way of the Lord? Did he fail at his job?

We said that men typically seek heaven by striving to be good externally, whereas John sought change in the heart through repentance of inner evil. Just so, men define power as position in politics, as victory in warfare, and as the miraculous in religion. Whoever succeeds in these ways is acclaimed great. The same is true in every field—economics, farming, art, sports, child-rearing—whoever can do the most with the least or rule over others is touted by the world as the greatest. But we learn in the New Testament (e.g. Matt. 18:1-4, Luke 22:24-27) that true greatness is none of these things. True greatness is an inner self-emptying humility which manifests itself in service to others, like washing the disciples' feet. We see it in John when he says, ". . . he that cometh after me is mightier than I, whose shoes I am not worthy to bear" (Matt. 3:11 or Luke 3:16), and "He must increase but I must decrease" (John 3:30). John was the first among men before Jesus to discover true greatness in self-emptying and humble service to others.

Real power is not to lord it over others (Luke 22:25), but to become as the least in order to upbuild others. "Greater love hath no man than this, that a man lay down his life for his friends" (John 15:13). In the kingdom, true greatness and power are not at all what the world supposes. John discussed the principle of meekness, to die to self for others' sake, as the way of the kingdom, and put it into practice.

John is, however, less than the least in the kingdom because he precedes grace. That is, John is the one humbling John. The Christian is humbled by the Holy Spirit and is born anew not by the will of man, nor of the striving of the flesh, but of God (John 1:13). Thus John is the greatest because, in that short span of time, he called men's minds to the new principle.

He did prepare *the way* of the Lord. The Lord Jesus carried this inverted way to its conclusion in His crucifixion. John did perform his task. He entered into and began the way which Jesus spoke of as His own and in which we shall forever walk as "followers of the way" (Acts 9:2).

What about the mountains and the valleys? Mountains symbolize prayer, and valleys speak of despair and humiliation. Scripture says, "He that turneth away his ear from hearing the law, even his prayer shall be abomination" (Prov. 28:9). Romans 3, quoting Psalm 14, tells us that every one of us has done just that. We have all turned aside from the following of the law, and our

17

prayer is an abomination, until the grace of Christ creates us anew. Since striving is fundamental to the old man, which must die for the new to be born, every mouth must be stopped (Rom. 3:19), even those of prayer! Aside from the cross, any spiritual success in prayer creates problems with pride, but in Christ we cease all boasting (1 Cor. 1:31 RSV). Therefore even the good prayers of men must be stopped, and every mountain must be brought low until prayer becomes an act of God in men undeserved, not a striving after Him by which He is manipulated.

So must every valley be exalted. All those who have utterly failed, not the succeeders, not the righteous ones, shall be saved. Jesus came to save the lost, those who go through the valley of the shadow of death. Not death itself but the shadow—the fears, the hurts, the failures—wreck the mind and bring down haughty pride. John's way might be the way of death, his way might tear down what is noble in the sight of man, but it is a comfort to those already down! Every person who has ever known depression would love and understand John the Baptist. Such people know his way to the fullest. His message was balm to the conquered multitudes. They were the ones who came in true heart to him to be baptized. The rich he sent empty away (Luke 3:8, Luke 1:53).

Whoever, then, would come in the power of Elijah must divest himself of visions of grandeur. The prophet of the New Testament is not the miracle worker, not the healer, not the teacher, not the evangelist. He does not stand in the limelight. The prophet is the enabler, the spark plug who gets others going. John's work was largely hidden, a wrestling in the desert with the unseen phantasmagoria of men's hearts. John's work was done in fasting and hiddenness that others might shine when Jesus came. He was the intercessor from the desert wildernesses that the inner prison doors might be broken and other men come to Jesus. That, too, is the work of the prophets of the New Testament.

This was the great change that made John more than a prophet.

Old Testament prophets shone as lights and leaders. They worked great miracles and signs. But we don't read of a single miracle done by a prophet in the New Testament, though prophets continue to exist. Paul, Barnabas, and Silas may be exceptions. Otherwise we hear of no Christian prophets being in the limelight as miracle workers. Philip had four prophetess daughters mentioned in Acts 21:8,9 but we hear of no works done by them. Agabus, the prophet, binds Paul's hands as a sign and warning, but we learn of nothing else done by him (Acts 21:11). There were prophets and teachers at Antioch, among them Barnabas and Saul (Acts 13:1). But their work is divested of its "fireworks in the night" prominence, not because the prophetic office has passed away, but because John, more than a prophet, and Jesus our Lord, have changed their course and thus their law. Now they, like John, do their work mostly in secret, or quietly within the body.

The further up the scale of both the gifts and offices, the less we see of open demonstration and the more of quiet hidden service. Of apostleship, the highest office, we know that he who is greatest must be the least.

The Christian prophet's power is to humble the mighty and to raise the destitute. When others are laughing, he weeps in his spirit, and when they weep, his spirit rejoices. For he is one step ahead in vision, and in the burden on his spirit. The Lord is the forerunner, but He is most often that forerunner through His prophets. They go before Him to prepare His way in the body. When the church is rejoicing and celebrating the victory of our Lord, the prophet is already called to the next battle, the next pit of sorrow. The next work of the Lord is upon him. When the body of Christ is groveling in pain and repentance, the prophet is rejoicing both that the body is repenting, and that the reward of the Lord's mercy is coming.

Though the prophet is one with the church, he yet always stands a little apart. The Old Testament prophet would have gone ahead to do all the speaking, or the healing, or whatever was needed. The New Testament prophet bows his spirit to prayer, unbeknownst to the rest of the body, and others find themselves healing or teaching or speaking. This is one reason why the prophets who are prophets by office sit in the meeting while others who do not occupy the office become the prophets of the moment. As John the Baptist's ministry, like an iceberg, lay nine-tenths beneath the surface, so is their power and work.

They are not manipulators, pulling strings behind the scenes. They are rather those who fight in the unseen against the real stringpullers, the devil, and the hidden forces of our own flesh. The prophets fight for freedom, that the inner man may be cleansed of obstructions for the working of the Holy Spirit.

Exorcists have a dramatic calling, seen of men. Evangelists, such as Billy Graham, are necessarily in the public eye—and they do a glorious, needful work. But whoever would stand in the spirit and power of Elijah must be willing to labor in unseen ranks, to be rewarded only at the end of life in heaven. St. Paul says this of apostles when he writes, "For I think that God hath set forth us the apostles last, as it were appointed to death: for we are made a spectacle unto the world, and to angels, and to men. . . . We are made as the filth of the world, and are the offscouring of all things unto this day" (1 Cor. 4:9,13). The same is true to lesser degree of prophets. In the Lord's inverted ladder, they are merely the next to lowest rung. The bottom of the barrel is the apostle, but next to him is the Lord's prophet.

This does not mean that a prophet or an apostle is never seen nor honored. Occasionally the Lord must call such a one to the surface of visibility, as was St. Paul. However, to receive honor among men is costly in terms of a prophet's quiet and humble service to God. We see a picture of the Lord coming to a school of prophets and saying, "One of you must now work in the public eye and be seen of men." All the prophets demur, for they know that to be

20

seen of men is to lose effectiveness in the inner prayer work. Finally one volunteers, for he sees even here the principle that to be dishonored for the Lord, to give up what we want for His sake, is always our calling. The prophet stands not only in the power of Elijah, now a hidden prayer work, but in the spirit of Elijah, which is death to self-wish and aliveness to obedience in His Holy Spirit.

Chapter Three

TO RESTORE
ALL THINGS

> And as they were coming down the mountain, Jesus commanded them, "Tell no one the vision, until the Son of man is raised from the dead." And the disciples asked him, "Then why do the scribes say that first Elijah must come?" He replied, "Elijah does come, and he is to restore all things; but I tell you that Elijah has already come, and they did not know him, but did to him whatever they pleased. So also the Son of man will suffer at their hands." Then the disciples understood that he was speaking to them of John the Baptist.
>
> Matthew 17:9-13

Jesus knew that men would forget the necessity of the Elijah task. We would all rather leap comfortably into the new without pausing painfully to remove the old. Therefore wherever He found occasion, Jesus spoke a few words to reveal His purpose for the end-time tasks of Elijah.

A few words, yes, but what a shocking, arresting, overpowering three words of prophecy! "Restore all things!" Obviously He could not have meant John the Baptist, even had He not used future tense. John did not restore all things. The Old Testament prophets never said he was to restore all things. To restore is a positive

23

command to build. John's commission was to prepare the way by lowering mountains and raising valleys, laying the axe to trees, reducing all man's pride to grass. None of this is a command to restore. Therefore again this could not be a reference to John the Baptist.

The Scripture does, however, speak of many who shall be restorers (Isa. 58:12; 61:4). The entire church is to act as Elijah. The church is not to flee to heaven before tribulation, but to restore all things in preparation for the return of its Lord. What glory is it to the Lord to carry away His army before the battle? The church is created for this very purpose, to restore all things that He may return in honor.

"But ye are a chosen generation, a royal priesthood, a holy nation, a peculiar people; that ye should show forth the praises of him who hath called you out of darkness into his marvelous light" (1 Pet. 2:9). We have been willing to celebrate being in the light. We have rejoiced over the mercy mentioned in the next verse. What about "showing forth the praises of him who hath called you"? That means standing as a peculiar and chosen people. That means victory in the midst of tribulation.

Isaiah prophesied about the nations being turned to the Lord, the earth's vegetation and animal life being healed and changed, and the wicked being unable to sustain their kind of life in the midst of such change (59:16-19; 60:1-5; ch. 62). Isaiah trumpets the victory of the Lord as He changes His earth *through* His chosen and peculiar people. We the church are the Elijah of prophecy "to restore all things."

However, the church does not become that Elijah of the end time until, as Jesus commanded, His specific messengers, His Elijah prophets, call the church to the Elijah task. "Elijah truly shall come first."

Elijah means, "My God is Yahweh." All else is idolatry. Elijah comes to proclaim the sole dominion of God in earth and heaven. That proclaiming is fire and destruction upon all that is not God. Elijah is thus called "the prophet of fire."

In Jude we learn that that fire is sometimes vengeance: ". . . just as Sodom and Gomorrah and the surrounding cities, which likewise acted immorally and indulged in unnatural lust, serve as an example by undergoing a punishment of eternal fire" (Jude 7). From 2 Thessalonians 1:7,8 we understand that God's fire has become vengeance to those "that obey not the gospel of our Lord Jesus Christ." We shall see, however, that before that final vengeance, while men still have time to repent and be saved, God's fire is for the dual blessings of refining and healing.

"He is like a refiner's fire . . . and he shall sit as a refiner and purifier of silver: and he shall purify the sons of Levi, and purge them as gold and silver, that they may offer unto the LORD an offering in righteousness" (Mal. 3:2-3). And Malachi prophesied a sun which arises for those who trust the Lord, as "the Sun of righteousness . . . with healing in his wings" (4:2), and for those who do not know Him, as "an oven . . . that shall burn them up" (v. 1). In one instance it blesses with healing, and in the other burns to destruction. This same fire acts differently upon men according to where they are in the Lord!

> The flame shall not hurt thee; I only design
> Thy dross to consume, and thy gold to refine.
> *author unknown (eighteenth century)*
> "How Firm a Foundation,"

Isaiah asked,

Who among us can dwell with the devouring fire?
Who among us can dwell with everlasting burnings?
He who walks righteously and speaks uprightly,
  who despises the gain of oppressions,
  who shakes his hands, lest they hold a bribe,
  who stops his ears from hearing of bloodshed
  and shuts his eyes from looking upon evil. . . .
33:14-15, RSV

It is not that the righteous shall escape the fire, but that they will know how to dwell blessedly in fire. The fire which is love shall have nothing of harm in it for those who know and trust that it is only burning away the dross. Those who do not trust God the Father through Jesus find themselves utterly destroyed by the outpouring of that same impartial fire of love.

John the Baptist said of Jesus, "He shall baptize you with the Holy Ghost *and with fire.* . . . Whose fan is in his hand, and he will thoroughly purge his floor, and gather his wheat into the garner; but he *will burn up the chaff with unquenchable fire*" (Matt. 3:11-12). The Old Testament Elijah would have wielded the fire himself, as he did upon the two captains and their fifties (2 Kings 1:1-16). John demonstrates the change in that he goes before to enable the Master to baptize with fire. Not John but the Master wields the fire. The first part of the Elijah task is to prepare the church for fire.

We have heard much of the baptism of the Holy Spirit. We should have. It was time for the baptism and still is. Now we need to hear the last part of those verses which prophesied the coming of the Holy Spirit through our Lord—"and with fire." Jesus wants us to have more than the baptism of the Holy Spirit. We are to be baptized with fire as well.

God may let Satan tempt. Satan has no power otherwise. God initiated the conversation which ended in His letting Job be tried in the furnace of affliction. "Then was Jesus *led up* of the Spirit into the wilderness *to be tempted* of the devil" (Matt. 4:1). Our sinless Lord had also to pass through the route of temptation and suffering.

God's love allows temptation and the church needs to believe it afresh. Satan is no longer the god of this world. He was a usurper and Jesus has deposed and exposed him. Jesus is Lord of all heaven and earth. Nevertheless, when we refuse to let the kind hand of the Lord minister to us, He opens the doors for Satan to teach the lesson (cf. 1 Tim. 1:20).

Sometimes, not because of stubbornness or sin, but simply because we, too, like the Lord, must wrestle with darkness to become strong, temptations will face us. That is why it is extremely important to know that Jesus Christ is indeed Lord and that Satan is a poor, demented, sick spirit whose dementia can sometimes act like a snake's venom to cure snakebite. We have many times fought for our very lives against the demonic powers and against Satan himself. We have been attacked, choked, nearly smothered, nauseated and unable to make a sound. From all this we learned that Satan had this power only if he could enlist our own energies in the battle. His only power is delusion. He truly is a weak, sick, old spirit who must flee when his victim simply praises the Lord! As the times of tribulation increase, let us have no more foolish exaltation of Satan's supposed power, no more projection of our troubles onto Satan as though he made us do what we have done, no more cavil under the hand of God as though He were not the one disciplining us, or as though contrary to all the promises of Scripture, Satan had somehow clutched us out of the hand of God.

Perhaps the most timely book in this age is Merlin Carother's *Power in Praise*. If the reader has not come across it, we suggest he put this book down and thoroughly digest it, for he cannot understand what this book offers without it. The church stands in its end-time tasks, "showing forth the praises of God," by praising Him throughout the afflictions and horrors of tribulation.

Jesus our Lord himself baptizes us with fire. Some of us have looked for sensations like burning upon the head or all over the body. God's wonderful love does truly pour over us in gracious flames of warmth. We too have felt again and again that fire. But such ephemeral feelings are not the full meaning of the baptism of fire. As tongues and gifts are not the fullest evidence of the Holy Spirit to those who believe (1 Cor. 14:22), so tongues of fire are mere passing signs in the flesh. The lasting evidence of the baptism of the Holy Spirit is a fruitful life, and the authentic evidence of the baptism of fire is a purged soul.

The church needs to understand its calling to be sons who, in the midst of the horrors, praise the Father for loving enough to discipline. It cannot judge by what its eyes see or its ears hear (Isa. 11:3). If pain and death and suffering are multiplied, the church is to see what God is forming thereby in the soul of man; or better yet, not seeing, to praise God in simple trust anyway. It is vital to our

Lord's coming to praise Him in the midst of the coming tribulations. He himself sends the fire in whatever form. Be it demons, devils, our own flesh, other men, shortages, natural disasters, death or sickness, whatever is the instrument in the hand of God, let us like Shadrach, Meshach and Abednego praise Him in the midst of it.

This is the first task of the Elijah prophets of this age, to prepare men for fire. We are not prepared by looking to escape. We are not prepared by Pollyannas. We are prepared when we praise God for all things. We are prepared when we see Jesus as the Lord of Glory in all things, and ascribe nothing to the instruments He uses.

We are prepared when we know that praising Him is accompanied by repentance on our part. By praising Him for all things without repentance we fail to face what is ours to face. Rather than ascribing too much to Satan, we can ascribe so much to God, that by so doing we hide from admitting what we have done or ought to do. These two, repentance and praising God, go as naturally together as night and day—one follows upon the other.

Elijah is the prophet of fire. He warns of the fire to come. He calls down fire by intercessory prayer. Elijah today will be the prophets of the Lord who warn of the onset of tribulation. Not only are they to warn generally, but specifically as the Lord gives utterance concerning families, churches, individuals, cars, planes, earthquakes, and tornadoes. A prophet of the Lord said to his friend, "Check your right front tire. The Lord just warned me something may happen to it." Before the man proceeded more than a few blocks, that wheel came off. Had he not been warned, had he been traveling at normal speed, he could have been killed. The Father takes interest in the slightest details of our lives. Prophets will be used of God to protect His own within the flames of tribulation in a pain-maddened world. They will call the body to pray most specifically to prevent or soften many tragedies. The prophets will speak God's warnings that ill may be prevented, or if not prevented, received in the knowledge that ". . . all things are for your sakes, that the abundant grace might through the thanksgiving of many redound to the glory of God'' (2 Cor. 4:15).

The prophets not only are to warn of danger ahead; in some cases they are to call for it to come. They are commanded at times to call down the fire of suffering quickly upon the body through intercessory prayer. Does that seem mean or foolish? Then why does a doctor give a patient a medicine which he knows will cast the patient into the throes of vomiting? He knows that the longer the poison remains unmolested within, the closer its victim comes to death. When God in His wisdom knows that we are unknowingly in the grip of evil, then in mercy He may bring discipline quickly, that death may be averted. Therefore God may ask a prophet to call for discipline upon a man, a family, a group or a nation.

End-time prophets must be thoroughly dead to themselves in our Lord and risen to perfect obedience. Their minds must be purely in Him, lest they cast water on fires God is building, or worse yet, call for fires of suffering out of their own hidden desires for vengeance.

The necessity of discipline is thus heavy upon us. Any fire, spiritual or earthly, is most difficult to control. Yet controlled fires have warmed our houses, cooked our food and driven our engines. Controlled spiritual fire is even more necessary and valuable. Men must learn, as Paul did, to let affliction work its weight of gold.

Sometimes, when we pray, we see in our minds a picture of peace, tranquility, and comfort. Sometimes that's God's wish too—and sometimes not. We may actually be worshipping an idol and trying to enlist God to help us. In that event His answer to our prayer may be the exact opposite of what we wanted.

The prophet may ask God to withhold the discipline, as Abraham pled for wicked Sodom and Gomorrah (Gen. 18). But he must also cease, as Abraham did, and let God go unhindered to the task of disciplining His sons for their own good. To a culture which has learned to wrap creature comforts about itself, and uses its science to rationalize away sharp truth, one of the most direly needed aspects of life to be restored is discipline (Prov. 13:18).

What more is meant by "to restore all things"? Is the whole earth to be transformed into Utopia before He comes? Scripture warns otherwise. What else can "restore all things" mean? If a man hires a management consultant for his office, he may say, "He will put everything in order; get us some efficiency around here." In that case, "everything" would be relative to the business of which he spoke. The man's home life, for example, might still be a mess, or his faith, or his life among his friends. Yet the consultant might indeed restore all things in his business.

Perhaps Jesus meant that everything in all the earth is to be restored by the church, and that these Scriptures which speak of ongoing warfare are a part of the fulfillment of that prophecy. Or perhaps, since He was speaking to the three inner disciples at that moment, He was thinking only of the restoration of the church itself. We have no conclusive word either way. Perhaps the Lord does not want us to know.

The Lord's prophet must learn never to presume to say a word on his own authority (Deut. 18:20). We know we are to continue to serve, to watch and pray with all the fervency of the Spirit in us until He tells us otherwise. Therefore it matters little at this point in history which meaning was His. Our work is the same. We pray for it every day as He taught us, saying, "Thy kingdom come, they will be done, on earth, as it is in heaven." Let us press on to be so fully in Him that His Spirit may have free reign to accomplish whatever He intends.

A word to the wise. The Elijah task is not to figure out precisely what certain prophetic Scriptures of the end time mean. This is busy work and accomplishes nothing significant in the heart of man, makes no real preparation for His return. It gives Him no real glory or honor. Romans 12, the entire chapter, tells us what it is to please Him and we hear nothing about searching the Scriptures for clues about how or when He is to return.

This much we can know: Whatever was lost or destroyed by sin needs to be restored. Christ was sent to destroy the works of the devil (1 John 3:8). Restoration not only destroys Satan's works but also transforms all things so that they work together for good to them that love God (Rom. 8:28). Every troubled situation is a forge in which God is working strength into His children. Whatever is amiss, whatever is a result of human sin needs to be restored; this is the work to which the Lord's servant is called.

However, the existence of trouble is not what moves the prophet of the Lord. Numbers of invalids surrounded Simeon at the pool of Bethesda. Jesus raised only Simeon (John 5:1-9). In other instances He healed *all* the sick (Matt. 8:16 and 12:15). Therefore the Lord's prophet is not moved by tragedy or calls for help. He should ask his Lord when he sees one or hears the other, but only the Lord's command moves him to action.

Whatever restoration God decrees in the given moment is the prophet's task, no more, no less. Jesus warned that many would go about doing great works, but not in His will (Matt. 7:21-23).

A good work is iniquity if we have done it outside the command of the Lord. If a sergeant fails to check with his captain, or worse yet, disobeys him, and captures a hill, that very bravery may expose a flank and jeopardize a whole army. So it is with the Lord's host. Obedience to the Spirit is being trained into the children of God. We restore what the Lord commands to restore, and nothing else.

This lesson infers one of the great tasks of this age, the return to unity. Unity already exists. We are in the Spirit, and He is in full

union with the Father and the Son, and with every other Christian.
Thus, in the Spirit, we tell no lie when we sing,
"Like a mighty army, moves the church of God;
Brothers we are treading where the saints have trod;
We are not divided, all one body we,
One in hope and doctrine, one in charity."

> Sabine Baring-Gould
> "Onward, Christian Soldiers"

In Him we *are* one body, however conflictingly we express that
one doctrine which exists and runs through our several spirits as
one river of faith. Whoever would set out to create or build unity as
though it did not already exist commits blasphemy. Whoever in
obedience to the Spirit acts within that unity to restore unity is a
soldier in His ranks.

Unity is vital. His army must act in concert. Unity is the very
ground of God's acting among men.

Behold, how good and pleasant it is
  when brothers dwell in unity!
For there the Lord has commanded the blessing,
  life for evermore.

> Psalm 133:1,3

There, where "brothers dwell in unity," is where God has
commanded the blessing. The inference is that where unity is
lacking, the blessing of God cannot be. You don't have to be
around the church long to learn that where there is unity God
blesses, and that where there is discord, He doesn't. Unity is the
prelude and primary condition for power in prayer (Matt. 18:19).
Unity always exists in the Spirit in the body, no matter how we fuss
and fight, but unity must travel from spirit to soul to heart and
mind and action before it bears fruit among men.

However, the quest for unity need not prevent discussion,
difference of opinion, or even sharp disagreement. It is one thing to
agree so deeply in heart and soul and spirit that we can violently

disagree in mind, without disturbing unity or breaking the agreement which profits prayer. It is another to so let disagreements enlist angers and party spirit that inner energies are drafted to unconscious battles and conscious debates. Paul and Peter battled heavily (Gal. 1-2), and yet the Father worked stupendous miracles in and through both of them, and wherever they went the church prospered! Men fought Paul everywhere Most of the letters of the New Testament are written about quarrels or are themselves involved in settling some dispute. Yet the early church was filled with power. We can fuss at each other strenuously without disturbing true unity. We must not so make an idol of unity that we drive necessary irritations of communication underground and so provide lip service to unity while we are inwardly frustrated into hating. The restoration of unity also means the restoration of honest communication. Anger, jealousy, spite, envy and the like tear the fabric of unity, not honest communication. If men's hearts are knit as one, the mental exercise of debate serves only to heighten respect and increases banter and fun. We need not fear to fuss and fight, as long as we immediately forgive and laughingly embrace. Unity moves from spirit to soul and heart by the route of openness, not tight-mouthed silence.

Each denomination contributes its learned strengths to the rest of the church. For example, some Protestants are now beginning to cherish what God has sustained and prospered among Catholics in such areas as the mass, concepts of authority, and liturgical devotion. Some Catholics are learning to value what He has revealed to Protestants in terms of reverence for the Bible, being born anew, and the free gift of salvation. For God intends to turn the age of division into the age of unity, causing each arm of His body to present what it has sculpted from the rock of truth in isolation as a gift to the whole church. Paul spoke of the unity of the faith. When it happens, we are no longer tossed about by every wind of doctrine, but are found speaking the truth to one another in love, growing as a body "fitly joined together" increasing and upbuilding itself in love (Eph. 4:12-16).

No one who toots his own horn and claims exclusive access to truth has a place in the army of the Lord, much less in the ranks of the Elijah prophets. Elijah cried out, "How long will you go limping with two different opinions? If the Lord is God, follow him; but if Baal, then follow him" (1 Kings 18:21). The issue wasn't solely that of choosing God, and only Him, but of having one opinion, unity in the body. Jezebel led away to Phoenician gods. Ahab should have led to God. Unity was destroyed, but God raised up a Jehu, through Elijah, to purge Israel until unity was restored. Today, God restores unity not by fire and death, but by the way of the cross, the fire of the Spirit, and the mercy of forgiveness and sharing. It is time for the wood, hay and stubble in our thinking to be burned, that His precious gems of wisdom preserved in each arm of the church might glisten in His light (1 Cor. 3:11-15).

The restoration of unity may be the one factor for which the Lord awaits the call to the last battle. In a chorus, chatter and horseplay go on until the choirmaster raises his baton. A hush ensues until all is silent concentration in that one man. Not until the choirmaster has that unity will he give the signal to begin. The Lord's great choir is coming together from its several walks, still slapping each other on the back, still gossiping and falling into criticizing each other's ways. But the baton is being raised. "There was silence in heaven about the space of half an hour" (Rev. 8:1). Then came the trumpets!

Daniel asked of the end time. "How long shall it be till the end of these wonders?" He was told, *"When the shattering of the power of the holy people comes to an end"* (Dan. 12:6-7). We are the holy people (1 Pet. 2:9). Our power was shattered by division. But now, the Holy Spirit is restoring unity among the hearts and minds of men; and we shall see end-time wonders accomplished by the Lord through the church, in concert with the angels of heaven.

Let no supposed prophet tell you that the rest of the body has gone wrong. Let no foolish prophet convince you that only those who discover the truth he has will be saved. "For there shall arise *false Christs*, and *false prophets*, and shall show great signs and wonders; insomuch that, if it were possible, they shall deceive the very elect" (Matt. 24:24). "For many shall come *in my name*, saying, *I am Christ*; and shall deceive many" (Matt. 24:5). Many people think these prophecies say many shall come claiming to be Jesus Christ, and since they don't see anyone who is claiming to be Jesus, they don't think that the words apply. But they only say "Christ" or "Christs." Christ means anointed one. Many are truly anointed. They truly have His unction upon them *in the Spirit*. But they have not sufficiently purified themselves (Dan. 12:10 and 1 John 3:3). Therefore, though the anointing is true in the Spirit, and they do really come in God's name, nevertheless in *soul* and *heart* and *mind* they are not true, and they lead astray.

None of us can escape this charge. False Christs and false prophets are among us always, because in one degree or another we are all false to Him, and so we exist within the body of Christ as checks on one another. He has raised up a new sense of unity and authority, that we might be subject to one another, receive one another's rebukes (Luke 17:3, Gal. 6:1) and live. Not only, then, is that brother unlikely to be true who stands off alone, claiming to possess the true revelation, but he is even less so when he refuses correction. That brother is least likely to be true who brings a divisive word. Sometimes the body does indeed split over the word of a true prophet, and for that he cannot be held responsible. But the prophet who directly calls for division between brothers as though he alone had the truth is least likely to be true. We are not to "go here" or "go there" but to stand in one unity of faith with our brothers, whether we can agree with their doctrinal opinions or not.

That which calls for separation from other brothers is most often born of fear, not of faith. There are occasions wherein we must not be mismated with unbelievers, but remember that the word is "unbelievers" (2 Cor. 6:14), not those with whom we disagree *in the faith*. If our brother knows Jesus as Lord and Savior, however contrary to ours his doctrinal opinions, we have no business judging him as an unbeliever. More importantly, we have no mandate to depart from him as a brother—unless as in 3 John he persists in denying Jesus Christ as Lord in the flesh while claiming to be Christian, or, as in 1 Corinthians 5, one persists in some heinous sin despite all we can do. The way of Jesus is to lay down His righteousness for others (2 Cor. 5:21). The way of the Christian is to accept the brother, whatever his condition, as Jesus entered the homes of Pharisees who hated Him, and ate with them. He let wicked women wash His feet with their tears. We who would walk after Him have no other commandment than to hold the heart open and to love.

An authentic prophet can admit that he may be untrue, and therefore wrong in many areas. He knows that his protection from error is within the unity of our Lord's body. Conversely, the false prophet confuses his anointing with what he thinks in his soul and heart and mind, so that he thinks he cannot be wrong.

The members of the Lord's army may have different spears (thoughts), different armor (customs and traditions), but they "do not thrust one another" (Joel 2:8). The time for talk is now. Now we pierce and test one another out of our several traditions as we sift and judge. But whenever we engage in prayer or service, we postpone such questioning.

We have examined the baptism of fire, and the unity of the Spirit in terms of the restoration of all things. A third and perhaps the most important area of restoration concerns the inner man.

Jesus repeatedly upbraided the Pharisees for observing exterior laws while refusing change of heart. The first three chapters of Revelation bear the constant refrain "To him who conquers. . . ." What is to be conquered more than our own flesh? The whole of Jesus' ministry from His first public reading to His death on the cross, points to and accomplishes cleansing and changing of the heart. The church is long overdue for an understanding of its inner nature and the consequent inner battle which must be fought. Again, sanctification *has been* accomplished *in the spirit*. It must be worked out in *heart* and *soul*. Whoever works to cleanse the inner being as though it were not already cleansed by the cross is on the wrong track. Nevertheless, what remains of the carnal nature within us must be dealt with. As John was called to turn the *hearts* of men to the Lord through repentance, now again the Elijah prophets need to be trained in the pathways of the human heart, and in the way of His inner deliverance through the cross and resurrection.

We see no more urgent need than the liberation of man from his own self. Perhaps nothing is more essential to the work of restoration than the sanctification of the heart, soul, and spirit. Some have come to think that the sanctification or healing of the inner man is all that our faith is about. It isn't. But it is so vastly important that we can see how many could be trapped in it. In any case, "to restore all things" includes the restoration of the soul, for what is more directly affected by sin than the soul which dies for it? (Gen. 2:17).

Also in need of restoration is the mind of man (Rom. 12:2; 1 Cor. 2:16; 2 Cor. 10:5; Phil. 2:5). Jesus was crucified on Golgotha, the skull. He was crucified on, by, and for the mind of man. The first sin was a mental sin (Gen. 3). How could there ever be full laughter and joy in the house of God until the erring mind of man is fully collared and harnessed to the Word and to the Spirit?

And the nations are to be restored. The Bible is replete with Scriptures concerning the restoration of the nations. They were first scattered in Genesis 11 (the Babel Tower incident). Their restoration is a grand theme of the Bible. Isaiah 65 and 66 and Micah 4 contain prophecies of the consummation of the Lord's restoration of true peace on earth. However, the travail of nations which began in Genesis 11 ends not until Revelation 22, the last chapter of the Bible.

Economics, politics, justice, education, race, the arts of drama, painting and writing, newspaper and TV production—all of these areas and many others need to be restored.

But fire and unity must come first. Mankind must be transformed. Then and then only can the nations live in peace. Whether the nations are restored before or after the *parousia* (the return of the Lord), we do not know. We do know that it is the command of the Lord that his prophets summon the body to the healing of the nations. We are the leaves of the tree that are for the healing of nations (Rev. 22:2). The tree is Christ. This task is most unequivocally prophesied as belonging to His body.

When all else is restored, what remains? Then it is that the sons of God are to heal the earth. In Genesis 3 the earth was cursed because of man's sin. "All the foundations of the earth are out of course," because we walk on in darkness (Ps. 82:5). God the Father plans to restore not only man but nature as well. "O LORD, thou preservest man *and beast*" (Ps. 36:6). See also Isaiah 11:1-9 and Romans 8:18-23.

Mankind must be fully restored before the earth can be, else through continual sin, the top of Carmel will wither again and the pastures mourn anew (Amos 1:2). Thus though this task is foremost in our own hearts by desire, it is last in the Lord's order of restoration. By then hopefully the Lord's new prophets will have arisen and we shall be one small tenor and alto in the mighty chorus of the Lord's hallelujah anthem.

One sees throughout that all restoration depends on man's learning the sweetness of obedience. And obedience depends upon accurate hearing. For how shall the army know to move if it cannot hear its Lord's commands? Thus the first and most presently urgent restoration is the resurrection of the church's capacity to hear its Lord. Every soldier on duty must hear his orders. Every soldier must learn how to put together what he hears with what those in authority over him hear, and how to submit to such authority.

Every citizen in the Lord's kingdom must know of dreams and visions (Joel 2:28,29), and yet each must learn to be afraid to speak against the Lord's servant higher in authority (Num. 12:8). All must learn to discern what is true and what is false (1 John 4:1). Some are given only to obey, but in the new kingdom we are not as servants who do not know what their master does, but as friends to whom all is made known (John 15:15). Therefore there must needs be now a discipline of listening. These three chapters of this book have been a prelude to that task. From here on our responsibility shall be to see what it is to be called and trained to be a prophet, how to understand dreams and visions, how to hear directly, and thus how to fulfill the functions of speaking God's Word within the body, and most importantly how to do and lead others in the most urgent and cogent work of intercession.

Chapter Four

THE CALL OF
A PROPHET

For many are called, but few are chosen.

Matthew 22:14

No one by deciding, or wishing it so, can become a prophet. The corps of prophets is not an open club. One cannot pay dues, or take training, or desire so intensely as to become a prophet. There is no membership roll, as in a church. One cannot inherit the prophet's mantle. It cannot be given by one man to another, though a man can be the Lord's instrument for such. Reading this and a million other books will not make a man a prophet. Hours of prayer, diligence in intercession, seeking the gifts of the Spirit, none of these will make a man a prophet. There is no way a man can become a prophet by the flesh.

This is not only true of the prophets; it is true of becoming a Christian. "Which were born, not of blood, nor of the will of the flesh, nor of the will of man, but of God" (John 1:13). Many have thought that they could choose to come to God in their own good time. They cannot. No one can. We come to God when He calls us,

41

or we come not at all. We are born anew of the Spirit, and not by man. If we choose Him, we choose Him by and only when He has chosen us.

Such election is far tougher for the prophet. Not only may a man not become a prophet unless God calls, he may become a prophet only by responding in obedience when He calls, as He calls, and in confirmed recognition within the body of Christ. Then he will be trained, and his training is like no other! It shall probably take no less than a dozen years. St. Paul underwent at least fourteen years' discipline and training (Gal. 2:1).

The call of a prophet is given solely by the Lord. It was His Holy Spirit who called and spoke through every prophet of the Old Testament (Heb. 1:1). It remained the same in the days of the New Testament. It remains so now. One difference pertains. Now the prophet's call must be independently confirmed by the Lord through the body, and that body must hold and keep the prophet both in his training and throughout his ministry. Apparently the people did not confirm a prophet's call in the Old. The Old Testament prophet stood over against everyone else. The New Testament prophet is not only called within the body, but the whole body is itself based upon the foundation of apostles and prophets (Eph. 2:20).

The call of a prophet usually but not always includes his job description. This was so with both Jeremiah and Isaiah. The call of Ezekiel, however, does not contain his job description. Ezekiel was unique. In him, prophecy entered a new dimension. Ezekiel performed special acts which were not mere signs as they had been with Isaiah, Jeremiah, and Hosea, for example, but a "burden bearing" for the house of Israel.

> Thou, also, son of man, take thee a tile, and lay it before thee, and portray upon it the city, even Jerusalem: And lay siege against it, and build a fort against it, and cast a mount against it; set the camp also against it, and set battering rams against it

round about. Moreover take thou unto thee an iron pan, and set it for a wall of iron between thee and the city: and set thy face against it, and it shall be besieged, and thou shalt lay siege against it. This shall be a sign to the house of Israel. Lie thou also upon thy left side, and lay the iniquity of the house of Israel upon it: according to the number of the days that thou shalt lie upon it *thou shalt bear their iniquity*. For *I have laid upon thee the years of their iniquity*, according to the number of the days, three hundred and ninety days: so *shalt thou bear the iniquity of the house of Israel*. And when thou hast accomplished them, lie again on thy right side, and thou *shalt bear the iniquity* of the house of Judah forty days: I have appointed thee each day for a year.

Ezekiel 4:1-6 (italics mine)

This was a new thing. No prophet before Ezekiel had consciously borne the people's sin. This was both prelude and preparation for the cross.

Ezekiel was called "son of man." It became a messianic title because Ezekiel initiated the burden-bearing which was central to the efficacy of the cross. Jesus indentified himself with that new work begun by Ezekiel. It would be His main purpose for coming to earth, to become sin for mankind and die in our stead. However, this task of being the initiator of burden-bearing was not contained in Ezekiel's call. Sometimes the Lord includes the prophet's job description in his call, and sometimes not.

Though the Lord is a God of principle, and we need to understand and follow His principles whenever possible, He has purposefully made those principles crosscurrent to each other so that we may neither reduce life to utter manageability nor lose the spontaneity of continual surprise in Him. God will not let us see small boxes and say, "This and this only is His way" until we have ruled out our Lord and all surprises from "interfering" with our control of life. Whenever we think we have life contained in predictable terms, God will shatter our too neat shapes. Who knows, there may therefore be true prophets whose call was never more than a subliminal hunch and who never yet have been confirmed within the body. What we lay down as biblical principles to be observed by the body are the general rule, for its safety. But none of these will confine God. He who gives birth through a virgin and brings ultimate victory for life through death will not stop at our understanding of the way life goes.

If principles are for safety, that there may not be confusion, but order in the life of the flock, we must nevertheless remember that Jesus, not those principles, is our order and security. Our safety is never confined to remembering which rule applies where. We are not dependent upon nor saved by knowledge. We are saved by the person of our Lord Jesus Christ. To Him we refer constantly, not merely to the written Word by and about Him. Thus we want to know and observe so far as possible His ordinances for the calling of a prophet, but with humility, lest He invoke some alternative principle far above our understanding. Whoever thinks this is too loose and confusing to follow is right, for we are not to follow after knowledge or principle first, but always to be dependent upon a Lord whose thoughts are not our thoughts.

That is the way of an Elijah prophet. For he must hold men to the Word, and then smash the hold of the word upon men, that Christ may be all to all and in all. Whoever finds this too confusing had better live longer with our Lord before continuing, for the axe of John must undercut any stance we assume that does not mean total dependence on Jesus. One must have learned that he needs nothing other than Jesus before he can continue to walk as an Elijah prophet. Many of God's children fasten onto pieces of Him. They hold to those pieces as though they were everything. But we must instead love and serve all of Him. When we stand clear in Him and in Him alone, not in some principle or law, then is our peace secure (Isa. 26:3).

Prophets are called in many different ways, at different times, and under different circumstances. "Moses was fourscore years old, and Aaron fourscore and three years old, when they spoke unto Pharaoh" (Exod. 7:7). "Abram was seventy and five years old when he departed out of Haran" (Gen. 12:4). Samuel, however, was only a child asleep upon the floor of the temple when God called him (1 Sam 3:1-10). Jeremiah was not only a child (Jer. 1:6), he was called and ordained from before his birth (Jer. 1:5). John the Baptist was announced before his conception (so was Isaac—Gen. 17:16), and was also filled with the Holy Spirit from his birth (Luke 1:13, 15).

Incidentally, that clearly refutes our principle that no one receives the Holy Spirit unless he has first been converted and has received laying on of hands. It is wise to try to observe good order, but God will not be confined to it. Do we see how the Lord will smash all our nice, neat, secure little ways? He simply will not be contained within our petty conceptions. It is good to know the principles of the Lord, but we too must never be confined to them. We walk by grace in the Spirit of our Lord Jesus Christ.

The call of the Lord may come upon a man directly, the Holy Spirit speaking to him in his own listening. Or the call may come indirectly, through another man, as Elijah called Elisha (1 Kings 19:19). The call may come while awake or sleeping, by vision or dream, or inner speech. Samuel was asleep, but was awakened and heard the Lord—was it aloud or within his spirit? Joseph was called to accept Mary while asleep (Matt. 1:20). Isaiah was in the temple, apparently on regular duty as a priest, for he seemed to be within the holy place when he had his vision (Isa. 6).

The Lord has not changed. He yet calls his servants in whatever way he chooses, though most often through visions or dreams. Paul was knocked off his horse in a vision (Acts 9:3,4). John the beloved was carried into heaven to be given the prophet's vision to write the book of Revelation (Rev. 1:1-3, 9,10). Peter was guided

45

to a new work by a half-awake, half-asleep "trance" (dream or vision? Acts 10). Cornelius, in the same chapter, was guided by a vision. Deuteronomy 13 speaks of a prophet as a "dreamer of dreams."

A man may hold some other office, and be promoted to the office of a prophet. Barnabas, Symeon, Lucius, Manaen and Saul (Paul) were teachers and prophets, when the Holy Spirit ordered Barnabas and Paul to be set apart to the office of apostle (Acts 13:1-3). Thus the word of the Lord was fulfilled. "His master said to him, 'Well done, good and faithful servant; you have been faithful over a little, I will set you over much; enter into the joy of your master.' " (Matt. 25:21 RSV). Pastors and teachers are often elevated to become prophets, and prophets to become apostles. In so doing, they do not always leave their former office. A prophet may yet, when called upon, be a teacher, a healer, an exorcist, or an evangelist; he may fulfill any function under him in authority. He may not act, however, as an apostle. An apostle may act in any capacity within the church.

Prophets may resist their calling—as Jonah did his—with dire results. During one period of time, several men, one after the other, came to Paula and me for counsel. Each one seemed to have a curse upon his life. Nothing would go right. Businesses failed, wives left them, or they could never find a good woman to marry in the first place. Storms in nature and inner storms continually overtook them. Each man had resisted and rejected an earlier call to the Lord's ministry. One, who was young, responded—and how the Lord has blessed him. He even brought a wonderful young lady to this young man's side. If the Lord storms over those who refuse His call to the pastorate, imagine how He treats those who refuse His calling to prophecy. We do not have to imagine. We have only to read the story of Jonah.

How shall we recognize God's calling upon us? It is often only afterwards that the call becomes clear, that the mind sees how incident after incident in our lives, like rows of toppling dominoes, ran climaxing to that moment. Later chapters will discuss how we hear the voice of God. The discipline of God does not fall unless we have persistently ignored His voice, either consciously or subconsciously. God will give us clear signs. And He will come again and again, patiently. He knows us well enough to start in plenty of time!

Once we have heard, He will confirm the call by personal signs, and then through others. Not all confirmations come from members of His body. The Lord has often brought the least likely angels as His messengers to us. Strangers and unbelievers have been used to tell us things, the depth of which they did not know. This sort of thing is not uncommon among the Lord's people. The Lord often guides or rebukes me through the mouths of children (Ps. 8:2). The Lord may speak through anyone or anything to confirm His message to His servants, the prophets.

Agnes Sanford tells of her move to California in her book, *Sealed Orders*. It involved me a little bit and I want to add some details she doesn't mention but which are pertinent. Agnes was living in Westboro, Massachusetts. I came to visit. One morning, while we were having devotions, the Lord prompted me to lay hands on Agnes and prophesy. Agnes's ministry was to be changed, I said. No longer was she to minister only to people. Now she was to minister to the creation, specifically to flowers and the earth. She would move, within six months, to California. I saw a specific and detailed vision of the house in which she would reside and described it aloud. The hillsides behind it were festooned with flowers, trees grew next to the house, it had a balcony and white stucco sides. A few months later her friend, Margaret Sedenquist, a real estate agent, talked with Agnes while she was visiting her children in Southern California. She said, "I have a house which I believe is just right for you." Agnes loved it upon sight, and moved in. Shortly after that I came to visit and recognized the house as identical in every respect to the one which I had seen in the vision six months before.

We then understood her call to be an order to pray for the area whenever earthquakes threatened. That's because the house stands on a hillside directly over the San Andreas fault. All this was just before the great scare which came to California concerning earthquakes. Hundreds of people saw visions of horrendous earthquakes and of Southern California sliding under the sea. Entire congregations, warned in such dreams and visions, picked up and moved to the Midwest. They understood neither the meaning of the warnings, nor the power of repentance. Agnes went to work calling others to join her in praying for California. A group of young people trooped over the mountains loving the earth and praying for its protection. I joined with her for a while, but then, like Elijah in 1 Kings 18:12, was carried off by the Lord "whither I knew not." Agnes slugged on in prayer, calling others continually. The Lord found His ten righteous ones (Gen. 18:32). To date, the prophecies of doom have remained unfulfilled.

The unbelieving will of course say, "That only goes to show it was all foolish superstition anyway. There never was going to be such a tragedy. Those people became alarmed over nothing." "But the wise shall understand" (Dan. 12:10). "If my people, which are called by my name, shall humble themselves, and pray, and seek my face, and turn from their wicked ways; then will I hear from heaven, and will forgive their sin, and will heal their land" (2 Chron. 7:14).

The prophet has little honor in this life. No one can know the amount of spiritual exertion which went into Agnes's and her cohorts' prayers. Prophets work in secret intercession.

Later, Southern California did have a mighty earthquake. When I could get a phone call through, I asked Agnes, "What's the matter, Agnes, were you asleep on the job?"

"That wasn't my patient," she replied.

"What do you mean?"

"That was the San Gabriel fault. I was sent to pray for the San Andreas fault. I didn't even know there was a San Gabriel fault. Don't worry, I've got it now!"

Whoever thinks Agnes is fooling herself is mistaken.

This story contains lessons worthy of note. The move to the beautiful California house, and the leading into the prophetic task, were a promotion of Agnes for work well done. For years she had been a faithful healer and teacher. Now she was called to the prophetic position. The reward of the Lord's servant is not, as in secular circles, banquets, plaques, and the congratulations of men. For Agnes it was to be given a beautiful new home, but more importantly, to be given new and greater works to do for Him. It is like a father on earth who says to his son, "Hey, you did a swell job hoeing those two rows of beans; as your reward, here are twenty rows of corn to hoe." Oh my! Yet that is precisely the glory and joy of the kingdom. To be put on the shelf or out to pasture is punishment, but to be given new and heavier responsibilities—that is joy and reward.

Agnes had been a healer and then a teacher for many years, prepared through much discipline and experience to be a prophet. Her training had been accomplished already before her call. Thus she stepped naturally and easily into the prophetic office.

She was anointed to be a prophet through the laying on of hands by another prophet. Neither she nor I had thought of any such thing before the prayer. It was purely an act of the Holy Spirit. Nevertheless, it would have been invalidated without the confirming signs of the house and the timing. Her call included the job description, yet only sketched in outline. The Lord gave the major strokes of the brush after she was in place.

Agnes was past sixty-six when the Lord gave her the new task. Most of her friends were in the East. The move meant a complete uprooting of her life. Old friends had to be left behind, perhaps hurt in the process. Little explanation for the move could be given to friends who felt they had a right to know. Like Abraham, at seventy-five commanded to uproot his life, and be rewarded for it, so Agnes was called to a hard obedience.

She really couldn't tell her friends too much. What would she say? "I'm going out there to save California from going into the sea!" A prophet's commission is usually not made public until after it is accomplished. Sometimes even the prophet does not know, until in retrospect it is revealed to him what the Lord has accomplished through him. Thus he often cannot explain to people why he does what he does.

Countless other prophets have been moved by the Lord to a specific place in a given time for His purposes. Elbert Jones was sent to the Fort Lauderdale area, and then to Ocala, for the Master's own purposes. He moved on sheer faith, knowing neither what income nor purpose would be his. The Lord revealed and supplied. Harald Bredesen was sent on a trip around the world, on naught but faith.

We share these few stories of calling and obedience to convey that the Lord works in our day as much as in Bible days. His dealings with Abraham, Moses, Jeremiah, Ezekiel, and every other Old and New Testament prophet were not different than with a Saint Francis or Sam Jones or Mary Brown. . . .

Paula and I were called, in many ways and times, from degree to degree. Our training spanned many years of both blessing and cursing. Like Agnes, I was a teacher and healer after I received the baptism of the Holy Spirit in 1958. At a Camp Farthest Out in Ardmore, Oklahoma, which is the one always held for healing, Agnes Sanford, Tommy Tyson, and I were the three leaders. One evening, under the anointing, Tommy could not present a regular lecture. He kept returning to old-time, fundamental, sawdust and tears revival preaching. At the end he gave a call for anyone who had never accepted Jesus as his own personal Lord and Savior to stand and do so. My heart was on fire—which was ridiculous because I had accepted Him many times before. Then Tommy extended the call to anyone who might have accepted Him before. Wayne McClain raised his hand and said, "I want to, Tommy." I stood and said, "I do too." Agnes stood, and all the audience stood! On the way back to my room, my heart was singing, "Hurray, I'm saved! Hallelujah!" Needless to say, I was more than a bit confused. Back in the room, I said, "How come you do me this way, Lord? What's going on? You know I've accepted you before." To explain the answer I heard I should first explain that when Agnes and I teach concerning the inner man, we often call the unconscious "Junior" because it is the storehouse of youthful experiences. The Lord told me that night in Ardmore, "Junior just got the idea."

Sometime later I had a vivid dream. Tommy Tyson was driving my car. I was alone in the back seat. Before I could protest, or do anything about it, Tommy drove right off the edge of the road over a high cliff. I was scrambling around in the back seat trying to figure how I could land on the cushions so I might have a chance to survive. Tommy had disappeared. The car kept plummeting down and down, like the poor coyote who has just missed the roadrunner again, sailing down to the desert floor! The car finally hit the bottom with a feathery, easy poof! I sprang out unhurt but somehow changed, and a voice said with great authority, "This is the birth of a prophet."

From that moment on everything went wrong in my life! My thriving church began not to thrive. Agnes and I split apart as a team. Missions and teaching tours spluttered. I fell into a spiritual delusion and was off the track for a while. Finances became tight. Then, when I got back on center spiritually, the work load had increased until Paula and I thought we could never survive. From week to week we kept promising our tired bodies, "If you'll just get us through these days, maybe we'll be able to rest." Paula had a major accident and was nearly killed. The children and the house were in turmoil.

The Lord was breaking every source of confidence Paula and I had. We were to learn that we could accomplish nothing by ourselves. These were our seven years eating grass (Dan. 4). Only the Spirit could thrive in and through us. I needed that strong spiritual delusion because my confidence had been in my ability to hear God, not in God's ability to overcome my sinful heart to speak to me.

All of this was that long fall in my dream, in which I was constantly sought some way to stop, or find a way to land without getting hurt. The final landing in death came when I let go and utterly died to my own striving. I let all my ambitions and desires, dreams and wishes, fail and die completely, in the bare hands of God. It took about six years, that fall, all of it a dying to more and more of my pernicious self. Doubtless there are many more deaths to go through. But the prophet was at last born. And so was Paula. Tommy, through whom the Lord called my heart to death, was the driver in the dream. He and Agnes and others, praying over me in Schools of Pastoral Care, had often seen me as a prophet of the Lord. Therefore I had received both the inner call and training, and the confirmation of the Spirit within the body.

But the Lord had long spoken of the two of us as a prophetic team. This was confirmed when several groups, setting up teaching and counseling series, requested that Paula come with me, and provided full transportation for her as well. She, too, was confirmed within the body.

Still lacking was a specific vision of our tasks. In *I Believe in Visions*, Ken Hagin says that there are four basic periods in the life of a servant of God. The third begins with the vision of the servant's field of labor. The servant must wait for that vision. So in the middle of that tumultuous period, the Lord began to say to both of us again and again that He would change our lives and our ministry. Then a young man came for ministry, and afterwards, filled with the Spirit, wrote for me the following long prophecy:

To John Sandford, October 17, 1971, about 4:30 p.m.:

My son, has not the Lord, your Holy One manifested himself unto you in ways and by means that the natural mind of man cannot conceive? For surely, says the Lord, I have made known unto you my ways and my works within you are so that your heavenly Father shall receive glory. I am a God of purpose and direction. I have not left man, any man, unto his own choosing and way, but all things are in my hands and by my sovereign design all things are working together for good. You have wondered 'Why has the Lord been so blessed to me? Unto what purpose has the Lord chosen me?' I have given you unto my people *as a sign, as a test*, and as a *wonder*, that they may know there is One who is high and lofty that inhabits eternity that dwells among the poor and broken and contrite in heart. Yea, in the past I have drastically changed your ministry twice and many times you have felt new waves of glory go through your body and enlighten your mind. But again I am changing you. There is a change, a deep and abiding change, that is taking place deep within your well and a new flowing of the rivers of my life shall arise within you. For you will touch more and more the throne of my grace and from within shall waters proceed unto many brokenhearted and wounded spirits with renewing and rejuvenating power. For you have found a key, and I *shall* unlock the doors of *opportunity* for you in the *near* future to *embark* upon the *great sea* of *adventure*. For you shall be released of your present situation in a way that wiil both startle and delight you, and you shall be free in me to do my bidding. Wonder not how the Lord shall perform His word. For in a way you know not you shall be relieved of your duties in your congregation! I say not how, neither are you to wonder how. But in a most startling way you shall be "free." Then, my son, you shall know the restraining power of the Lord upon you. For you shall have one thought of as to where the Lord would have you go, but you shall quickly know it is not there, but in another place. But unto another pastorate in the near future you shall not go, but "shepherd" you will my people, though not in the way of man's understanding. For a great cleansing shall spread over the land as you train my servants in the ways of my healing. You shall not touch the surface but penetrate to the core. You shall become quite controversial and many shall despise you, condemning themselves, for they shall not want to be exposed. For my light in you shall *expose* the hidden works of darkness in others, not to condemn but to deliver the oppressed ones. In all this remember, I do this, and be sure to give me the glory. This work shall begin soon and I shall hasten the day—says the Lord.

We had never met this young man before he came that one time for counseling. He knew nothing of my life, yet the Spirit spoke accurately of the two drastic changes, and of the glory passing through, and of my wonderings. We never saw the young man again—to this day.

Two more years of the fires of tribulation followed, climaxing in June of 1973 when I was invited to be one of the speakers at the Seattle Charismatic Clinic. There Costa Deir laid down his life in intercessory prayer for me. Winston Nunes called me to die to all my ministering to others in every way, prayed for separation of spirit and soul, and for renunciation of all the past, people and events alike, that I might be free in Christ. Paul Gordon and Bob Heil supported me greatly and brought healing to me. Les Pritchard gave me advice and counsel. Bob Arrowsmith helped me. Others too numerous to mention gave me strength and encouragement. The "dark night of the soul" was ending in the dawn of a new day.

Yet the vision of the new tasks had not come. In July the Lord ordered me to resign from Wallace United Church of Christ as of August 31. In that denomination the pastor must give the church ninety days service beyond resignation, and the church is to keep him on full salary for that same period. That meant that salary would end November 30. But the Lord would not let me circulate papers to enter another pastorate. Here was part of that prophecy being fulfilled. Raymond Huddleston had come by earlier, wanting me to enter a work with him of founding Christian youth ranches—which work he has indeed begun. We did have a thought to go that way, but felt immediately the Lord's restraining power. Nor would the Lord let me contact anyone to find a position. We were forbidden to do anything to find work in any way. "After they were come into Mysia, they assayed to go into Bithynia: but the Spirit suffered them not" (Acts 16:7).

Two of our six children were now independent. But we had one son in college, one in junior high, one in grade school, and a girl in kindergarten, in addition to a seventeen-year-old girl living with us. After November 30 there would be no more income. October missions proved unusually generous, and many bills were cleared away. But October came and went with nothing other than "wait" as a message from the Lord. Friends fussed, tried to hold onto faith, and worried for the Sandfords. November came and still no word. Faith was being tested. We were learning obedience in new dimensions.

Not until November 20 did the vision come. Part of it was, "You are to write, lecture, and counsel. I will provide." Immediately came a letter from Elbert Jones, with a small gift, saying he was delighted to give in support of our mission. No one had told him anything—unless the Holy Spirit had! The Lord was confirming His word.

Then came the command to move to Coeur d'Alene, Idaho.

Then a friend called to tell us about a lovely home to rent. We looked and were pleased, but rental would mean pouring $175 a month down the drain. We thought, "If only we could use the camper for a down payment, perhaps (a wild thought) we could buy a house!"

So on Friday, November 30, we walked into Northwest Real Estate and by one of God's coincidences, out of twelve men there, talked to a Christian agent who had moved only a few months before to Coeur d'Alene on sheer faith. He understood. The first house we looked at, we fell in love with. It had everything—three bedrooms, full basement, two baths, two fireplaces, two-car garage, rear covered-deck, built-in dishwasher and electric range, fully carpeted floors—and the boys could have a large downstairs bedroom so that I could use the smaller upstairs bedroom for writing and counseling. We returned home full of hope and prayer.

Then we found out that the bottom had fallen out of the camper sales. One could hardly give away a camper, due to the energy crisis. Our down payment disappeared. We prayed for the house anyway.

On Saturday morning I walked back into the real estate agency and said to our agent's boss, "I'm a pastor without a church. I don't have a job. I don't have any money. And I want to buy a house."

He smiled, and said, "We'll see what we can do."

Sunday, a lady from the Catholic charismatic Lord of Love Community in Spokane, prompted by a nun whom I had counseled, called to say, "I have six thousand dollars you can use for your down payment!"

Monday I went with Ken Campbell, then manager of the local savings and loan, to see a Coeur d'Alene banker. Ken told him the Sandfords had the down payment but no other money, no guaranteed income, and only the prospect of entering into counseling, using the home as an office. The banker responded favorably and said, "We're going to move on this for you, John." Tuesday at eleven in the morning the banker called. The bank had already checked our credit rating (a task of several days, usually), already appraised the house favorably (another task requiring days) and already agreed to make the loan. We moved in Tuesday night and the deal was all closed a week later. Our praise of God knew no bounds.

Starting on Friday with no money and no job, by Tuesday the Lord had provided a glorious, brand-new house—and thus confirmed a new ministry.

The calendar is full of counseling appointments each afternoon, and I write and Paula types each morning. The Lord's timing is something marvelous. On that Monday I told the banker I intended to charge twenty dollars an hour for counseling. On that basis the loan had been granted. On Wednesday, after we moved in, the Lord reminded me of Luke 6:38 and commanded me not to charge. Counseling is *given* to all who come. Some people give nothing, but others give as the Lord prompts. Can you imagine what the banker would have done if I had received that command earlier and had to tell him, "Oh, we aren't going to charge anything; the Lord will provide for us"?

The walk is still one of faith, hand to mouth financially. But He has promised, and He is faithful to provide.

Such was our call, not more dramatic than those of many of the servants of the Lord, but certainly fulfilling the prophecy of "delight" that "you will be set free in a startling way . . . to embark upon the great sea of adventure." And the commission is as prophesied, specifically, "to train my servants in the ways of my healing."

He has called, and He will surely perform His word. We pray that these testimonies may give others encouragement to respond to the call of the Lord. "Faithful is he that calleth you, who also will do it" (1 Thess. 5:24).

Chapter Five

THE DISCIPLINE AND TRAINING OF A PROPHET

And Jehoshaphat said, "Is there no prophet of the Lord here, through whom we may inquire of the LORD?" Then one of the king of Israel's servants answered, "Elisha the son of Shaphat is here, who poured water on the hands of Elijah."

2 Kings 3:11 RSV

Elisha poured water on the hands of Elijah. The training of an Old Testament prophet was done by placing him under the care and discipline of an older prophet. Lessons were not merely formal classroom sessions, though the prophets did at times literally sit at the feet of the master. The more cogent teaching happened wherever incidents in life brought opportunity. The modern TV program, "Kung Fu," pictured the way eastern wise men actually were trained. Life was the teacher, the master was the assistant.

At present there is no special college for the training of the Lord's modern day prophets. Seminaries and Bible colleges train pastors, priests, teachers and missionaries. The Lord, and men like Billy Graham, provide for and train modern evangelists. So far, to the best of our knowledge, there is no school specifically for the discipline and training of end-time prophets. We hope that this book is the beginning of the raising up of such a school.

Prophets today are trained primarily by the Lord Jesus Christ himself through His Holy Spirit. Their training is as much in life as in the classroom. Consequently, when we speak of a school for prophets, we mean only that kind of training ground which can prepare the church as a whole to understand and nurture the budding prophets in its midst. The Holy Spirit is the master teacher, raising His prophets. No longer does He take them apart to sit under a single teacher as in the Old Testament. The prophet is now integral within the body; the body becomes his matrix and training arena. Many prophets miss their calling or fail to understand their training for the lack of the church's support. The church needs to recognize its prophets and provide the milieu in which they may mature.

It is difficult to recognize a budding prophet, yet there are clues which should alert elders. Great tragedies *may* signal God's special preparation in a life. People who are dreamers and visionaries upon receiving the Spirit should be watched, for among them *may* be a prophet. Burden-bearers, or those who often take into their own beings empathetically the burdens of others, *may* be fledgling prophets. Those with teaching gifts may be chosen by the Lord for prophecy. But these are only hints; nothing can be conclusive apart from the Holy Spirit's call and confirmation.

A pastor may or may not be a prophet. A prophet may or may not be a pastor. But it is nearly impossible to wear both hats at once. A pastor must necessarily have the flock upon his heart in a special way. He must not feed his flock swift waters or expose to them what they cannot yet swallow. Yet the prophet is often called to do those very things. The prophet should realize how what he says will affect the pastor, but that must not silence him. If both callings are in one heart, he is nearly torn apart.

I used to feel set free whenever I was called to leave the local pastorate to speak elsewhere because it was easier to act as a prophet away from home. I loved the pastorate, but God was readying me to accept another call.

God may touch anyone—a garbage collector or mayor, janitor or senator. But whoever, it's often hard to see them because the Lord often hides them. Moses was hidden in the bulrushes and then in Pharaoh's household. Jesus had to be hidden away in Egypt. Both our own flesh and Satan would destroy His elect if they were discovered too soon. So, when the Holy Spirit reveals a budding prophet, the church should be alert and ready to protect him or her.

Elisha poured water over the hands of Elijah. To pour water over another's hands was women's work. People ate with their fingers. Women servants then brought washing bowls. One bowl was set under the eater's hands, and water was poured from another over the guest's hands. A towel over the server's arm was for drying. This task was considered very menial, and was always done by women.

An older prophet trained a younger prophet by humiliating him, crushing and breaking his pride, defeating him and revealing his smallness and incapability before God. Test after test was put upon the neophyte. The test was a success only if he *failed* to pass it! To learn that he could not succeed by his own soul's resources was the first building block and constant checkpoint of the prophet's study course. Whatever showed the prophet his inner rotten core and brought him to despair of conquering it was a success for it had taken away another "reason for confidence in the flesh" (Phil. 3:4). Watchman Nee has written well of brokenness in *Release of the Spirit* and *The Spiritual Man, Volume 1*. They are excellent, although Nee wrote before the Lord's word through Merlin Carothers. And, for that reason, *The Spiritual Man* can become overbearing.

The prophet's training reveals and undercuts, one by one, all the false and hidden motivations of his life. When I was not allowed to seek another position upon resigning from my church, and could do nothing to insure that I might bring home the bacon for my family, it was a death, at the heart level, not merely in my mind. I had to look at my pride, a thoroughly cultural thing, about being the provider for my family. What people thought of me was also a humiliation to bear and learn from.

Speaking to an audience has always been easy for both Paula and me. But the Lord has purposely confused and broken some of our speaking, or worse, let us speak brilliantly only to discover that what we said brought no life to our listeners. Both of us are singers and the Lord has, on occasion, broken our voices to teach us to rely totally on the Spirit. I, an athlete, was given humiliating "leaning tower" back trouble every once in a while. Bones in Paula's back were broken in an auto accident. All of my dreams and visions became confused until I could trust nothing in myself. Given sensitive natures so that we could readily feel God's presence and soar into devotional heights, both of us were shut down until we could feel nothing.

Name any area of natural success—sex, communication, intelligence, friendships—and, if the Lord has not already smashed it in his servants until all their confidence is in Him alone, He soon will. Agnes Sanford, one of America's greatest in the healing ministry, had a breast cancer, and despite the prayers of all—and waiting almost too late—suffered the humiliation of a radical. The greatest teacher on depression and how to heal it, she then went into depression. The hand of God was preparing her for the task of prophecy.

When humiliation is complete, we are ready to graduate to prophecy. Western men think little of pitching in to help with the dishes. But not so eastern men. To be asked to do a woman's work is an unacceptable loss of face. To pour water over the hands of Elijah was thus the final degradation, the graduation test and ceremony.

People will not recognize prophets in training as having wisdom and sound judgment. The Lord frustrates even their common sense. Agnes used to say in despair of me, "I declare he is the wildest man I ever knew. He can swing wider and farther from pole to pole than any person I ever saw." Another friend described me as an Indian scout who wanders off into the hinterlands and comes running back, hair standing on end, eyes bugging out, yelling, "Not that way, boys, not that way!"

Prophets in training make fools of themselves more times than they make sense. The Lord characteristically gives a young prophet two or three true visions, and the prophet in turn speaks warnings to the congregation. And it works! About that time the tyro prophet begins to take "his stand on visions, puffed up without reason by his sensuous mind, not holding fast to the Head" (Col. 2:18b, 19a RSV). He becomes strongly deluded and, the next thing you know, he is utterly abased and humiliated before his fellow parishioners. God arranged it that way and, even if the prophet has abundant common sense, he cannot escape the process of humiliation essential to his training.

It is not that the Lord ever tempts anyone. James says that "every man is tempted, when he is drawn away of his own lust, and enticed. Then when lust hath conceived, it bringeth forth sin: and sin, when it is finished, bringeth forth death" (James 1:14,15). The Lord does try our hearts (Ps. 66:10-12). But that should not be confused with the temptation to sin. God's trials come in the form of afflictions and hardships; temptation is another matter. Temptation can never be blamed on anyone but ourselves. Whatever the instrument, wielded by whatever hand, the scouring is because the blemish is upon the pan, not the hand.

We've met some people whose entire lives have been a series of tragedies. The details were often agonizing beyond belief, but we often found that behind it all lay the gem God's rough hand was polishing. A prophet was being trained.

Behind all of the prophet's training runs one basic theme—death of self in order that unity may blossom and the prophet may enable others to shine.

It is to that end that all of the prophet's training proceeds. He must learn how to hear God speaking in dreams and visions. He must polish his gifts of perception and knowledge by practice. He must learn to combine bold forthrightness and reticent courtesy. He must know the law—and when and how to follow the Spirit beyond the letter of the law in mercy. He will above all learn the power and ways of intercession, and how to call the body to it.

All of these are objective, exterior forms of knowledge, which only secondarily involve the prophet's character and personality. Nevertheless, his character will strongly affect the way he does these things, unless he dies to self.

Until a man dies to himself, he is an idolater. He worships an image which is subtly and unconsciously nothing more than himself. And he spends his life and energy seeking to get people to love, honor, worship and adore him. We are all Nebuchadnezzars at heart and, like him, we have our fiery furnaces into which we cast those who refuse to join in our idolatry. Our carnal natures, though undercut by the cross, still rule too much of our lives. Therefore the Holy Spirit must continually bring us a Daniel and his three friends to show us, by our angers, what we are cherishing which is not of God—though we think it is. Because we are living from our unconscious picture of life (idolatry), we tend to think that everyone who fails to agree with us is false. We are trying to program others to be like us. Others, sensing they are being swallowed up into our world, flee from us. Until we fall into the earth and die, we remain alone (John 12:24). Even if others join us we remain alone because by joining us they have ceased to be independent sons of God who freely choose us—they have become instead extensions of us, satellites in our orbit.

Often a counselor's work is to set people free from each other. Idolatry can be very deeply entrenched in family relationships and it must be broken. We need to be separated from each other's unconscious demands, which is why Jesus said He had come not to bring peace but to divide by a sword (Luke 12:52,53). Those demands often have great power because they are backed by years of mutual family idolatry wherein husbands and wives, and parents and children, have idolized each other and thus controlled one another. They have come to unspoken agreements by which they mutually affirm what splendid people they are. It is, in fact, hatred masquerading as love.

When a person falls into the earth and dies—daily—he dies more and more to his own idolatries, as well as to those imposed upon him by others. He thus becomes free *from* others, and free to be *to* them. At first this causes trouble, for all around are forced to change the way they relate to him. But gradually needy people begin to seek him out. He is no longer alone, for they sense and want his freedom. They can tell they will not be forced into his mold, nor judged nor condemned. With him they will begin to find themselves rather than to become a copy or shadow of him.

Thus a prophet becomes an enabler. Because he has fallen, and sees himself not as a god but as a creature, others are set free around him (2 Cor. 4:11-12).

The prophet of the Old Testament called people back to the law. He called them to accept and return to living up to a way exterior to them. Thus he was necessarily an imposer. He upheld and defended a way of life, a picture, a mold which was outside the person and to which he must conform. The prophet of the New Testament, however, stands beside his brother, speaking God's word to him, that each brother may experience God's inscription of the law uniquely in his own heart. This stance fulfills Jeremiah's prophecy: "I will put my law in their inward parts, and write it in their hearts; and will be their God, and they shall be my people. And they shall teach no more every man his neighbor, and every man his brother, saying, know the LORD: for they shall all know me, from the least of them unto the greatest of them, saith the LORD: for I will forgive their iniquity, and I will remember their sin no more" (Jer. 31:33-34).

In the Old Testament, idolatry was understood largely in

external terms (Isa. 45:20), but in the New it is an internal malady (Col. 3:5). Thus the prophet of the old covenant thundered against sin as something that needed to be shed like a garment. But the prophet of the new covenant must look into men's hearts. He knows that there alone can the critical transition take place. Sin no longer incenses him as it did his Old Testament counterparts. Sin has had its fangs pulled by the mercy of the cross. Now the prophet stands by, that the Holy Spirit may enable each man in his own trek, so that the process of recognizing sin, asking forgiveness, and being changed may write God's character into each man's heart. Behind the Old Testament prophet's warning not to sin was the compulsion to obey, to live up to a picture of glorious Israel. Behind the New Testament's warning not to sin is the love of a Father God coaching His sons as they grow up in Him. Sin is still horrendous, but in the New it is transformed to glory by His mercy.

Jesus, by entering into and conquering death, has made death the joyous route to life. Self-death itself is that strait gate which, Jesus said, few ever find (Matt. 7:13-14). Everything God says in the New Testament is meant either to maintain the milieu of heaven and earth in which He can birth and raise sons, or to raise, teach, and chastise those sons. The prophet of the New is therefore called to die to every picture he might entertain of the good life, that he may stand selfless beside each brother, tribe and nation, that God may be unhindered in the saving and raising of His sons. This is what Paul was telling the Romans (see Rom. 14:10-15:7, especially in the Living Bible's version).

The calling of a prophet demands years of self-death. No one can become a prophet quickly. The age of instant coffee and instant-on TV cannot produce instant prophecy. The apostles and prophets are foundational to the church because they have been brought to more death of self than others not so chosen, and to rebirth in Him.

Prophets and apostles have no less sin than other people. Far from becoming so sinless that he has confidence in his righteousness, the prophet has rather been made so aware of the deceit and villainy of his inner heart that he has come to utter despair of his ever becoming true to God. That awareness of helplessness is what God wanted.

When St. Paul began his ministry, Jesus told him he was a sinner ("why persecutest thou me?" Acts 9:4). Later he preached that "all are under sin" (Rom. 3:9). At the end of his ministry, while such healing virtue was flowing through him that handkerchiefs were taken from his body and placed upon the sick so that they became well (Acts 19:12), he wrote to Timothy, "This is a faithful saying, and worthy of all acceptation, that Christ Jesus came into the world to save sinners, of whom I am chief" (1 Tim. 1:15). Mark the tense. Not that he was once a sinner, but that he presently recognizes himself as the greatest of sinners. Every apostle or prophet has this as his hallmark, that the Lord continually shows him the villainy of his inner being that he never ceases to be a beggar pointing other beggars to where food is. Whoever is rich in himself has learned nothing and has nothing to give.

God's call to high office in the church is never an elevation to honor. It is rather always an invitation to humiliation (1 Cor. 1:26-31).

The church needs not to be affrighted nor affronted by those who seem to be thrashing around most wildly on the Lord's line; that fish may be the one whom the Lord is preparing for highest office. The church needs to cease to be afraid of sin (not to run out and do it more freely) and to love its sinners (which means discipline, too) that God may use everything in life to raise His prophets to their task.

Sadly, the church has often been too stifling an atmosphere for the production of prophets and apostles. Bob Mumford speaks of the way we reward and honor a soldier wounded in battle, but when a soldier for Christ falls wounded in battle, "What do we do? We finish him off!"

How we praise and thank God that the church did not cast us out or reject us while we learned. America is literally strewn with the wreckage of my mistakes. Others, however, have not fared so well. They have been haunted out of the church, or stunted, or capped off and shut down, and did not rebound to mature into His fullness.

The training of a prophet or apostle is the hardest, most excruciating discipline to be endured anywhere in the universe. Let the church become a part of the solution rather than the problem.

My son, if you come forward to serve the Lord,
   prepare yourself for temptation.
Set your heart right and be steadfast,
   and do not be hasty in time of calamity.
Cleave to him and do not depart,
   that you may be honored at the end of your life.
Accept whatever is brought upon you,
   and in changes that humble you be patient.
For gold is tested in the fire,
   and acceptable men in the furnace of humiliation.
Trust in him, and he will help you;
   make your ways straight, and hope in him.

                                   Ecclesiasticus *2:1-6 RSV

---

* Ecclesiasticus, or The Wisdom of Jesus the Son of Sirach, is part of the Old Testament apocryphal books which are not printed in most Protestant editions of the Bible, although they are included in Catholic editions. For more information see B.M. Metzger, *An Introduction to the Apocrypha*, New York: Oxford University Press, 1957.

Chapter Six

LESSONS IN PROPHECY FROM THE STORY OF THE WOMAN AT THE WELL *(John 4:1-42)*

Within this story is one of the greatest miracles of conversion ever recorded. In somewhat over an hour, our Lord awakened a total stranger from sudden chance acquaintance to full and glorious recognition of himself as more than the expected Messiah, all without overriding her free will and stubbornness of heart.

We are convinced that this woman was not a wicked woman at all, but a prophetess of the Lord. See what you think as we proceed. It may be of little import what we think of her now, but it is fun to entertain new thoughts. Meantime, we shall use this story as a springboard to many lessons in the art and practice of prophecy—and other ministries.

Hostility between Jews and Samaritans had long been intense. After the death of Solomon, the ten northern tribes of Israel seceded from the united monarchy established by David. The capital city of the secessionist tribes was Samaria (the biblical writers generally referred to the northern kingdom as Israel and the southern as Judah). After the successful siege of Samaria by the Assyrians in 722 B.C., the Israelites were deported en masse and replaced by other Near Eastern captives of the Assyrians. Although these captives were mostly Gentiles and polytheists,

69

they adopted the religion of the region to which they had been sent as colonists. Thus, by New Testament times, they worshiped Yahweh, acknowledged Moses as the supreme apostle of God, accepted the Torah (Genesis-Deuteronomy) as canonical Scripture, recognized Mt. Gerizim (not Zion) as the chosen place of God mentioned in Scripture (e.g. Deut. 14:23), and expected a final day of judgment.

They were obviously very close in faith to their southern neighbors, but, since we always fight more viciously with our brothers than with strangers, that closeness only heightened the hostility. Geography served to acerbate the problem further. By the time of the Roman occupation, orthodox Jews inhabited the regions both north and south of Samaria. Their feelings against Samaritans were so intense that a pious Jew generally traveled around Samaria rather than pass through it on a trip between, for example, Jerusalem and Nazareth. The resultant racial hatred between Jews and Samaritans made our modern racial tensions seem like a tea party.

However, Jesus decided to pass through rather than around Samaria. He had walked some twenty to thirty miles, in how many hours or days we are not told. The disciples had gone ahead into the city to buy food. Jesus was alone, hot, tired, and thirsty. There was no container with which to draw water. The city carefully provided none, that strangers might not defile nor carelessly use all their water, for this was a sacred well in Israel's history. Jesus therefore was dependent upon whomever might happen to come to the well to draw.

No one likes to be dependent upon others. It hurts our pride very little to give to others, even if we give until it hurts deeply. We can always be proud that we gave. It is much more humbling to *receive* gifts from others, except, perhaps, at Christmas or on birthdays, when we feel that gifts pay us honor due. To receive gifts daily, however, is humiliating. Add to this that a man will receive gifts from others only as God prompts, and one is being taught the lesson of dependency implicit in the words, *"Give* us this day our *daily bread."*

A prophet's task may also complicate this part of his life. God may command him to speak an extremely hard word to people, for which the people are likely to hate the prophet. These same people are the hand of God to feed him. Every pastor knows this.

Jesus had commanded His disciples, "Take nothing for your journey, neither staves, nor scrip, neither bread, neither money; neither have two coats apiece. And whatsoever house ye enter into, there abide, and thence depart. And whosoever will not receive you, when ye go out of that city, shake off the very dust from your feet for a testimony against them. And they departed, and went through the towns, preaching the gospel, and healing everywhere" (Luke 9:3-6). Prophets must learn to live by the Lord's people. This is a two-edged lesson. First, it teaches the prophet humility and faithful dependence upon God. Second, it creates the kind of relationship among men in which prophetic ministry can have fullest effect. Whoever gives to a prophet opens doors to the Lord (Matt. 10:40-42).

The Shunammite woman, seeing the prophet's need, prepared a room for Elisha. Therefore she was to receive a prophet's reward. The prophet promised to her a son, which in due time she did have, ending her disgrace among her kindred (2 Kings 4:8-17).

God intends to do good for his people. But He is polite; He will not invade; He must be given our permission. So He comes in many ways, one of which is in the person of His prophets. If people give something to a prophet, it opens the way for the Lord to give to the people. In the same way the Lord makes his prophets dependent upon the people. It does not hurt if the people realize this, and subsequently give with selfish motives. "For whosoever shall give you a cup of water to drink in my name, because ye belong to Christ, verily I say unto you, *he shall not lose his reward"* (Mark 9:41).

On the other side, prophets must always *give* their services.

71

They do not charge. As they give, the Lord gives back to them through men (Luke 6:38). Likewise a church should never speak of "hiring" a pastor, or a traveling prophet, teacher, or evangelist. Such men are not hirelings, that they should flee when the wolf comes. Such men lay down their lives for the sheep as a free gift from God (John 10:11-13). The pastor is never paid a salary. He, like the Levite, lives from the offerings given to God. They are his to eat.

It is unwise for the businessman to say, "Let's get this thing into business terms. What are we going to pay this man if we bring him here?" Business terms do not belong. The servant is freely given by God to the people. The people are to give freely to God's servants. No servant of God can legitimately lay down salary terms as a demand before he will come to a people. If the businessman wants to insure that the holy man is rewarded adequately, let him give generously, and see to it that others do. The pastor and the church may agree beforehand what is to be set aside for him, but that amount should not determine whether he will accept the pastorate or not.

God has not changed His *modus operandi*. He still commands His servants to depend utterly upon Him. It is still good for the church and good for the prophet. The Lord's servant needs none of the world's assurances, however comforting they may seem. God is His sufficient supply, never men.

Jesus had no real need of the Samaritan woman. He could have commanded the water and it would have flown to his lips. But "though he was in the form of God . . . he humbled himself . . ." (Phil. 2:6,8). In this sense Jesus needed the Samaritan woman's help. Many times God arranges it so that others do for us what we think we can do for ourselves.

Soon after we moved to our new house, two young men came by with a cord of chopped wood on their truck, offering to put it into the garage for what I later learned was a ridiculously low price. I

72

owned a pickup, knew where to go to cut wood, used to be a professional chain-saw operator, and had planned to go out to get my own. I turned the men down. At that moment a feeling of having erred struck my heart. Yet I remained stubbornly unaware that my heart was full of confidence in my own flesh to get that wood. Sure enough, when I took a neighbor to get the wood, the whole trip was entirely frustrated! Snow had fallen and we had to turn back because the old chains did not fit the new truck tires. Once we remedied that and were back in the woods we came across a car stuck in a ditch. We pulled him out, losing valuable time and breaking many links in the chains. Finally, in place to cut wood, the new chain saw would not work. I knew in my heart that these were not all simply coincidences. The Lord frustrated my efforts because I was supposed to have accepted the help of those two young men. The lesson was the important thing. The lack of firewood was a cheap price to pay for it. I was humbled before my new neighbor because I had failed to humble myself.

But, for all this humility, Jesus did not ask the Samaritan woman politely. He boldly commanded, "Give me to drink" (John 4:7). Elijah commanded the widow of Zarephath to give him a morsel of bread (1 Kings 17:8-16). But she was making a loaf for her son and herself, the last they were to have. They were, she grimly explained, preparing to starve to death. Nevertheless, Elijah insisted, "Fear not, go and do as thou hast said: but make *me* thereof a little cake *first,* and bring it to me, [not even, "I will come and get it"] and *after* make for thee and for thy son" (v. 13). The world would expect more courtesy under such circumstances. But we must obey God no matter what looms before us. We must despise our own wisdom in order to choose His. That is true humility. Human humility is inevitably outward. We say, "What a humble man he is." The prophet must surrender that kind of humility. His reward is not from men, but from God.

Thus Jesus disregards the Samaritan woman's tiredness, the heat of the day, the exertion required to haul the water up, the fact that she is a stranger, and that she is a hated Samaritan. He *commands* her to give him a drink. This alone ought to have begun to tip her off that she is in the presence of a prophet—probably it did. Incidentally, had she been a wicked woman, she most likely would not have been allowed to come to this well. It was sacred, and her sins would have defiled it.

Normally, if a man spoke to a woman in public in that country, the woman would consider herself shamed, and either say nothing or run to the men in her family, who could be counted on to demand apologies of the offender. Only two kinds of women would answer back to Jesus—a harlot or a prophetess. Her response shows that she is the latter. "How is it that thou, being a Jew *askest* drink of me, which am a woman of Samaria? for the Jews have no dealings with the Samaritans" (v. 9). For the moment she has disregarded that he has not asked but commanded. She is not yet ready to recognize Him as a prophet.

She is standing before the Lord of glory, in the confidence of her own flesh, changing His command to an asking, as we, too, often do. She has encountered a prophet unawares. Her question, however, shows that she is a prophetess among her people. And Jesus immediately moved to call her to see Him as her Messiah. "If thou knewest the gift of God, and who it is that saith to thee, Give me to drink; thou wouldest have asked of him, and he would have given thee living water" (v. 10).

We generally delight to tell others things directly because it is self-exalting. And the learner has not been invited into the process of discovery. However, a man dead to self teaches whenever possible by parable and analogy, that others may learn by discovery. Though Jesus could have announced, "I am the Son of God," He did not take such a short cut. Men must go through inner stages of learning, voluntarily, on their own. More than the Samaritan's head must retain what she learns. Therefore He moved indirectly.

The woman continued to miss the point, "Sir, thou hast nothing to draw with, and the well is deep: from whence then hast thou that living water? Art thou greater than our father Jacob which gave us the well, and drank thereof himself, and his children, and his cattle?" Another valuable lesson is wrapped up in her not seeing. Why did she not see? Her mind was good. She knew the prophet's way, which Jesus was using with her. But Jesus has offered her a gift, "If you knew the gift of God. . . ." He himself is the gift of God. It is beginning to dawn on her that He may indeed be the Messiah. This would mean an indescribable blessing to her to have found the Messiah! But that was too awesomely good to be believed easily and quickly. People can far more easily believe bad news than good! Lying at the root of most troubles in Christians is the inability to believe "Jesus loves me, this I know, for the Bible tells me so."

This woman has been through tragedy repeatedly. She has lost five husbands. (There was almost no divorce in those days—her husbands most likely have all died.) She has learned to expect trouble, not blessing. To find the Messiah would capsize whole mountains of living into a sea of blessing.

Jesus waits while her inner heart convulses in surprise and alternate joy and terror. Bearers of good tidings must learn not to rape this process of discovery in another. If one helps a chicken to break its shell, it will die, for it needed the exercise to find its strength. That is no less true of us.

Jesus tried again with the water analogy. But the woman was too frightened to claim the good news her mind had already sensed. She fled into "practicality." "Sir, give me this water that I thirst not, neither come hither to draw." It is not that we are actually that practically minded. But we have fled to the surface meaning to hide. This woman, disbelieving still for joy (Luke 24:41), is fleeing. Her heart, however, does believe.

Therefore Jesus answered her with a sign. The messenger in the Lord learns to sense when the heart of the other has opened to belief, and when it has closed. Zacharias and Mary were both

75

visited by the angel Gabriel. Both asked Gabriel a "practical" question (Luke 1:18,34). But Gabriel knew that Zacharias disbelieved and Mary believed. So Zacharias was disciplined and Mary received signs to confirm her way.

If a man believes, God will give him signs, that he may know that he has heard rightly. He will then be sure that he has not followed his own imagination. But if a man does not believe, God will not give him a sign. If he were to give the unbeliever a sign, He would be proving himself to him that he might believe in God. God would be jumping to his tune. Who then would be God? God will not give a sign to an unbeliever in order to convince him to believe. He must believe first; then God will confirm.

The Lord's servants are often tempted to think, "Oh, if the Lord would only work this or that stupendous miracle, then these people would *have* to believe." But a sign will only show His servant that it cannot compel people to believe. One of the most tragically funny things in the Scripture happened when the Pharisees and Sadducees came to Jesus, immediately *after* He had healed great multitudes—the lame, the blind, the deaf, the demon possessed—then fed the multitudes from seven mere loaves and two fish. These all were the very signs given in prophecy by which to recognize the Messiah. At that moment they asked Him to work a sign from heaven that they might believe (Matt. 16:1). Only the Holy Spirit gives the grace of belief—otherwise nothing, neither persuasion nor miracles, will bring about true belief.

Since Jesus proceeded to give the Samaritan woman a sign, we know that in her heart she had already believed. First, knowing that she has no husband, He says, "Go, call thy husband, and come hither." In effect she has been lying to Him, acting as though she does not believe when she actually does. A seventeen-year-old girl came to live with our family. When we talked she would repeatedly say, and be convinced in part of her mind, that she did not understand what was said to her. We learned at last to detect when she was only fooling herself, and did in truth understand. The Samaritan woman has been fleeing from Jesus. Therefore He gives her opportunity to leave Him, acting as though He is not a prophet and therefore does not know that she is not married. He will not force her to believe. If she wants to flee, He will invite her to do so.

Paula and I have often listened to preachers get carried away and shout, "Whoever does not come down here to this altar denies God," or, "If anyone leaves this building without leaving his sins at the altar, God will discipline him!" But the servant of God should never threaten (1 Pet. 2:23). A true prophet must stand mute and meek before the will of another. He must never force another to do his own will. Sensitively, Jesus was saying, "Okay, I won't force you. Go get your husband and come here—knowing either you won't come back or I won't still be here by that time. I'm letting you off the hook."

Had the Samaritan woman actually wanted out, she would have seized the opportunity to flee from His presence. Instead she answered that she had no husband. *What* she answered is of little import—that she *remained* at all is what matters. It said that she had decided not to honor her fear. She would see it through.

Real faith is a matter of what we do, not what we think or say (James 2:18). Doubts and reservations don't bother God, when a person is nevertheless living his faith. The woman made no oral confession of belief, but she stayed when given opportunity to flee.

"Jesus said unto her, Thou hast well said, I have no husband: for thou hast had five husbands, and he whom thou now hast is not thy husband: in that thou hast said truly." From this sign, whereby He shows her that He sees into her life by the power of God, she knows that He is a true prophet. Many people have misinterpreted what He said, and thought that she was a wicked woman. But an entirely different explanation is possible. The Old Testament law (Deut. 25:5) required that a widow's brother-in-law succeed her husband if she was childless, so as to guarantee an heir. Thus Boaz could not marry Ruth until Elimelech refused to do the part of a kinsman for her (Ruth 4). The woman at the well has had five husbands

77

because each has died. The sixth relative has taken her into his household (guarded from immorality by dozens of chaperoning relatives) but has not yet entered into marriage with her.

If a woman was not married, or lost a husband, she was thought to be cursed of God (Isa. 4:1). If she lost a second husband, she would be considered doubly reproached. But if she lost a third, then a fourth and a fifth, people began to regard her as being prepared for high service as a prophetess. Prophetesses could speak to men in public. Men and women alike would seek their counsel. Anna was neither embarrassed nor out of place when she gave thanks over the infant Jesus and "spake of him to all them that looked for redemption in Jerusalem" (Luke 2:38).

What Jesus said to the woman was no reproof to her. Because she stayed despite her fear, He rewarded her with the sign that He knew her private life and said, "I honor you as a prophetess. I know your sufferings, and the work they have wrought in your heart." She felt welcomed and received by Him.

She now has had two signs, His brusque manner and His kind words. She knows without a doubt that He is a prophet. Jesus, however, wants her to see more. But she is still half afraid to believe. Like so many of us, she immediately raised a nagging but impertinent question for the prophet to resolve. "Our fathers worshiped in this mountain; and ye say, that in Jerusalem is the place where men ought to worship" (v. 20).

We learn in Jesus' answer another technique or attribute of the Lord's prophet. The prophet comes with a word of revelation from God. His problem is always how to get us to receive that word. We are not prepared and often do not want to receive the stern words of God. Because of this, Amos, for example, used an extremely clever gimmick. He began his tremendous speech by excoriating Israel's traditional enemy, Damascus (still today Israel's enemy). Then he scolded another enemy, Gaza, a Philistine city. Then all the major cities of Philistia came under his thundercloud. Then came Tyre, a Phoenician city. Then Edom. The people delightedly listened to the prophet scold their enemies. Next he attacked Ammon, then Moab, then Judah, their bitterest rival and closest neighbor. The trap was now sprung. They were listening raptly. Now he could turn his guns upon Israel and they could not but hear. Likewise, when David sinned with Bathsheba, Nathan called for David to judge a case. David found himself judged by his own words.

The prophet enters upon whatever ground is given him, in order to meet the person. Then he expands or turns the subject to cause his brother to open his heart to the new revelation he brings. "For though I be free from all men, yet have I made myself servant unto all, that I might gain the more. . . . I am made all things to all men, that I might by all means save some" (1 Cor. 9:19,22). We walk in on the grounds where people are, in order that we may walk out with some.

The body of Christ must learn to stand by His prophets, for He may send His prophets to coexist with strange people. The Lord may strike up a friendship between His prophet and a Sikh, or a Hindu, or a Moslem, or a whore, or a bartender. Men complained of Jesus because He ate with sinners and publicans (Mark 2:16).

More importantly, the body needs to learn to stand by the prophet while he enters into the mentality of his friend. A leader of a nearby charismatic group met a girl who was caught up in eastern meditations and philosophies. The leader was winning the girl to the Lord. In the process, God was bringing new truths to the leader from the girl's eastern sojourn. The leader indeed was walking in where the girl was, to walk out with her. The Lord was using the occasion to bring to the leader biblical truths, hidden in eastern garb, which had been blocked from the leader for some time. In due time the Lord would have shaken and sifted these new thoughts (Phil. 3:15). Whatever was not perfectly congruent with Scripture would have fallen away. However, the rest of the group did not understand the process. Nor did they comprehend the faith required to let their leader be exposed to new currents, trusting the Lord to reveal in time what was true and what was not. They were afraid and impatient.

Jesus was not bothered by the woman's questions about where men ought to worship. It was His opportunity to expand her thought with fresh revelation, "But the hour cometh and now is . . ." (v. 23). *What* He teaches her is important in itself, but more important to her is that by using those words of fresh revelation, He has intimated that He is more than a prophet. Meanwhile, His glorious presence is flooding over her spirit. Gone from her now is the fleeing. She suspects that He is the Messiah. In the polite indirect way of the east, she offers, "I know that Messiah cometh, which is called Christ: when he is come he will tell us all things" (v. 25). But He has come as more than the Jewish expectation of the Messiah. He is the Son of God, which none had yet understood, though the prophets had prophesied it. Therefore He used a phrase which could not be anything else than a major sign to her, "I that speak unto thee am he" (v. 26, the Greek is *Ego eimi, ho lalon soi—I am,* the one speaking to you).

In the garden of Gethsemane He would use those same words, "I am he"; whereupon the soldiers, priests, and all fell back from Him on the ground (John 18:6). Because God revealed himself to Moses as I *AM*, pious Jews carefully avoided using that phrase or the related word, Yahweh. A superstition had grown up that whoever spoke His name would be struck dead. Therefore no one said, "I am." Various circumlocutions were devised to avoid it. God would strike dead the person who said I AM. And so they all fell away from Jesus, thinking God's thunderbolt would hit Him. Never mind that this was only a superstition, not a part of God's Word. When nothing happened, they were convinced that the one they were taking before Ananias and then Pilate was the Son of God.

Just so, Jesus used those same words, "I am," to tell the woman that He was more than the Messiah. She got the message. She now sees not merely that He is *a* Christ, but that He is *the* Christ. And the Holy Spirit quickly confirmed this revelation to her with sure signs. The disciples return. She sees the amazement on their faces that He is talking with a strange woman in public (v. 27). Yet none of the disciples said, "What seekest thou?" (to her) or "Why talkest thou with her?" (to Him). The disciples showed perfect courtesy and deference to His authority. Both of these were signs to her. It is still so, that we in our deportment are the signs which vouchsafe or destroy faith in others. Ghandi said, "I would accept your Christ were it not for you Christians!" These disciples are the signs.

Therefore the woman gave a sign that she believed, *she left her waterpot*. The westerner, who is used to dashing down to the hardware store to replace cheaply any lost or broken water pails, says, "Okay, so she left her waterpot, so what?" To the easterner that is a clear sign of faith.

Water is sacred. Water containers in biblical times became associated with the sacredness of life. Thus they were never to be lost, left behind or thrown away. If a waterpot were dropped and broken, that was a shame and a tragedy. Even the pieces were not thrown away. Larger pieces were used as mixing bowls or cutting boards. Smaller pieces were used to scrape boils because they had become so associated with healing virtue (Pillai). Job 2:8 says, "And he took him a potsherd to scrape himself withal; and he sat down among the ashes."

The woman came to the well looking for earthly water. In Jesus she found heavenly water. Therefore she left her water jar as a sign that true holiness and religiosity is not to be found in the forms of Samaritan or Jewish worship, but in the person she has just met. Had she only found a messiah, she would have kept the forms of worship, she would have kept her waterpot. But she has found more and does not need the forms any longer.

When a person receives a call from God, he must leave behind whatever has been his form of life up to that moment. When Jesus called James and John, "They immediately *left the ship and their father*, and followed him" (Matt. 4:22).

Elisha took his oxen, slew them, hacked up and burned his plow and harness for the barbecue he then held for his friends and relatives. He has thereby given three irrevocable signs. His oxen are slain; he cannot return to his farming. His instruments are burned. All his family have eaten salt with him to witness to his departure from farming to the service of God. There is no way he can return.

Whoever receives a call from God to high service—evangelism, prophecy, ministry or priesthood, whatever it may be—should renounce whatever has formed him. This is not to insult his heritage. It is to cut apron strings. It is to deny any further formation by the old carnal life. Now he will be formed by and serve only the God who has called him.

Many servants, not knowing this, have fled to their homes from service or seminary, thinking to obey the call of duty to help the folks. Thinking that they are yet to obey the fifth commandment, to honor the parents, they do not realize that they have been given a call which transcends that. For example, the Pharisees and scribes wanted to label Jesus as a false prophet. They told Him, "Thy mother and thy brethren stand without, desiring to see thee" (Luke 8:20). Had Jesus turned from the present work of the Lord to honor His mother or His brothers, they would have cried, "You see, He is no true prophet. He has not renounced His mother. See, He turns back from following God." Jesus used the occasion to teach a deeper lesson by saying, "My mother and my brethren are these which hear the word of God, and do it" (v. 21).

One word of clarification may be needed here. The Pharisees and scribes began to make false use of this principle. They said that "If any one tells his father or his mother, What you would have gained from me is given to God, he need not honor his father (Matt.

15:5 RSV)." Jesus told them that for the sake of their tradition, they had made void the word of God. Every Christian should beware of this trap. We are all to renounce the continuing carnal influence of parental holds upon us when we become adult Christians, so that we may become free in Christ; but that freedom is not license to reject parental duty.

Once again it is a matter of truly hearing and obeying God. When He calls us apart, we have to turn our backs on much, if not everything that has been important to us, which may include our parents. Certainly the Holy Spirit will seek to destroy idolatrous relationships with any family, in order that He might instate true love and honor. No human being, by his own powers, can possibly discern fully the difference between idolizing and honoring one's parents. As always, we are dependent on Jesus who alone can guide us along this narrow way.

Lazarus was a friend Jesus loved. "Now *Jesus loved* Martha, and her sister, and Lazarus. When he had heard *therefore* that he was sick, *he abode two days still in the same place where he was*. Then *after that* saith he to his disciples, Let us go into Judea again" (John 11:5-7). To the carnal mind, how can that be love? Hearing of a friend's sickness, to remain where He was? Martha said it, "Lord, if thou hadst been here, my brother had not died" (v. 21). Mary said the same thing (v. 32). He had to bear the reproach of His dearest friends.

If Jesus had rushed to His friend's side, it would have been disobedience and idolatry. That would have jeopardized His friend. True love would not do that. No call had come from Lazarus, but his sisters were not above "using" the friendship—"behold, he whom thou lovest is sick" (v. 3). What they did was wrong. To inform Him that Lazarus was ill was a true duty. To remind Jesus that "he whom thou lovest is ill" was to put a burden of friendship upon the call for help. It was an attempt to control and manipulate Him. The words were insulting, as though they had to remind Him of His love. Fear had overcome Mary's and Martha's walk in the Spirit.

Similar kinds of things happen today in the church. Mary Jones is sick. The pastor is informed, but does not come. Mary's family is indignant. How ashamed we should be of our demands when, at heart, they are idolatrous. Friendship is wonderful, but it can be a cloak for idolatry and, as such, will try to supercede God's bidding. This thing has happened countless times in the church. Our friendship and our labors must not place any special demand upon a servant of God. We have not bought anything by our labors. God's servant owes us nothing. He must, if he is true to his calling, come or go only where the Holy Spirit directs him. If he answers a need other than our own, it does not mean that he does not care for us. Our supposed righteous demands upon his time mean that we're only hungry for attention, not God's glory.

Some time ago I was in California at a teaching mission. One of my dearest parishioners was suddenly and tragically killed. Now the question lay upon my heart. Should I, as pastor, rush home to Idaho to comfort the family? Or should I stay where I was? Had not the Lord known when the man would die? I was in California as a prophet and teacher. I believed that the Bible taught that that call should take precedence (1 Cor. 12:28). Nevertheless, I repaired to the Lord quickly to discover whether the law prevailed or the Holy Spirit had some new word to me. The word was to stay in California. That could mean a church in uproar, and friends greatly hurt. Praise the Lord, those few who tried to fuss were simply heard without response. The Lord protected me as I obeyed and supported me through His loving body. I talked with the friends by phone, they were ministered to by a brother pastor, and they understood. God is faithful, and so was His church.

The church sometimes wrongly thinks it pays pastors or evangelists and therefore has "a right to its money's worth." How out of order is this thinking. No servant of the Lord can be purchased and remain God's man or woman. He must be responsible to his duties, yes, but not so that the people may have *their* money's worth. He lives from money given to God. The church should learn not only how to support His servants, but how to check them lest their liberty become license. The Word gives guidelines. The Spirit must rule afresh in each instance.

The woman in our story has well learned the lessons of prophecy. Not only does she leave her waterpot, she leaves the Lord. Peter, James, and John wanted to stay on the mountain top with Jesus (Matt. 17:4). The church often falls prey to the notion that it is primarily in worship services and prayer group meetings that the real presence of Jesus is to be found. The *feeling* of His presence may truly be strongest in group meetings. Perhaps that is as it should be, but the church must not live by feelings for the feelings of which people speak in this context are always good feelings. But Jesus is wherever suffering is (Matt. 25:40). Where people ache and need, that is where He is. That is where the church is called to be. Worship services are refreshments and training between true labors of love. The worship service is neither the first labor nor the primary place of His presence. This Samaritan woman does not fall into the error of making an idol of His euphoric personal presence. She immediately thinks of others, leaves His presence as she should, and goes to others who do not yet know Him.

We can forgive her for hyperbole—it seems unlikely they had time for Him to tell her *all* things she ever did (v. 29). Weren't we all pretty enthusiastic when He first came into our hearts?

Observe one final prophetic lesson in her behavior. We might expect her to blurt out, "This is the Christ himself!" But the Spirit's check is upon her lips. Therefore she puts it, "Is not this the Christ?" (John 4:29). Her certainty has not entitled her to abrogate her fellow man's search. And her restraint bore fruit. They came back to tell her, "Now we believe, not because of thy saying: for we have heard him ourselves, and know that this is indeed the Christ, the Savior of the world" (John 4:42).

Many brilliant prophets, preachers, teachers and evangelists have magnificently laid out the truth time and again, then puzzled when their hearers seemed to get it at the time only to fall back into unbelief and forgetfulness. Has the devil come and snatched away the word? Do we need to pray harder for protection? Perhaps not, maybe we have never learned the lesson of transparency. We have done too much, not too little. We took away their right to discover. Our hearers fail because the search has not become their own. Wise is the servant of God who has learned to invite others into the search rather than to tell others too many answers.

Behind the story of the woman at the well is one final lesson. The neophyte becomes preoccupied with making things go, whatever they are—healing, preaching, teaching, etc. He doesn't really believe that God is doing it. He is striving.

The mature prophet is, as we said before, mute and meek before the will of the other person, and he is a silent observer of what God does. It is God who acts. To be a watchman or a witness is to see what God is doing. We use the word witness too often only to describe our speaking to others. Rather it means one who watches God in operation among men. To be "in the Spirit" is consequently to be one who is not acting within his own energies or his own flesh, but as one attuned to the wind of the Spirit, turning as a weather vane to point where He moves.

Such watching involves all our energies, for God's love is flowing through us to the other, while the other's sin, sickness and death are flowing past us to the cross. Unfortunately, what should flow *past* us to the cross often flows *through* us. In this way burden bearers become overburdened. How great is the weight of carrying too much for the Lord.

How blessed it is when the Lord's servant learns these two lessons: "Behold, the former things are come to pass, and new things do I declare: before they spring forth I tell you of them" (Isa. 42:9) and "There remaineth therefore a rest to the people of

God. For he that is entered into his rest, he also hath ceased from his own works, as God did from his" (Heb. 4:9,10). When I first saw my responsibility to intercede for others, I couldn't turn it off. It became excruciating. If I walked downtown, I saw and felt so deeply the need of every person that it absolutely wore me out. People thought me aloof because I rushed on past, seeming not to see people—indeed for a while I did not at all—it was too painful. What relief it was to learn that the Lord's servant is blind. The Lord's servant sees nothing occult. He actuates no psychological sensitivities. He sees no visions or perceptions unless the Holy Spirit reveals.

This fact distinguishes the prophet from seers. A seer, like Jeanne Dixon, is not a prophet. The seer sees by exertion of his own considerable psychic powers—and possibly by the assistance of demonic spirits of divination. A prophet sees only what and when the Lord opens his eyes to see. He will not peep. A seer commits the first sin of forbidden knowledge. The seer peers wherever he can and often publishes what ought to be kept secret. Not so, God's prophet.

The Lord's servant has no labors. Only the Spirit labors; and what he does is done with "no sweat." The first relief of redemption is to restore men to that free walk with the Lord whereby they do nothing while God's Spirit works through them. St. Paul testified, "Whereunto I also labor, striving *according to his working*, which worketh in me mightily" (Col. 1:29).

All through the talk which Jesus held with the woman at the well, we see Him restfully following the wind of the Spirit blowing upon her. His cleverness and insight are solely those of the Father through Him. We learn these things consciously with our minds, not in order to become stuck with, "Now I've got to remember all those things," or, "I'm just too stupid to serve Him like that," or, "How could I ever be that clever?" We have all seen the most stupid people minister mightily, in great wisdom and learning. Knowledge is important, but it is not what we strive for nor is it our power.

Chapter Seven

THE PROPER DISCHARGE OF THE PROPHET'S DUTY

Only Jesus is truth. He has embodied truth, lived it, expressed it, and contained it within his own gracious character and personality. In Him, truth has become a way, *the* way, and life. This means that, for the Christian, truth has ceased to be confined solely to logical fact. Truth is either done within the character and personality of Jesus, or it has failed of fulfillment as truth, no matter how factually accurate. *A man can present truth so arrogantly that men will not listen. That man's truth has failed to find expression in our Lord's way; therefore, however factually true it may have been, it has failed to become truth to his fellow men.* Men may stubbornly resist truth, however well presented, but our concern here is the way in which the messenger presents that truth. "A bad messenger plunges men into trouble, but a faithful envoy brings healing" (Prov. 13:17 RSV).

For example, suppose a prophet is told by the Holy Spirit that farmer Jones is putting rotten apples in the bottom of his boxes. And the Lord commands the prophet to warn farmer Jones. How shall the prophet discharge this duty? If he arrogantly scolds the farmer, the farmer is unlikely to repent in his heart, even if he removes the rotten apples. The true facts will then have been made untrue to God's purpose. If, however, the prophet visits the farmer and acts as though he knows nothing, and casually tells him a story of a man who was putting rotten melons in the truckload he was sending to market, and how God's discipline regrettably had to fall on the man, the message has been conveyed well enough. We are to be " . . wise as serpents, and harmless as doves'' (Matt. 10:16).

Between 1956 and 1961 we served a small church in Streator, Illinois, while completing seminary in Chicago. We were also accumulating heavy debts, some of which were needless, but we had become so used to the pinch that we were ignoring the fact. Some of the parishioners, hearing of it, informed the conference minister, the Reverend Frank Edwards. He called us to Chicago for a visit, and took us out to lunch at his own expense. There he talked about how so many student ministers had fallen into the trap of ignoring their heavy debts. We could not help but hear and feel his love for the young clerics in his charge. There was no anger or condemnation in his tone. His spirit was weeping for us. We could find no excuse in his behavior to leap to our own defense. Instead he helped us to look at our own sin, and determine to change. And the impact of that help was so great that we kept our credit rating A-1 from then on. And we could not help but love Mr. Edwards—and other conference ministers after him.

So a prophet needs to know more than *what* to say. He needs also to discover *how* God wants him to say it. Courtesy and kindness can, however, become idols, as though if one were always gentle, that would always accomplish God's purpose. Elijah was not gentle with the widow of Zarephath (1 Kings 17:11-13), nor was Jesus with the Samaritan woman (John 4:7). Moses, on the other hand, was disciplined because he struck the rock twice (Num. 20:11,12). Methods and rules (like, always be kind) will inevitably get us into trouble. We must depend on the Holy Spirit alone.

The prophet must rebuke. He has no other choice.

Son of man, speak to the children of thy people, and say unto them, When I bring the sword upon a land, if the people of the land take a man of their coasts, and set him for their watchman: If when he seeth the sword come upon the land, he blow the trumpet, and warn the people; Then whosoever heareth the sound of the trumpet, and taketh not warning; if the sword come, and take him away, his blood shall be upon his own head. He heard the sound of the trumpet, and took not warning; his blood shall be upon him. But he that taketh warning shall deliver his soul. But if the watchmen see the sword come, and blow not the trumpet, and the people be not warned; if the sword come, and take any person from among them, he is taken away in his iniquity; but his blood will I require at the watchman's hand. So thou, O son of man, I have set thee a watchman unto the house of Israel; therefore thou shalt hear the word at my mouth, and warn them from me. When I say unto the wicked, O wicked man, thou shalt surely die; if thou dost not speak to warn the wicked from his way, that wicked man shall die in his iniquity; but his blood will I require at thine hand. Nevertheless, if thou warn the wicked of his way to turn from it; if he do not turn from his way, he shall die in his iniquity; but thou hast delivered thy soul.

Ezekiel 33:2-9

Not only must he rebuke, he will also be held accountable for the way he does it. For instance, "He went up from there to Bethel; and while he was going up on the way, some small boys came out of the city and jeered at him, saying, 'Go up, you baldhead! Go up, you baldhead!' And he turned around, and when he saw them, he cursed them in the name of the Lord. And two she-bears came out of the woods and tore forty-two of the boys" (2 Kings 2:23,24 RSV). Bethel was a favorite place of prayer for the prophets. The children shouted, "Go up. Go up." The place of prayer was high upon the mountain top. Times were hard; people had fallen away

91

from prayer. Since children often express what is in their parents' hearts (no matter what the parents say with their lips), these children were taunting Elisha about prayer. They were expressing their parents' doubt.

Elisha may not have been bald at all, and most likely was not. A man of age and wisdom, whose hair had turned snowy white, was honored among men, and was called an "almond tree," because his white hair was like unto the blooming of that tree (Eccles. 12:5). Baldness was taken to be a sign of defilement and disgrace (Lev. 14:8, Num. 6:9, Deut. 21:12, etc.). Samson lost his power when shaven (Judg. 16:19).

The term "baldhead" was a double taunt. It meant both one who is silly, disgraced, and outcast because he believes in prayer, and one who has become a Nazarite set apart for God (Num. 6:18). The children were actually taunting the Lord through His servant. Perhaps they meant no more than foolish children usually do by their taunting. But that kind of behavior cannot be tolerated by the Lord, for the sake of the children's souls if for no other reason. The prophet must rebuke, or God's discipline will be upon him.

Elisha did not do the disciplining. He only turned and "cursed them in the name of the Lord" (v. 24). In the next chapter we shall study the operation of the law. The curse will then be more fully understandable. For now suffice it to say that he asked the Lord to arrange for these children to reap quickly what they had sown by their actions. But he did it in the name of the Lord. Knowing we should pray in the name of the Lord, we carefully tack His name onto the end of our prayers. But that doesn't really do the job. The name of a person stands for his destiny, purpose, and character. The name Jesus means "God saves." His destiny is salvation; His purpose is to love us to heaven; His character is gentleness, kindness and love. Therefore Elisha called for this discipline not only in the authority of the Lord but within His loving nature, His purpose, and His will.

Elisha then left. It would take two she-bears a while to make their way out of the woods and down to the city walls. It was up to God to discipline His children in His own way. Elisha most likely had no idea how or when the Father would discipline, only that He would. As the Father later commanded the fish with the shekel in its mouth (Matt. 17:27), and again the one hundred and fifty-three fishes (John 21:11) for Peter's sake, He then commanded the two she-bears.

We see even heavier discipline acted out in the New Testament. Peter saw the hand of death fall upon both Ananias and Sapphira (Acts 5:1-11). Had Peter acted in his own anger, God's wrath would have been upon him. Peter asked his questions to allow both Ananias and Sapphira ample grace, and every possible opportunity to repent. Nor did Peter call for death upon Ananias. Ananias simply died. Peter knew that the same would happen to Sapphira if she did not repent. Therefore he tried to give her chances to confess truth and repent.

Whoever sees only harshness and stern judgment in Peter or God, has most likely imputed into the situation only his own judgment and fear. Worse, he has missed the loving nature of God. We do not believe Ananias and Sapphira went to hell. They were Christians. Christ had died for them. God knew that since they had set their souls to do evil, they would eventually become so corrupt of heart they would turn to reject their salvation. Therefore it was mercy to take them home out of the body before they were lost entirely. Do we not see the same in St. Paul's command, " . . . to deliver this man to Satan *for the destruction of the flesh,* that his *spirit may be saved* in the day of the Lord Jesus" (1 Cor. 5:5 RSV). To God the death of the body is not the worst thing. He weeps for death of soul and spirit. Therefore sometimes He must take life in order to save it.

God's nature has in it both wrath and mercy, both sternness and gentleness. We therefore have no business judging the prophet's work from the standpoint of the flesh. What seems unkind and unfair to us, or out of place, especially because of the manner in which it was done, may be the action of the Holy Spirit, not the flesh. We are called only to obey God, not to judge the prophet's manner. God will judge the prophet.

In 1960 Paula and I attended our first School of Pastoral Care conducted by Agnes Sanford. One incident stands out in my memory. During the question and answer time one afternoon, a gentleman of imposing mien stood to ask a question. Agnes answered gently and fully. He was not satisfied. He asked another, an unnecessary detail of the same question. Agnes answered again gently, but with an edge in her voice, and tacked on a kindly warning that he had been answered and there were others who had questions. The man did not take heed. Disagreeing, he took it upon himself to remonstrate with her. He could have disputed with her later, in private. Never have we seen a man so humbled, humiliated and put in his place as he was by the sharpness of her answer. He never said a word the entire remainder of the school.

Some did not understand. They thought Agnes unfair. But the Spirit immediately checked me, and opened my mind to the Scriptures about rebuke. A quick check in the concordance will show that it is firmly within the realm of possibilities for Christians who walk in the Spirit.

The prophet should be careful to walk in the Spirit all the time. He is to pray constantly. This often means silent prayer in tongues. St. Paul said, "I thank my God, I speak with tongues more than ye all" (1 Cor. 14:18). Praying like this edifies (builds up) the one who speaks (1 Cor. 14:4). It gives him rest when weary (Isa. 28:12). It keeps his spirit tuned to God's Spirit. Therefore the Holy Spirit can quickly check him when needful. Secondly he must have so read and reread, so devoured the Bible that the Spirit can recall to his mind those parts of the Word most appropriate for the fire of the moment. The Lord's prophet is a man of the word. If he does not know the Scripture, there is great danger of his being deluded.

On the other side, while there are occasions when the prophet must rebuke sharply, we often are guilty of shooting canaries with shotguns. How often have we blasted some poor little Christian with a cannon when a pebble would have done? Therefore, that he occasionally has a right to express God's anger gives no license to the prophet, rather it gives him a grave responsibility to sense and follow the spirit's leading and to deny himself.

The joint tasks of building up and unifying the church are never spelled out as the commission of any Old Testament prophet. This, however, has become the ground of every New Testament prophet's charge, whatever specific commission may be his. If what he has been told to do or say would jeopardize or attack edification or unity, the Christian prophet should ask for confirming signs before he takes any action.

Much of this upbuilding will be done in secret. The command to pray in secret (Matt. 6:1-6) is to all of God's children. To the prophet the command has distinct application. Much of what is revealed to him could create unnecessary fright or turmoil if told abroad. One day I saw a vision of my friend, Ken Campbell, caught and being sucked down in a whirlpool. I had no idea whether the pool could be a literal pool of water or a set of circumstances or both. I had no feeling that I should say anything at all to Ken. This was distinctly a call to intercessory prayer. The Lord, seeing what lay ahead, did not want Ken drowned nor sucked under by problems. I prayed for Ken's protection, and said nothing. The next day, Ken went fishing with his son, Greg. It was too early in the season to wade the streams; the high current could sweep a man away. Ken was standing on a rock by a deep pool, watching a great whirlpool forming in front of him and thinking, "Man, if a fellow got caught in that, he would never get out." Just then, Greg floated by! There was nothing to do but throw down his pole and jump in after him. Greg was carried easily by the current to safety. But Ken was caught in the whirlpool. To this day he does not know how he managed to get out alive. Would Ken have drowned if God had not warned? Would he have gotten out anyway? No one, including me, can answer those questions. I merely praised God for saving my friend.

On another occasion, in a dream, I saw a miner being caught and crushed under rocks in a mine tunnel. Again, I was not to tell anyone. It was a call to prayer. The next week, the head deacon, a faithful man, was barely missed by tumbling boulders, which made a little nick in his thumb. A member who seldom attended church was barely missed in another crash of rocks, and a gash was cut in his leg. A third member, who never attended, was hurled by an ore car against a wall, breaking several ribs. I praised God that none was killed. To this day the speculation is not answered: was there less possibility to protect the men who were less obedient to the Lord? Were these men further out from under the under-shepherd's care? Did prayer have anything to do with their protection? We *believe* so but we do not *know* so.

The prophet may also be told of some great blessing coming to the church. Unless the Lord tells him to make public the glad news, or orders him to summon the church to believe what is coming and to pray for it, the prophet probably has no mandate to speak. An old proverb says, "Do not talk away your good fortune." God usually keeps blessings hidden until He springs them upon us, lest we do something to block them, or claim credit to ourselves. "I have declared the former things from the beginning; and they went forth out of my mouth, and I showed them; I did them suddenly, and they came to pass. Because I knew that thou art obstinate, and thy neck is an iron sinew, and thy brow brass . . . " (Isa. 48:3-4). Often if God foretells something to the entire community, it is so cryptic we do not see it clearly. Has not almost every charismatic church received prophecies of blessing? And did not we usually misinterpret or fail to understand completely the good that was to come to us? God planned it that way, for there is something of Herod in all of us, something that would kill the Christ child coming into our midst, if we could discover enough details.

The prophet can be tempted to congeal God's revelation into too concrete terms. To what God has said, he may add what he only thinks His words meant, and not realize he has confused the striving of his mind with God's word. Jesus said, "Take heed . . . how ye hear" (Luke 8:18).

An entire prayer group stood at the grave of a dear lost member, sure that the Lord had prophesied that he would return to life. Probably the Lord had spoken but with quite different intentions. Martha carefully ruled out such misinterpretations when she said, "I know that he shall rise again in the resurrection at the last day" (John 11:24). Jesus told her He had far more than that in mind. One man we know announced that a certain blessing was coming to him. It did not come. Instead, a great rebuke fell upon him in another area. That rebuke turned him about and became the greatest blessing in his life. That was the blessing the Lord meant.

Prophets should not only be careful how they hear the Lord; they also need to learn that people's wishes can affect their hearing. One friend called me, long distance, in great consternation. "My son just took off with three friends to fly from Seattle to Sun Valley. A squall came up. They haven't been heard from. Search planes are up. Can you give us a word from God?" We need to be careful not to be placed in the position of seers or wizards. Saul thought Samuel was a seer who could tell him where to find his lost asses. This is not the primary function of a prophet. (1 Sam. 9:9). But my friend wanted to know where her son was. So I asked the Lord anyway. The answer was immediate. They had flown north, not south, and were lost. There was no hope. I tried as gently as I could to tell her over the phone. Unbeknownst to me, the woman had such confidence in me, she persuaded the searchers to switch the operation to cover the northern area indicated. Then she called me again and again. Her importunity worked upon me and then upon my clarity with God. I began to think the Lord was telling me good news through various visions, which I passed on to my friend. I was not sufficiently aware how our connections with others in our spirit can affect our channel with God. The next summer, when the snow melted, the crashed plane was found, in the area I had first indicated. The falling snow had immediately hidden it. The four had died instantly.

Prophets must learn to adhere to the first word God gives them. During the reign of Jeroboam in Israel (the northern kingdom) a prophet came from Judah to Bethel to work a sign for Jeroboam. He was commanded to return home without turning aside and without eating bread there. But a local prophet in Bethel heard of his performance that day, came to him, and persuaded him to eat. The prophet of Judah was then slain by a lion. Not only did the prophet lose his life, but all of the dire things he had prophesied came to pass. The inference of the story was that had he obeyed, God could have spared Jeroboam's house (1 Kings 13).

There is a delicate balance between two seemingly contrary commands of the Lord. First, the prophet must not listen to the voice of other men. He must hear God only. Second, he must check all things with his brothers and not stand apart as a renegade. How can the prophet observe both of these principles?

David Wilkerson made public a vision of five warnings given to him by the Lord. One was that charismatic Catholics would have the welcome mat pulled out from under them by the hierarchy of the church. Some of the leaders in the charismatic movement have said that perhaps Wilkerson did not check with the body before presenting this divisive word; and some have said that perhaps the vision reveals some unconscious biases in Wilkerson.

Let us see whether we can bring some clarity. First, warnings call to repentance or preparation. They do not have to happen as prophesied. God warns us to protect us from dire consequences or to strengthen our resolve. For example, a few years ago a servant of the Lord whom we know well was warned by a prophetess that she had seen his plane crashing in flames as he flew to speak in Australia. Unfortunately our friend saw this in only one light. He decided not to go. It did not occur to him that he might use the warning to pray that the accident be averted. Moses and Elijah appeared on the mount with Jesus, ". . . and spake of his decease which he should accomplish at Jerusalem" (Luke 9:31). That did not keep Jesus from going; it prepared him for what He should endure. Agabus, a prophet of Judea, bound Paul's hands and feet with his girdle and warned Paul that he would be bound by the Gentiles in like manner if he went to Jerusalem. Paul's company and the people at Jerusalem pleaded with Paul not to go to Jerusalem (Acts 21:8-14). Paul, however, was ". . . ready not to be bound only, but also to die at Jerusalem for the name of the Lord Jesus" (v. 13).

Both Jesus and Paul had received prior orders as to where they were to go. They would not turn from their original courses, no matter what the company of the Lord said to them. The warnings given to Paul were not to deter him. They were a preparation and a call to prayer. Praise God that neither Jesus nor Paul turned from his assigned course. Our faith would not exist had Jesus let the disciples deter him. The book of Romans would never have been written had Paul not determined to go to Jerusalem.

Even before the transfiguration Peter had tried to keep Jesus from going to Jerusalem (Mark 8:31-33), but Jesus rebuked him. The body of Christ is never to preempt the prophet's original order. Remember also what we said earlier about surprises. The prophecy was that the *Gentiles* would bind Paul's hands and feet. It was, however, the *Jews* who caused the trouble. Paul's appeal to Rome resulted in his being bound by the Gentiles (Roman legionnaires) who escorted him safely out of Jerusalem and later brought him, as he had hoped, to Rome.

Both Jesus and Paul had received their own private orders to go to Jerusalem. In both cases, confirmation from the community came in the form of talk about sufferings ahead. Neither thought that his orders would always have to come through the body. Neither thought that what God had told them in private had to be agreed to by the body. Confirmation by the Lord through the body may not mean agreement. The prophet, having an assignment from the Lord, should check with his brothers for advice as to how to discharge his duty, but he must not let that advice deter him from it altogether if his guidance is clear and has been otherwise confirmed. "For by wise counsel thou shalt make thy war: and in multitude of counselors there is safety" (Prov. 24:6).

David Wilkerson has been charged with not consulting with the brethren before presenting his warnings. Perhaps. We do not know. We presume that he did check. Perhaps David could have been wiser in presenting his five warnings. Perhaps not. But the church is *not* called to quibble about the way a servant of the Lord discharges his duty. The church is called only to respond. Praise God that David Wilkerson had the courage to risk his own personal popularity to give God's message.

Wilkerson has also been charged with presenting a divisive message. Nonsense! He did not order anyone to separate from anyone. He warned that division could occur. This is the Lord speaking for unity. Let the church respond humbly, alertly, and quickly on its knees before the Lord.

What David foresaw does not have to happen. God warns in order that it might not. Nineveh was not destroyed when Jonah finally obeyed and gave warning. Paul's bane was turned to blessing. If none of what Dave Wilkerson saw happens, that will in no wise prove him a false prophet, just as Jonah was not. It will only mean that the Lord's own have heard and responded and God has turned to heal their land (2 Chron. 7:14). At this writing several of the political and natural disasters predicted by David have already happened.

Does this mean that prophets never make mistakes? Of course not. God tells us they will, and that He himself will bring it about

(Deut. 13:1-4). Too often the church wants to assure itself that there are some things God will never allow to happen. Such thinking is presumptuous and inevitably dangerous.

If every prophet spoke only absolute truth, whom would the people follow? Not the Lord but the prophets. To prevent that, God uses cracked and foolish vessels. Every man must therefore check his own spirit, heart, and mind according to the word, whenever a prophet speaks to him in the name of the Lord. God uses cracked vessels for this very reason, that we must ever turn to Him to ask, "Lord, what does this mean? What do you want me to do?"

A prophet must do all that he can to assure that his word is truly from the Lord. Jeremiah and Ezekiel both warned of horrors for the prophet who does not (chapters 23 and 13, respectively). And the prophet should counsel with his brothers, and let God confirm His word to him. Once these are done, the prophet must not be deterred from his task by either friend or foe.

If he were a video or a phone, the prophet could glibly say, "Whatever I say is all of the Lord. I have no responsibility. Take it up with God." But he is a person, and speaks for the Lord as such. He must learn to rejoice that however wrong he may be, it is God who speaks through him. But he must also learn to stand in without using God as a dodge, and say, "Yes, I said that, and I will take responsibility for it. Deal with me, brothers, that I may learn." Under the new covenant the prophet's errors are not dealt with as they were in former days. Deuteronomy 13:5 commanded that erring prophets be put to death. Under the new covenant the gentle mercy of the cross brings first death, then life (Gal. 6:1). Let us not fear either to speak or to hear the word of a prophet. In either case, God will deal with us, and comfort us after affliction (1 Pet. 5:6-11).

The prophet does not address the general public. Insofar as he is an evangelist, he may also work to convert outsiders. But he and his works are given *as signs* only to believers (1 Cor. 14:22). Unlike the Jeanne Dixons, et al., true prophets do not announce

This man just brought Prophecy to nothing wind Default

what they know to the general public. They speak to the church. If the public hears, well and good, but the prophet's address is to the Lord's own.

"Give not that which is holy unto the dogs, neither cast ye your pearls before swine, lest they trample them under their feet, and turn again and rend you" (Matt. 7:6). "Dogs" in biblical countries meant anyone who was an outsider. Pearls stood for wisdom or revelation. If a man had a greedy, unbelieving, rapacious streak, it was called "a pig of the mind." We should not give holy revelation to outsiders, nor cast pearls of wisdom before people who have such pigs of the mind that they will turn and scoff at the speaker, rending the Lord's thoughts by their unbelief.

About four years ago, the Lord warned Paula and me that unless the entire Silver Valley (Shoshone County, Idaho) repented of its sins, judgment would come upon it in the form of fire and smoke and cause many deaths. Much confusion and hurt would result. The Wallace United Church of Christ was to stand as a rock in a sea of confusion. None of our own people were to be hurt in any way. The Lord told me to warn the body of Christ to take heed, repent and pray.

However, I was too young in the prophetic calling. I should have gone quietly to the various prayer groups of all the churches and called the Lord's elect to stand in prayer. Rather, I misjudged the spiritual maturity of my own church. Too many of my parishioners were not ready to understand such a vision, nor to know what to do about it. I warned that great tragedy would come in the valley if it did not repent of its ways. People in and out of the church rose up in great anger at me. "If he doesn't like the valley, why doesn't he get out of it?" "This is a good place to live." (Never mind that five open houses of prostitution existed in a town of 3,000 at the time.) "This valley isn't any more sinful than any other place; where does he get off? . . ."

The Sunshine Mine disaster happened on May 2, about two years later. Fire and smoke were the agents of destruction as prophesied. Carbon monoxide poisoning took the lives of ninety-one men. Great confusion and hurt prevailed in the valley. The church did stand as a rock in a sea of confusion, operating a nursery for all visitors and miners' wives and families, serving as a Red Cross center, making sandwiches and refreshments in its kitchen to supply the people at the mine, sending many of its men into the mine to rescue work, and eventually serving as host to many funerals too large for other churches to contain. None of our congregation's members were lost or hurt in any way. Our head deacon, who was foreman of the electricians, had been in the mine that morning and had come out. One young man had been switched from day shift to night shift the week before. Another had broken his ankle the week before. And so it went. The prophecy was fulfilled in every detail. Some members remembered the warnings and remarked about how specifically they had been realized.

A prophet must give his warning to the right people. Had I gone to the other pastors and to their prayer groups, they could have joined in prayer. That way, every pastor would have had opportunity to protect his flock from the impending peril. The warning was to the entire valley; therefore it should have been presented to the right people throughout the entire valley. I confused the positions of pastor and prophet. I gave the warning to my own flock, and through them word got out—haphazardly and frantically—to the rest of the valley. Thus they heard and were responsible, in spite of my immaturity.

Disasters do not necessarily impugn the characters of their victims (Luke 13:2-5). Our miners were not any more or less sinful than those in any other mine. Men's sins pile up like rocks on a ledge. Eventually that pile will break the ledge and cause a landslide. The man who happens to be walking by at that moment and is crushed is not more or less sinful than those who do not. Thus the relation of sin to tragedy is more likely corporate than personal. That may seem unfair but it actually works to our advantage in that just as only a relative few die in any disaster, so only a relative few need to repent and intercede in order to avert disaster.

Nor was the valley, though copiously sinful, perhaps any more sinful than other places. The call was for the valley to repent *of its own* sins, but the harm that came upon the valley may have been due to the sins of mankind in general as much or more than for its own sins.

Many may not be prepared to see any relation at all between such disasters and human sinfulness. They may want to attribute such things entirely to chance, and scoff at any other explanations. The relation between sin and sickness, or sin and tragedy, is gone from the minds of too many of us. But we need to regain it. For that reason we regard the next three chapters, "The Good, the Acceptable and the Perfect Will of God," "The Stopping Place," and "The Creative Power of the Word in Prayer" as pivotal. If this understanding is not accepted, then the whole purpose and function of prophets cannot be grasped at all, much less fulfilled. So, if your mind is reeling with questions, or disgust, or fear, hang on.

I happen to be a friend of the then vice-president and superintendent of the Sunshine Mine. A few days before the disaster, I was playing basketball with him in his back yard. As I drove away, the Holy Spirit said to me, "There is a fire in the Sunshine Mine. Something can still be done about it. Go back and warn Marvin." I thought, "That's crazy! How can there be a fire in a hard rock mine? Marvin would think I'm nuts. And what if nothing were found? Good grief!" So I prayed, "Lord, I can't believe I heard rightly. But just in case there was something to it, please protect the men, and help them find that fire." But we cannot ask God to do what He had told us to do. We can pray for good crops, but He won't plant our corn or harvest our fields. Later I learned that Marvin would have believed me and checked, had I given the warning.

The Father's first will is not always done among men, or Jesus would not have taught us to pray, "Thy kingdom come, Thy will be done on earth as it is in Heaven." My heart was crushed when the fire broke out and men began to die. For days I reeled under the impact of my responsibility. I eventually learned that God's mercy is always bigger than my capacity to goof. And God does not want a prophet to fold up because he failed, but to let the lesson of it be scored deeply into his heart.

Scored deeply into the heart. . . . A prophetess once told me, "John, you don't let anything really get to you. You block everything out. If you start to feel a real emotion, you catch it with that quick, analytical mind of yours, jump on it, cut it up into pieces, put it in boxes and shut it all off. Why don't you just live something all the way through once?" In twenty years I had never raised my voice or a hand to Paula. In a few days, I blew up at her. Paula giggled and blurted out, "Hallelujah, you've become real!"

The Lord's servant must not rationalize too soon. He should live whatever is upon him all the way through, then let the mercy of the cross release his heart. If he goes too quickly to the cross, it becomes a cop out. He must repair instantly to God, of course. But the Lord will sometimes not let him come to Golgotha without Gethsemane. To flee to the cross and claim resurrection victory prematurely can be self-deceiving for the heart needs time for sorrow.

God knows our failures before they ever happen and has His grace always ready to help us past them. Realizing this helped me, one day, to up and resign the general managership of the universe. What a relief! Together Paula and I then learned that much of our frantic praying and caring for others had not actually been born of His love as we assumed, but of unbelief. We did not fully believe that God truly does have everything in His hands. Consequently we had become melancholy Danes.

The time is out of joint; O cursed spite,
That ever I were born to set it right!

Hamlet, I,V, 188

105

We pour the oil of comfort on the tragedy God's hand was using to bring His child to the desperation which is prelude to salvation. As Bob Mumford says, "If we fix the fix God has fixed to fix us, God will only have to fix another fix to fix us!"

So we began to learn not to take ourselves too seriously. One of the surest signs of inner healing is that the person can look back and have a good belly laugh at himself. Conversely one of the surest signs of inner turmoil and unsettledness is the inability to chuckle. Most of a new prophet's mistakes come from doing too much rather than too little. Though our freedom to fail is not to be used by us as license to escape from responsibility, a part of a prophet's sanity-saving armor is the happy knowledge that if he goofs, God is big enough to take care of it. Isn't it a wonderful relief to know that our sin is not omnipotent?!

God knew all along precisely to what depths our sinfulness would carry us. And He knew just how much and how little we would let Him enter to comfort and prevent. Therefore we fall no further than the moment we needed to "come to ourselves" (Luke 15:17). Right there, in the middle of the mess, is where the Lord has His prophet. He learns to relax in the mess. His freedom is not to go right on in whatever the mess is. His freedom is from the tension of the mess.

I have learned, in whatsoever state I am, therewith to be content. I know both how to be abased, and I know how to abound: everywhere and in all things I am instructed both to be full and to be hungry, both to abound and to suffer need. I can do all things through Christ which strengtheneth me.

Philippians 4:11-13

Chapter Eight

THE GOOD, THE ACCEPTABLE, AND THE PERFECT WILL OF GOD

A father wants to raise his sons in love and gentleness, within the happiness of understanding and cooperation. Sons, however, have a way of going astray. They are full of mischief, capriciousness, and laziness. And there comes the day in every father's life when he has to face this rude fact and decide what to do about it. He may try to control or manipulate them, but usually with disappointing results. What many fathers finally settle on is a combination of acceptance and discipline. He permits them to goof, but not to escape discipline. He chastises, instructs, exhorts and scolds that his sons may grow strong in righteousness.

If, however, his sons will not heed his instruction and discipline, if they leave his house as did the prodigal, then his sons can no longer be protected by his corrective hand. They must therefore reap unprotected whatever they sow. A son can ultimately fall to such disgrace that, for the protection of the rest of the family, a father must act against every other level of his will, disowning and disinheriting his own son.

Consider then the problem of God. He would have sons. Unlike human fathers, He could make them in an instant, all perfect. But what would He have? Robots. Sons, however, are companions.

Sons love because they choose to. Delight of heart to heart and mind to mind can occur only where one freely chooses to cherish another.

Thus God limits himself. He must not break the rules of the game, or He will not have sons. Even God must pay the price. That price is the prize and thorn of human free will, sticking like a diamond needle into all the web of God's planning, necessitating that all of creation and history weave the fabric of life around it.

The tears of God splash about this one heartrending fact, that the loving Father God restrains His omnipotent saving hand. The heart of the Father weeps for His sons even as He casts them into the earth (Matt. 13:37-38), while the wisdom of God, looking to the long morning of joy, rejoices to see the celebration beyond the sorrow of the night (Ps. 126:6).

From before creation it was ordained that the Son should come, and suffer, and die (John 17:24; Eph. 1:4-7). Evil was inevitable because of free will. Reparation and restoration, healing and forgiveness were also therefore built into the creation from the beginning. But even so people had to choose; nothing was automatic. So the Father must give time for men to discover the effects of the law of sowing and reaping. Though the Father would love to straighten up every child's mess instantly, He must not, or His sons will never learn. Burnt fingers are thus the inevitable price of learning.

Forgiveness, therefore, could not be automatic. The heart of our gentle, loving, perfect Father could not but forgive. But as sometimes an earthly father greets a wayward son with a forgiving heart, yet knows that he must restrain and talk, so that the son may grow by seeing his error, and confessing, so even He whose heart bursts with tenderness must bristle with wrath for His child's sake.

While forgiveness awaits conviction, confession, and the cry for mercy, men stumble about God's ordered universe, setting in motion forces which can do naught but redound to destruction. Men become like boys set loose with ball and bat in a china shop, or worse, like infants pushing buttons in an automated cement factory. They would for the most part remain blissfully unaware of what they had set in motion, while machines formed fiery messes to pour over their own heads. Thus from the beginning Christ paid for sin in its every ultimate legal demand of all the forces of the universe, seen and unseen! Mankind's nursery had to be so designed that men could have horror enough to learn, but safety enough to continue.

There are three distinct levels of God's will: ". . . that ye may prove what is that good, and acceptable, and perfect will of God" (Rom. 12:2). The first level is His perfect will which has not yet come on earth. For it we pray, "Thy kingdom come, thy will be done, on earth, as it is in Heaven." Heaven shall some day descend to earth "as a bride adorned for her husband" (Rev. 21:2). That prayer, for the coming of His kingdom, which has ascended out of the throats of countless millions, will some day be answered.

The Father's perfect will cannot come in fullness to any individual. One person may become so obedient to the Spirit that he often moves as a finger of God inseparable from hand and wrist. But can a perfect violin solo be a concert? Can an aria comprise an opera? Without our brother, none of us shall be complete. "For what is our hope or joy or crown of boasting before our Lord Jesus at his coming? Is it not you? For you are our glory and joy" (1 Thess. 2:19,20 RSV). "For now we live, if ye stand fast in the Lord" (1 Thess. 3:8). No man can become all that he should without every other brother whom God has designed to be part of him.

But we can be in that perfect will which is His plan for our lives. "For we are his workmanship, created in Christ Jesus unto good works, which God hath before ordained that we should walk in them" (Eph. 2:10). That does not mean that we become perfect. We remain corrupt so long as the kingdom has not fully descended. And we are in peril the moment we forget this. Rather, to be in His perfect will means that for the moment He has overcome our wayward tendencies, and we are walking hand in hand with Him by grace alone. He goes before us to dispossess nations greater and mightier than ourselves. He is opening the doors before us, and we are continually delighted with those little coincidences that bring order and fruitfulness to our lives. We find ourselves putting our foot on the brake; only then to discover the car we never saw which would have clobbered us had we not stopped. We meet accidentally the one of whom we thought earlier in the day. Thoughts flow from heart to mind to speech without interruption. The heart leaps in joy or weeps as is appropriate, for we are walking in the Spirit. We are continually surprised at what we have said or perceived—because we fail to know how we could have had such wisdom. Miracles and signs follow upon what we have said and prayed. Others seek us out and find peace in our presence. The Lord himself dwells with us and blesses us.

Most of the time, however, we are living within His acceptable or permissive will. We are saved. We are accepted as sons, adopted into His family. But we are like an aborigine at the queen's banquet. We little understand the graces of the kingdom, and worse yet, have little power to live that which we do know. Therefore we are also under the hand of discipline, and being fainthearted, we often misunderstand the approaches of God which would bring healing.

The Father may discipline us in order to awaken us from this dull state. He may take direct action, so that if we say an unkind word, we suddenly feel the flush of fire and are wrapped in instant embarrassment. Or the Father may speak through a friend or relative such words that we know the Father has reproved us. Hundreds of ways the Father has to discipline us—our car won't start, or we fall down in the mud. Whatever, it comes quickly on the heels of our offense, and it teaches us to hate our sin. But God may reprove us quite differently and more severely by absenting himself from us. In the other instances whatever caught our conscience was God's active intervention. Whereas now we are caught by impersonal, cold and efficient laws of cause and effect. We sow to the wind and reap the whirlwind.

3) This brings us to the third level of the Father's will, the good will of God, the law. It is good, utterly good, but inexorable. The whole Psalm 119 is an anthem to the goodness and perfection of the law. St. Paul says, "Wherefore the law is holy, and the commandment holy, and just, and good" (Rom. 7:12).

The law is not merely the ten commandments. Nor is it all the ordinances given throughout the Torah. These are but laws given to men. Law has its source in the nature of God. It is principle and order, the very structure and discipline of the entire universe. Nothing operates outside it, for chaos is but departure from sane principles to principles operated in a jumble. The ten commandments, indeed all of the moral laws given to man, are what God has chosen to reveal of His whole scheme of order which is far beyond our ability to comprehend.

This law is impersonal to us. But it can never be impersonal to Him, for He is love and personal in all. But we do not and cannot comprehend that mystery of love. Therefore we speak of the operation of the law as impersonal, for to us it is.

That law is relentless, for nothing changes it. Even God himself does not break His own principles. If He did, His name would be Chaos rather than Father. What seems miracle and mystery to us is in truth operation of principles beyond the principles we know.

"Whatsoever a man soweth, that shall he also reap" (Gal. 6:7). That is the good will of God. He has built the universe to operate upon principles of balance and retribution. "For every action there is an equal and opposite reaction." All of our science and technology are based upon the certainty of God's principles. If His laws were not immutable, no architect would dare to build a skyscraper, no astronaut would venture beyond earth, no electrician could wire a house.

We have somehow lost hold of the basic principles of life, the good will of God revealed in the Bible. Men who have better sense

Faith rest on revelation

than to violate business or engineering principles, somehow think they can hop into bed with any man or woman with impunity. They are like a criminal who, having not been apprehended within a week after his crime, believes he has evaded the law. The laws of God are enforced more perfectly than any criminal code in the world. There is nothing relative about them. *They describe the way reality works.*

Our faith rests upon revelation. Christians believe that the Bible contains God's moral law. Prophets must stand firmly on that belief, because all our power of intercession, our authority to forgive, and our ability to understand God's will among men is rooted there and nowhere else.

We have stressed this point because the prophet must know that there are sure girders for the tower of imagination. When man builds from his imagination, Babel is the result. When God builds, it will be within the absoluteness of the principles of His Word. Whoever is not willing to let go the prides of his own imagination to admit that some things are fixed forever, is not only not qualified to step to the plate as a prophet, he has not even entered the ball park! "Heaven and earth shall pass away: but my words shall not pass away" (Luke 21:33). Too many men, who observe physical laws to comfort and protect their lives, think they ought to be "free" (lawless) to try anything spiritually. The prophet of the Lord must have surrendered every thought captive to obey Christ (2 Cor. 10:5). He is not thereby given license to force any man to agree with him. God will convince whom He will. It is a man's business to hold whatever opinion he wants, but the prophet of the Lord who insists that he is free to experiment according to his own pleasures will nevertheless reap what he sows.

So, if a man steals from his brother, God and the brother may still love him. All of life may go on normally. Yet the boomerang he threw swishes to its inevitable return. It has nothing to do with the way God feels toward the man, except that in that specific area, God sees, has compassion and wants to warn him in order that the

112

man may repent and be spared. When God speaks so often as He does in the Old Testament how He will punish so drastically, He is not speaking of His own first will, which is always to forgive and heal, but of the way in which His good will, His unbending law, will bring retribution. He says, "I will do this thing," because His law is His law and all things are personal to Him. But from our point of view, let us see it as the reaping of what we have sown, not as God's capricious vendetta.

Whoever casts a crumb upon the waters receives a loaf of blessing. God built His entire universe upon the principle of blessed increase. His first command to mankind was to "Be fruitful and multiply" (Gen. 1:28). Whatever we do sets in motion forces which not only return but increase before they do.

"And whosoever shall give to drink unto one of these little ones a cup of cold water only in the name of a disciple, verily I say unto you, he shall in no wise lose his reward" (Matt. 10:42). There is no way a man who does this can lose his reward. But many of us have gotten the notion that if we give with wrong motivations, that somehow disqualifies the law from working. Nonsense! The law is immutable. It is no different than saying, "If I really love this girl, though we are not married, sex couldn't be sin, could it?" Let us once for all clear our heads. Sin is sin. Law is law. We reap what we sow no matter what we feel or how we're motivated.

Look at the goodness of God's law: we are continually reaping blessings from what others have sown. We reap the good results of others' inventions—wheels, tires, lights, batteries, ignitions, safety devices. Homes, appliances, clothes, TVs and radios, surgery, and medicine—what have we enjoyed which is not a reaping of the good others have sown? Madame Curie made one discovery, and all men benefited. The law is both impersonal and general. We reap what has been sown by men whose names and faces shall ever remain unknown to us. And what we sow they reap. We reap personally the good we ourselves have sown, and every man reaps the good every other man has sown. So we share in the blessings of life.

However, by that same impartiality, the criminal and the good man both use the phone and watch the TV. All reap what all have sown. God sends rain on the just and the unjust (Matt. 5:45).

Ten-year-olds demand a fairness which is puerile. I say to my son Timmy, "You go to bed when I say you go to bed. Never mind what Johnny does. I'm the daddy. You do what I say." Our demands upon God are like that. In fact our cries for justice often are no more than cloaks for our covetousness. That's what Jesus meant when He asked, "Is thine eye evil because I am good?" (Matt. 20:15).

The prophet should carefully remember to cherish God's faithfulness, no matter what awful things he sees. For if he walks now in blind faith, he shall some day graduate to hear his Lord say, "Henceforth I call you not servants; for the servant knoweth not what his lord doeth: but I have called you friends; for all things that I have heard of my Father I have made known unto you" (John 15:15). Faith must come before understanding. God will explain himself to no man that he may believe. But if a man believes, God will grant him wisdom and understanding beyond measure.

The good law of God works not only to bring blessing. It works equally impassionately and immutably to bring evil.

God has made the principles of the universe neither void nor invalid for the Christian. The same laws still operate. But Christians have been guilty of elitist feelings about themselves from the early days of the church. And at various times groups, called antinomians, have actually formed to propound the doctrine that the law is a matter of indifference for believers. How subtly we can use our freedom in Christ as a pretext to sin. We shall explain this more fully later. Suffice it now to say that as a man repents of the evil he has sown, our Lord pays the price by reaping his debt. Thus we are set free. Without the shedding of Christ's blood, there is no escape from the law.

Whatever we do can be likened unto a man throwing a rubber

ball against a wall. Physicists, knowing the weight and composition of the ball and the force of hurling power, can compute with what force that ball will return. That is law. It does not matter what the thrower thinks or feels, that ball will return according to the way he threw it.

Add to this picture the law of increase. Imagine that ball growing in size and weight the longer it flies. If it starts as a Ping-Pong ball, it grows steadily, unless it is stopped, into enormous proportions, so that the Ping-Pong ball becomes an aeronaut's balloon. Thus, when a farmer sows a single grain of wheat, it may produce a hundred more like itself.

Therefore Jesus told us not to seek our reward from men, but to lay up treasure in heaven (Matt. 6:19-21). The longer we are willing to wait for our reward, the longer the law of increase has to work and the greater will be our reward. This calls for quick confession of sin, but great secrecy and patience about our good works. Christ warned that the hypocrites "have their reward" (Matt. 6:1-6). Since they prayed or gave alms, they were to receive reward. Nothing could stop that. But they sought and received their reward too soon, on their own unfaithful terms, and from men. Therefore it was as though they had cashed in their stocks before they could appreciate in value.

A foolish notion is taught from time to time as though it were wisdom. "Don't do anything for reward. That's selfish and wrong." That's a pious fantasy that exalts human nature rather than God. Jesus *commanded* us to lay up treasure in heaven. But we think so highly of ourselves that we feel demeaned by the idea of reward. Perhaps it reminds us of an animal learning tricks for a treat. The difference may not be so great as we would like to think. We need the motivation of rewards to spur us on to righteous living (Rom. 2:4-11).

Salvation and eternal life are free gifts. But what else we receive is determined by what we have sown. "For there is no respect of persons with God." The law of reward is an impersonal, unchangeable principle. Some will find little reward waiting in heaven, whereas others will find great reward. This is part of God's justice, that the sinner converted at eighty and the faithful servant of a lifetime look not to the same rewards. The goodness of God is that He manages to prompt us to do something good—and then heaps reward upon us as though it has been entirely our own doing.

Because we have become evil, we can operate the law unto our own death. Every sin unrepented and full grown is the same as the man who throws a Ping-Pong ball, reaping in due time enormous consequences. Unfortunately, not only he but countless others reap the evil that he has sown. Shall we say that it was fair for us to reap the good, vastly multiplied, which every man has sown, and unfair if we reap the evil? It is the same impartial law. "Then desire when it has conceived gives birth to sin; and sin when it is full-grown brings forth death" (James 1:15). The longer a sin goes unrepented, the greater the danger. For the blessing of reward, the longer we wait the better. For the bane of reaping evil, the sooner we get at it the better. Therefore God's kindness is meant to lead us to repentance (Rom. 2:4 RSV). God would have us repent quickly, lest what we have sown destroy us.

Now perhaps we are prepared to understand the efficacy of the cross. In countless hymns we have sung that He paid the price for us. Did we understand the weight of what we sang? Every time any man in all the universe has sinned, he has set in motion forces which must come to resolution. This is impartial inescapable law. Full and exact payment had to be made for everything. God, knowing all the horrible things men unconsciously had set in motion, let alone what was due for conscious sin, gave, and constantly continues to give unmerited deliverance. In Jesus, on the cross, the law was not abolished; it was fulfilled (Matt. 5:17).

That cross is effective throughout all time. Time is a dimension of space. This means that that cross is like a light shining through the halls of departed time to the present. It makes little difference whether one is fifty feet removed from the cross or a million light-years; that cross is a present reality, drawing sin to itself. Full resolution for every sin is paid upon the cross. What happened on Good Friday is a part of history and yet it transcends all of history. For this reason our Lord says, "For I am the LORD, I change not; therefore ye sons of Jacob are not consumed" (Mal. 3:6). Had not God drawn everything which is BC forward to the cross, and everything AD back to it, we would all have been consumed by the fierceness of what we have sown.

Nevertheless, that mercy is not automatic. It waits upon confession. If we live outside the cross, we must reap accordingly. The moment we repent and confess, the Lord takes the due results of our sins to the cross.

Whoever understands this, and loves his Lord, never wants to sin again for he sees that grace, though free, is not cheap. The price for every sin is excruciating upon the body and within the eternal soul of Christ. Whoever commits apostasy (or any other sin knowingly) will "crucify the Son of God on their own account and hold him up to contempt" (Heb. 6:6). The mystery of time is such that our present sins crucify Him anew.

If all of us were to go out into the street, pick up handfuls of gravel and throw them into the air, each pebble would have to come down. Some would fall on the earth. Some would fall on people. One might get hit by six pebbles, another by none, another by four, and so on. Just so, people are continually sinning, knowingly and unknowingly, and reaping accordingly. However, that reaping operates on principles unknown to us. We cannot say why one man is hit, and another not. It often seems to us that there is little or no relation to the receiver's spiritual condition. A believer can be so protected that all of the promises of Psalm 91 come true for him. But if a man reaps evil, that does not mean that he himself deserved that evil more or less than any other man (see Luke 13:1-5). There are things far beyond our understanding.

God always knows when even the smallest sparrow falls (Matt. 10:29). He does not want His children hurt unnecessarily. He may, in His acceptable or permissive will, allow a man to reap some of the harm he or others have sown, that men may learn. But He does not want tragedy. Therefore He moves to prevent. Then it is that He needs a listener, for man has free will. If the man and woman next door are having a loud fight, we do not have a right to interfere. But it's different if they pick up the phone and invite us to help. God the Father observes that same courtesy.

This is where prophets come in. The sins of men, not allowed to go to the cross, are mounting to crescendos of tragedy in this age. God does not want tribulation to become tragedy. When it does, the Bible calls it rightly "the wrath of God," for it is the good law at work in His ire to purge and correct and balance His creation. But He prefers to have mercy.

As the times worsen, the Father will call those who have matured to understand His ways, to intercede that He may have mercy instead of wrath.

When we call out to God for mercy, we move from the fierce play of impersonal law, the good will of God, to the acceptable will. Through His Son, we have been made acceptable; our case can be heard; the Father can deal with us according to what is best for us and all others in the situation. But if we do not ask Him to help, He must let the inexorable cycle of events bring the discipline of the law upon us. When we call, He immediately takes the full guilt of our sin to the cross and we are cleansed. He may then allow some or none of what we deserve to come upon us, determined only by the mystery of His perfect knowledge of what is best for us. In this way He writes His laws upon our *hearts*—not merely upon our minds.

We do not mean to imply that every sin must be consciously remembered and confessed or the weight of each particular sin shall come upon us. No one knows why in some cases deliverance cannot come until particular sins are remembered, whereas in other instances general repentance seems to be enough. Nevertheless, when the Father is prevented from acting until specific sins are seen and confessed, He often will call in a prophet to speak to His suffering children. If all men could and would hear, prophets might be unnecessary. But not all men will hear.

When David sinned Nathan the prophet knew what was going on without help from the palace grapevine (2 Sam. 12). Elijah knew from the Lord what Ahab had done to Naboth; no one needed to tell Elijah (1 Kings 21). It is the same today. The moment that a dearly beloved parishioner fell into adultery, Paula and I not only knew it (more than fifty miles away), but grief broke my health in that moment. The exact same thing happened in Paula when another dearly beloved parishioner fell into the same sin. When parishioners were gossiping and slandering, we both knew it, and sometimes we were informed exactly who. I was working in my office one day, making out my income tax and worrying about where I would obtain the money to pay the year's social security tax in one lump sum. The phone rang. A prophetess from Texas did not so much as say hello, but said brusquely, "John, you are not to worry about money!" Sure enough, all the money I needed was soon on hand. Countless Christians could share similar stories. God is able to inform His children and call them to each other's aid.

When people receive Christ, they enter into a new dimension of protection. The more they receive of Him, the more He is able to bring the blessings of Psalm 91 to them. It is not that God plays favorites. Suppose a man had ten sons, who all wanted to play in a most dangerous area. He warned all ten. Some heard and obeyed. Some refused to hear. He talked to those who heard, and asked them to warn those who refused to hear. They did, and still some refused to hear or obey. Is it therefore the father's fault that some of the children stayed in safety and some were hurt? God could by His power override our free will to protect us, but He will not.

Sometimes things are not quite that simple. Our will is not always that sharp and clear. Sometimes part of our will wants one thing and another part another. If we are walking close enough to God that we are completely given to Him, He can and will often violate a portion of our will, to respond to another portion.

Agnes Sanford one day was suddenly in great consternation for her daughter Tookie. She prayed for her protection. Later she learned that at that moment Tookie had grabbed her friend by the hand and had dashed off her train at the wrong stop, on purpose, not knowing why. The train crashed before its next station. The Father necessarily violated Tookie's will to be at her planned destination in order to protect her.

If a person walks closely enough to God He is free to violate that person's conscious will in response to the deeper will of the person's heart and spirit. People with unsurrendered wills give Him little or no opportunity to save them from tragedy. But when a person surrenders deeply (and that requires time and suffering) there will be a blessed marriage of will and life, such that goodness and mercy surely do follow the man all of his life. Then it is that one begins to experience daily that "A man's mind plans his way, but the Lord directs his steps" (Prov. 16:9).

Outsiders sometimes pity the prophet because he is not free to do what he wants. But the prophet rejoices in a freedom of which the unbeliever knows nothing. Friends of ours, happening to visit us when prophets called with detailed knowledge of what we were doing, or seeing myself or Paula know something happening at a distance, have said with widening eyes, "I couldn't stand to live in such a goldfish bowl!" But it isn't an invasion of privacy. It's the love of God protecting His children. Unless a child of God has entered into trust deeply enough with the Father, his rebellious sense of privacy will prevent the Lord from protecting him.

As a servant learns the blessedness of walking in revelation, trust increases, intercessory tasks increase, and he moves more and more towards walking in his Father's perfect will. He presents his body a living sacrifice that he might prove or discover or demonstrate the good, the acceptable and then the perfect will of God.

Too long have we slept. The power of the cross too often languishes for lack of confession. Tragedies multiply that could be prevented. There is work to do. Let us arise and be at it. The needy world cries for intercession.

Chapter Nine
THE STOPPING PLACE

Intercession invites God to come between man and his sin with the stopping place of the cross. For the cross is the ultimate stopping place of everything in the universe. If intercessors lose this rootage in the cross, they become like Cain and Korah, offering wrong offerings, "fruitless trees in late autumn, twice dead, uprooted; wild waves of the sea, casting up the foam of their own shame" (Jude 12,13).

Intercession must not be the work of man. Paul said, "How shall I benefit you unless I bring you some [fresh] revelation or knowledge or prophecy or teaching?" (1 Cor. 14:6 RSV). We pray that God may "Give us this day our *daily* bread." We shall not intercede properly with yesterday's task or man's idea. Fresh bread must come from the oven of God's love.

Intercession is accomplished by more than words. When God touches a man through the handshake of another, the cross touches from spirit to spirit. For instance, when a man and a wife kiss, since they are "subject to one another out of reverence for Christ" (Eph. 5:21 RSV), His cross may stop animosity within the kiss. When couples have once experienced this they may be deceived into thinking that sexual affection was the source of healing. They

121

failed to see that mutual confession had prepared the ground for the power of the cross to enter from kiss to kiss. For this reason men have rushed to men and leaned on the flesh, only to fail, for they did not realize that at those times when healing occurred in an encounter, it was not the encounter that brought healing, but that somehow their spirits had been open to God that His intercession might flow through their hearts one to the other. The best intercession may be the avenue of prayer, but often what follows is the work of the cross active in the humble daily bread of living.

Intercession must be done *through* men, but it is accomplished only by the Lord (Heb. 4:15; 7:25).

The call to intercession is not license to manage and direct God. Compare these two prayers. Prayer one, "Oh God, please save my brother from tragedy." Prayer two, "I praise you, Lord, that you are entering in to save my brother from tragedy." The first leaves the question, "I wonder if He will do it?" And if He does do it, the petitioner will have to wrestle with pride because he may think that he has prevailed on God to move in his behalf—as though God didn't want to, or had to be jarred into activity by prayer. Preachers too often tell their congregations how "to get God to move on your behalf." That is blasphemy. The second prayer is the way of faith. It must not be used as a gimmick. To say it, one must first ascertain the fresh, present will of the Father in the situation, and then describe what God is doing, affirming that He is the one who loves, not we. True intercession asks only the question, "What sins of mine or the other's may yet block God's saving action?"

Other kinds of prayer may begin with man, such as thanksgiving, petition or praise, but intercession has this one distinctive hallmark, that it always begins with God, not man. If it begins with man, as though God had to be awakened out of the stern to calm our storms, it provokes that same, "O ye of little faith" (Matt. 8:26). Intercession when God has not called is born of fear and unbelief, not faith. Intercession born of faith is the Spirit moving through the cross to stop every mouth, to quell every rude and unruly wind, to curse every falsely blooming fig tree, to stop every rampaging illness, every march of death, every greed and coveting, every gossiping tongue set on fire of hell (James 3:6), every hate-filled heart, every fainting spirit.

Intercession moves first by the route of repentance. God's kindness is meant to lead us to repentance (Rom. 2:4). Repentance, also, therefore, is not a work of man, but a gift of God. What passes among men for repentance is often only remorse. We feel remorse when we fail to live up to what we think God has asked of us. Remorse is self-centered and born of self-pity. And it shows how deeply we worship at the false shrine of the idol of self. We are hurt that we could not be the gods we imagined ourselves to be. Striving is the hallmark of remorse. It is born and dies within the flesh only. It does not lead to freedom, for it never comes to the cross (John 6:37; 14:6).

True repentance is just the opposite. It is a gift of God in which He lets us see ourselves as we are, not as we would like to think of ourselves. It is a decision empowered by the Holy Spirit who convicts us so that we see how we have hurt earth or man or God and are truly sorry for their sake, not ours. It is not even primarily important that we may be the one who hurt the other. What is solely important is the condition of the other, for his sake. Repentance is born of love, remorse of idolatry. Repentance produces change through death to self on the cross with Jesus. Remorse never gets beyond the walls of self. Depression is the result of remorse. Life is the result of repentance.

Repentance is born of God-given disgust (Amos 5:15; Luke 14:26; Rom. 12:9). Some time ago I was trying to overcome a particular sin. I would pray and pray and pray about it, only to go out and do it again. Finally, in desperation and some anger at God, I cried out, "God, why don't you help me with this?!" The answer came back quickly and easily, "You aren't disgusted enough yet." God *was* helping; He was helping me to become more and more disgusted. It is truly a gift of grace to learn to hate evil.

Without that gift we shall either continue to foolishly enjoy sin or, failing that, feel remorse. This disgust, or godly sorrow (2 Cor. 7:10), should produce despair as we feel the hurt of the one against whom we have sinned. That, not our failure, must be the focus of our attentions. That hate born of love for the other is surely a distinct gift, for man does not have it in him to love. Only God gives the grace to love.

Repentance brings us to the cross, and Gethsemane always precedes the cross. Gethsemane is not our travail. The flesh can and often does have a grand and glorious time weeping and moaning before God at His altar in tears. But since it's the flesh, we can be sure no real change will occur. When the Spirit travails, joy enables the depths of sorrow to well up. And we break and cry. We did not turn our tears on. It was of the Spirit.

How often have we heard old-time preachers calling for travail, and we dutifully got down and tried to wail before God? Sometimes it brought glory; and somtimes nothing but weariness. Those preachers had the right idea. Gethsemane precedes deliverance. But it is the Lord's Gethsemane, not ours. We cannot promote it or prod it into action. If we try, it will only be fake. When the call was of the Spirit through the preacher, the Spirit moved. When the idea was of the flesh, He did not. If we are amenable to the Spirit, He will move us to weep before the tomb that the power of Christ may call our Lazarus to life (John 11:35). The Lord's death will be at work in us and His life in the one for whom we intercede (2 Cor. 4:11,12).

We cannot fake this dying of the Lord in us for others, though the flesh may try. We cannot truly weep and wail, though the flesh may stage a soap opera for all to see. Only Jesus goes to Gethsemane in us for others.

When we intercede, then, we speak the words, but the Lord does the real work. We have the joy of participation, but the Holy Spirit bears the burden and fulfills the law of Christ (Gal. 6:2).

What is the law of Christ? It is love. 'Greater love has no man than this, that a man lay down his life for his friends" (John 15:13 RSV). We sometimes mentally mistranslate that to mean "Greater love hath no man than that he should lay down his selfishness for his brother." Or "his own ambitions" or "his own wishes." None of these things are life. They are death. We do not have life to lay down until we receive Christ's life. That is the life we are called to lay down.

When someone comes to us reviling someone else in gossip, or speaking lust, or prejudice, we are legitimately afraid we may join them—"considering thyself, lest thou also be tempted" (Gal. 6:1). We shudder in spirit and soul and say inside to ourselves, "I want no part of this," which is okay, but to protect ourselves we withdraw from our brother and thereby become like the Pharisee who congratulates himself that he is "not as other men are, . . . even as this publican" (Luke 18:11). However, if we are walking in the Spirit, Christ will hold our heart open to our brother. We will identify with him. We will recognize that we and he are caught in the same rottenness. We do not protect our righteousness.

If we hug our righteousness to ourselves, and are afraid to risk the purity of our inner being, we will die (Luke 17:33). We become Pharisees. If, however, we are continually, daily, willing to become loaded with the rottenness of others, to "watch" with Jesus in Gethsemane, then the death of the cross will be at work in us for others, that His life may be at work in others. Thus we save our lives by being where that life is. Jesus is that life, and He goes continually to Gethsemane for others through us. If we fear pollution and hug purity, we wind up with an empty snipe bag, and life is an evil joke upon us. That kind of pollution was not what we were called to come out from and be separated from.

The law of Christ is intercession. To do it we must lay down our lives for our brothers. Burden-bearing is the central work of prayer, the work of the Spirit in us. Only three verses later, however, Paul puts the balancing word, "For every man shall bear his own burden" (Gal. 6:5). When Paula and I caught the idea of burden-bearing, we characteristically went to work at it—apart from the Spirit. Some weeks later, barely able to put one foot in front of the other, we decided maybe that wasn't such a good idea.

In counsel we have repeatedly discovered the Lord's natural burden-bearers staggering around bowed by the weight of centuries. It often happens that we leap to perform our mission in life, unguarded by the wisdom of the word. We need to change our perspective—again, away from ourselves and onto God who is our sufficiency. He doesn't need our help but He grants us the privilege and joy of being part of His glorious healing of the earth.

We must not close our hearts against our brother who sins or hurts. "He that saith he abideth in him ought himself also so to walk, even as he walked" (1 John 2:6). "As he walked" means in the joy of hearing the sweet and solemn music of humanity. Jesus laid down His own righteousness by letting a woman of ill repute wash His feet with her tears, while the Pharisees thought Him therefore no holy man at all (Luke 7:36-39). He ate with publicans and sinners, becoming, in the manner of the East, one with them by sharing their salt. Our calling is to become one with every man, especially those who curse us (Rom. 12 and 1 Pet. 3).

This unity with sinners is a matter of the heart and soul, but not of the mind. We do not agree with the thoughts of sinners. We are in the world but not of the world (John 17). If we let our identification with the other so corrupt our thinking that we think as he does, we have become Jehoshaphats, whose ships are wrecked because he joined himself to a heathen king (1 Kings 22:48,49). Our heart is to love the sinner and our spirit to bear his burden, while our mind hates the sin which destroys our brother. The Lord is then allowed to bring our brother's sin to the cross to set him free.

This work of burden-bearing and intercessory prayer has too long been obscured in sentimental thinking. And a burden-bearer will fall into heavy emotional strain if he does not know the stern and unbending principles behind intercession.

If we train a rat to respond to a light by rewarding it with food, it will eventually learn to salivate at the appearance of the light. After approximately seventeen generations, rats will be born already knowing to respond to light for food. If a dog is trained to bark, he will do so upon stimulus, or will not bark if so trained. This is called conditioned reflex.

However, animals with more elaborate brains can overcome this pattern of stimulus and response, stop their response and originate their own personal decision. Thus humans have been known to exhibit heroic or self-sacrificing behavior.

However, whenever man chooses to suppress his ordinary response to a given stimulus in favor of a different response, he will have to pay a price. For instance, a mother screams at her child. The child, stimulated, would scream back. But, intimidated by his mother's size and anger, the boy checks his response. He acts meek and respectful, but inside he's burning with anger. The stimulus he received demands a response, and, later, he'll find ways, perhaps unconsciously, to punish his mother, like wetting his bed. This, in turn, may anger his mother who also hides her anger behind a mask of concern, since that seems more acceptable. Thus the stimulus-response cycle grows into a monstrous conflict that smolders with buried resentment which keeps coming out at the most inopportune moments. Such is the "web we weave when first we practice to deceive." And who has not gone round and round this barn?

Social psychologists have discovered that if too many counterbalancing conditioned reflexes are built into a trained rat, he will finally have a nervous breakdown. The same regularly happens to us, the more elaborate our system of ethics. If our ethics work in us without the stopping place of the cross, we head for nervous breakdowns. No wonder Jesus said, "Come unto me, all ye that labor and are heavy laden, and I will give you rest. Take my yoke upon you, and learn of me; for I am meek and lowly in heart: and ye shall find rest unto your souls" (Matt. 11:28,29).

Christians often adopt elaborate ethical codes in an effort to control their behavior. This is, however, only a form of self-righteousness since the strong inner drives are merely suppressed. But we are not saved until we see those drives as humanly uncontrollable, confess them and ask Jesus to have mercy on us. There is no stopping place other than the cross. Sin begets sin. Stimulus engenders response. If a man stops anger and bites his tongue, that anger goes somewhere else. It may become self-pity or depression, or it may get dumped in a more "acceptable" place, like at home on the wife and kids. So the anger cannot be truly repressed. It will inevitably set more and more conflicts into motion, unless it is halted by the cross, which does not mean repression but cleansing. If a man can repress a response more thoroughly, it ricochets inside of him until he has ulcers or high blood pressure or something else. "When I kept silence, my bones waxed old through my roaring all the day long. For day and night thy hand was heavy upon me: my moisture is turned into the drought of summer. Selah. I acknowledged my sin unto thee, and mine iniquity have I not hid. I said, I will confess my transgressions unto the Lord; and thou forgavest the iniquity of my sin. Selah" (Ps. 32: 3-5). There is no escape from the operation of law, other than the cross.

This means that no one ever gets away with anything, ever, anywhere. But not everyone believes that. In fact, many people are totally oblivious to the inescapable operation of law, unaware that they must pay for every misdeed. Most TV viewers actually think that if a criminal escapes man's justice, he has altogether escaped, whereas the reverse is true—if he does not pay quickly, he will pay more heavily later. This does not mean that God stands in heaven with a heavy fly swatter just waiting for us to get out of line. Rather it means that like begets like and thus sin and injustice excite ever increasing cycles of evil. God, knowing that fact, wants to bring mercy. Otherwise, given the principles of reaping and increase, man and the universe would self-destruct.

128

The most dangerous thing we have done in the world is to teach men the moral law without Christil. No people who have ever learned the law have ever kept it. In one sense it was never meant to be kept. God knew in giving it that man could not keep it. Adam and Eve in effect had said, "We are not going to let you raise us. We are going to raise ourselves." God said, "Okay, try it. The sooner and harder you try, the sooner and harder you will learn that you cannot do it." This is why St. Paul wrote, "What then shall we say? That the law is sin? By no means! Yet, if it had not been for the law, I should not have known sin. I should not have known what it is to covet if the law had not said, 'You shall not covet.' But sin, finding opportunity in the commandment, wrought in me all kinds of covetousness. Apart from the law sin lies dead. I was once alive apart from the law, but when the commandment came, sin revived and I died; the very commandment which promised life proved to be death to me. For sin, finding opportunity in the commandment, deceived me and by it killed me" (Rom. 7:7-11 RSV).

People who try to be perfect according to the law are brought to defeat in direct ratio to the determination and strength of their attempt. They set into motion ricocheting forces of counteracting laws until there is no relief. God has designed the law to bring us to death. "Now we know that what things soever the law saith, it saith to them who are under the law: that every mouth may be stopped, and all the world may become guilty before God. Therefore by the deeds of the law there shall no flesh be justified in his sight: for by the law is the knowledge of sin" (Rom. 3:19,20).

Christians need to understand that their sins bounce not only from man to man but through all nature. The ground is cursed on our account (Gen. 3:17) and "all the foundations of the earth are out of course" (Ps. 82:5b). The end-time prophecies speak of earthquakes, tornadoes, the raging of the seas, famines and pestilences. We have set in motion forces that must increase to the total destruction of mankind and earth. The Bible calls such end-time tribulations the wrath of God, and truly they are, for all

129

His law is personal to Him, but they are not His preference.

We do not see what we have set in motion. We do not therefore hate sin as we should. "Were they ashamed when they had committed abomination? nay, they were not at all ashamed, neither could they blush: therefore they shall fall among them that fall: at the time I visit them they shall be cast down, saith the Lord" (Jer. 6:15).

To repeat, only the cross can put a stop to this otherwise endless chain reaction of death. Nevertheless, that cross does not work automatically. We must ask for help and thus convey its effect to every cycle of emotions, every circle of thought, every degree of passion, every consequence of human sin, every aspect of nature. Only as we respond to the urgency of God acting in and through the Holy Spirit to bring the filth of all man and earth to His Son's cross does anything ever come to full resolution and thus to full stop. This is an inexorable principle. And no amount of sentimentalism can make it otherwise.

The Elijah task is foremost the offering of our bodies upon the altar of God in intercession, that the stopping place of the cross may have effect in human and natural life. That will mean death to self, that what is done may be accomplished by the purity of Christ's blood rather than the striving of men.

Early in the nineteenth century the French village of Ars received a new parish priest. His name was Jean Baptiste Marie Vianney and he was neither very intelligent nor handsome. But his heart was great and soon began to break in response to the wickedness that prevailed in Ars. Of course he said masses, heard confessions and visited the people, but, most of all, he began to intercede for his flock.

So intense were his feelings that he even flagellated himself on account of their sins. Protestants may debate the propriety of flagellantism, but God is not so interested in how right we are as He is in how fully obedient we are in our hearts. Certainly the Holy Spirit honored his intercession. In time the entire region around

130

and including Ars had become deeply affected by the gospel of Christ. In fact, so notable was what happened there that the village became a place of pilgrimage, even during the lifetime of the Cure d'Ars (as Vianney became known). And he was canonized by Pope Pius XI in 1925.

What happened in St. John Vianney, as we understand it, was that he allowed the Holy Spirit in him to identify with his parishioners. He let their sinfulness become part of him. He repented in the spirit on their behalf. If he went too far in this, that mattered little. What did matter was that he let the Holy Spirit bring this repentance for sin to completion at the cross of our Lord.

Believing he could find that release in the power of the blood and body of Christ in the Lord's Supper, St. John Vianney came each day to the Eucharist with the burden of his people's sins in his heart. God honored the cure's faith and began to shed His grace on the people of Ars. God honors faith, not rightness in externals. So, however we expect the Lord to meet us, He will. We know one lady who imagined people's burdens put in helium filled balloons and floating to heaven. For her, it worked.

A friend of ours went to pray for a stranger. In the process of visiting, he found himself quite stumped, but as he started to pray, his spirit suddenly broke with grief. He could not utter a word. He sobbed and sobbed. The Lord then took that grief to the cross and the stranger was brought to his own repentance and salvation. Though the Holy Spirit will do the repenting and sin-bearing, and go to Gethsemane in us for our brother, He will not thereby rob our brother of his own coming to the cross. Each man truly will have to bear his own load (Gal. 6:5). One time I came home loaded with people's problems, found no relief at communion, nor in the prayer group, nor by talking with Paula or others—nothing seemed to help. Finally I felt it lift while watching a Disney comedy with the children. The Holy Spirit picks the times and the places, and varies them often to keep us from making a religious rite out of watching Disney comedies.

131

It's wrong, in the broad sense, to say that an intercessor repents for another man's sins. He doesn't. But since repentance is a gift of God, the intercessor is often called upon to make himself a channel for the grace of repentance by acting out that repentance before it comes to the one or ones for whom he prays. In addition, intercessor-prophets are frequently aware that sin is a corporate matter, that they share in the guilt of the one for whom they pray. Otherwise they offer their prayers from a lofty rather than a lowly position, which will never work since God draws near to the humble and contrite (Isa. 57:15).

The Holy Spirit intercedes for us with unutterable groanings (Rom. 8:26), and, since the Holy Spirit generally works through people, it shouldn't be surprising to see a prophet interceding with groans and tears.

Unfortunately, some Christians want to use the cross to flee from the work of the cross. They do not want to face their own sin or to become sullied by their brother's. These people make a selfish and divisive celebration of the mystery of salvation. They do not want to obey the command, "Let him deny himself, and take up *his* cross daily, and follow me" (Luke 9:23). Many in the church of St. Paul's day continually fled back to the old laws and traditions. The circumcision party still finds adherents among us today, when we fear the full life and choose rather the forms.

It is the Holy Spirit who brings man home to the cross. When men get stuck in neutral, the Holy Spirit can help them to get in gear through the intercession He prompts in others. As we intercede, He teaches us in our hearts what our Lord felt and suffered among us. The work of intercession thereby increases our love for Jesus.

When we accept Jesus Christ as Lord and Savior, He comes to abide in us. Implicitly the Trinity is therefore with us. However, each member of the Trinity is to be experienced separately and uniquely. It is Jesus who baptizes us in the Holy Spirit and who likewise introduces us to His Father (John 14:6,21,23). His commandment was "that ye love one another; *as* I have loved you" (John 13:34). We have seen that this means we are to lay down our lives continually, daily bearing our crosses for our brothers. Thus are we "builded together for an habitation of God through the Spirit" (Eph. 2:22). So by obedience in intercessory prayer we are prepared for the life of the Father in us.

One evening as I was driving home from Spokane along the freeway, the Lord came and tapped me on the shoulder—a very real tap—and said, "John?"

"Yes, Lord."

"I have someone I want you to meet."

"Oh? . . . Yes, Lord."

"I want you to meet my Father."

The next second, there came over and into me the most loving, gentle, sweet, tender, gracious presence I had ever encountered anywhere. I knew instantly in the spirit there could never be any presence more so. The most telling mark of the Father's presence was the sense of utter blessed safety and security. Even the words "peace that passes all understanding" would not convey that sense of gracious sweet wholeness, completeness and safety I felt. Praise God He came when the highway was empty. I clung to the wheel and whispered, "Oh, Father" all the way home and for days thereafter. I knew why St. Paul had cried out, "Abba, Father" (Rom. 8:15).

The fear of God may be the beginning of wisdom (Ps. 111:10), but only the beginning. Love—sweet, perfect, full and tender love—is the ending. Awe continues, yes, but dread, no. Fear which is respect, yes, but how completely, wondrously, overwhelmingly good and gentle, sweet and tender our Father is.

There is more to experience. Experience is not God, but we want always to know Him more. As we count all things but loss (Phil. 3:8), and present our bodies as living sacrifices (Rom. 12:1), interceding daily for every man we meet, letting the Holy Spirit bear His burdens in us, we are built into an habitation for God.

133

Therein comes to us the indwelling of His fullness. We are to receive more than Jesus and the Holy Spirit, more than the Holy Spirit and fire. The stopping place of the cross becomes, by the life of intercession, the final stopping place of all life, in the gentle loving arms of the most perfect Father who ever was.

Chapter Ten

THE CREATIVE POWER OF THE WORD IN PRAYER

My word . . . that goeth forth out of my mouth . . . shall
not return unto me void. . . .

Isaiah 55:11

God created everything by His Word, Jesus (John 1:1,14; Col.
1:16). Nor has He ceased to create by Him. Today God plans and
speaks and life begins, always through Christ. Thus the cross did
not happen *to* Jesus. Satan did not win a victory which God then
had to overcome by raising His Son. The Father from the
beginning planned *both* the cross and the resurrection.

Creative prayer begins with God, who moves through His Word
and Spirit to accomplish all that is. Whoever thinks it begins with
man is not prepared for this dimension of prayer. God speaks His
re-creation of the new heaven and earth through His praying sons.
Nothing exists outside of God. There is a sea of the Spirit of God
the Father in which the Father, the Son, the Holy Spirit, and all
creation, men and angels exist. The energy of the being of God is
one Spirit, in which everything lives and moves and has its being.
This energy is not the light that pulses behind and through all
matter; God is the Spirit within which that light is itself manifested.
It is crucial to our understanding of prayer to comprehend that this
Spirit or energy flows in and through *all* things.

135

We now know that matter is not solid, being composed of electrons, protons, and neutrons in which there is a good deal of empty space. That elusive energy behind the electron is the very Spirit of God. The Spirit of God is pervasive in everything that is. Matter is not something apart from spirit. There is no such dualism in the Judaeo-Christian faith, as in Greek philosophy. Spirit and matter are one, though the Spirit is far more than matter. Matter could be likened to ice floating in the water of the Spirit—different only in degree. Matter is some form of expression of spirit. *It did not become something outside of Spirit by entering into the form of matter.*

Judaeo-Christian thought is dualistic, in that it speaks both of spirit and of matter. But these two are not apart from one another and opposed to each other, as in Greek dualism. Rather matter is in, a part of, and one with spirit. We shall someday understand scientifically as well as by faith that neither space, in which exists what we perceive as matter, is void of spirit, nor is matter. Both matter and space are within the sea of God's Spirit, and nothing is without it.

If we do not hold firmly in our minds both this distinction between Spirit (as transcendent and impersonal) and the Holy Spirit (as immanent and personal) and the fact that God's Spirit pervades and is the energy of all that is, we are not qualified to understand either the creation or the healing power of re-creation in intercessory prayer. Therefore we need a proper biblical understanding of the relation between matter and Spirit.

Throughout history mankind has held, for the most part, a dualistic view of life. Spirit was something apart from matter. Matter was evil. Spirit was good. To be in a body was a defilement. Hinduism asserts that man has fallen into the body; through many successive incarnations a person is to put to death the body with all its desires in order to escape the body into the Nirvana (nothingness) of absorption back into spirit. One earns or merits this Nirvana through great labors from life to life. Christians, on the other hand, seek not to escape the body, but to be fulfilled within it. Heaven is fullness of human life within a new and glorified body. We believe in the resurrection of the body, not merely the immortality of the soul.

Hebraic faith contained an explosively unique revelation that earth and the body were created by a holy and loving God whose Spirit pervades all that is. No other creation story expressed such faith.

The Babylonian story of creation was that the god Marduk fought with the goddess Tiamat. Marduk stuffed the four winds of heaven into her mouth, whereupon her belly distended and she died. Marduk then slit her belly and lifted up the top half. The top became the stars and the heavens. The blood and intestines falling out below became the earth. That was creation. What kind of respect for life would that create? The Egyptian story of creation was that there was a flood of slimy mud. In that slime a hillock arose. On that hillock a man arose, and spat. That spit was creation. How could men respect the earth or their own bodies with that story foundational to their thinking?

Such mythical elements of conflict are absent from the biblical story. A holy, gentle, perfect, loving Father said, "Let there be light, and there was light." And "God saw that it was *good*." He brought order by His word rather than by primordial conflict. Our gracious Lord created with tender loving care, each day observing that "*it was good*." On the sixth He took that good clean earth and formed man, breathed His own holy breath into him, and man became a living soul, and "God saw that it was *very* good" (Gen. 1:31).

Life is not a battle between light and dark forces. This is the Zoroastrian belief, expressed among ancient Christians in the Manichaean heresy. Many Christians today, elevating Satan too far, have fallen into that heresy. Life is governed by a good God raising His sons in a world into which evil has been allowed to come that the sons may be disciplined, tested, and strengthened.

Nor does the Hebraic Christian faith monistically coalesce spirit and matter as though there were no distinction of any kind. Hebrew faith simply holds that spirit and matter, though different, are one in essence. Life is not split. God's Spirit flows according to His principles within the Spirit in and through all that is, like electricity within its laws.

Human sin has corrupted everything, nature as well. But since Jesus has shed His blood, all the earth and the physical body are clean and holy. "What God has cleansed you must not call common" (Acts 10:15 RSV).

However, the Christian faith was born within the climate of prevalent Greek influence. The New Testament was written in koine Greek because of that influence. The Greek mind followed Plato, who saw reality in extremely dualistic terms. For him genuine knowledge could not be ascertained through the physical senses because reality does not consist in physical existence but in the idea or essence behind the form, and which each form, to a greater or lesser degree, exhibits. Thus what is important is not the dog but the idea of dog, not the table but the essence of table. Ideas and essences cannot be grasped by sight, touch, taste, hearing or smelling, but by the mind which he regarded as immortal.

This may sound a bit abstruse but anyone can see that such ideas clearly elevate the nonmaterial above and separate it from the material. Platonic love therefore means a relationship between two people without physical expression, since what is important is the nonphysical idea of love. The man on the street has made jokes about this for centuries, but he and most of Christendom—especially Western Christendom—have been more deeply affected by it than he might suspect. The joke is on us.

Christian thinkers, most notably Augustine and Aquinas, have adopted the Platonic framework almost unchanged as a vehicle for theology. The results have been far-reaching and pervasive. We have seen them in recent times in Victorian prudery and in hyper-Puritanism. But the most pervasive and sinister result has always been an inability to see that all of life is a walk in the Spirit and a proclivity to divide life into the "natural" versus the "spiritual." People hold up a largely unattainable goal for themselves (it amounts to little more than a fantasy) while the reality of their lives serves only to depress and discourage them.

St. Paul wrote 1 Corinthians 15 because the Corinthian church fell into abhorence for the body and therefore felt scandalized that Jesus would come back in the body after His death. To them, that was the sole reason for dying, to escape the defilements of the body and return to the purity of being a spirit. Still today, Christians stumble when they think of Jesus' resurrection, a little unsure whether they want to say, "in the body." So they say, "in His *glorified* body." We know that spirit wars with flesh, and we are afraid that flesh means the body. But that is not so. The flesh speaks of the whole person—body and soul—in his rebellion against God. Jesus and Jeremiah did not inveigh against man's body, but against his heart. Body desires must be subdued to the Spirit, but the body is holy and clean and good. Jesus was raised in the body.

Because this Platonic lie that disparaged the body was so widely believed, it was unthinkable to many that God would be born in the blood of a womb, be suckled at a woman's breast, and have His diapers changed. Fleeing from that, they argued that God instead found a grown man and adopted him as His Son. It is probably significant that Luke addressed his Gospel to a Greek, Theophilus, and was so careful to fully document the nativity. Perhaps the adoptionist heresy of Cerinthus had already begun to raise its head by that time.

In a similar vein men claimed that God did not come in the body, but only appeared to have a body (because the Greek verb for appear was *doceo*, this was called the docetic heresy). Docetist documents said that the Christ (Spirit) left the body of Jesus shortly before the crucifixion, and that it and the resurrection were illusions.

Because of this split way of thinking, the Apostle John wrote, "Beloved, believe not every spirit, but try the spirits whether they are of God: because many false prophets are gone out into the world. Hereby know ye the Spirit of God: Every spirit that confesseth that Jesus Christ is come in the flesh is of God: and every spirit that confesseth not that Jesus Christ is come in the flesh is not of God: and this is that spirit of antichrist, whereof ye have heard that it should come, and even now already is it in the world" (1 John 4:1-3).

Many modern Christians have failed to heed his warning and have believed the spirit of antichrist. They think their dualistic assumptions are the Christian way. They regard contrary Hebraic concepts as superstition or animism. That fact is very destructive not only to the creative power of prayer but to the totality of our Christian life.

Plato's thinking came into the hands of the church largely through the mediation of Aristotle, when Aristotle was reintroduced to Europe by Arab and Jewish scholars in the early Middle Ages. Aristotle stated his rules of investigation in his treatise on logic (Latin title: *Organum*). He saw God as the prime mover, the first in a great chain of actions and reactions, who was not organically involved in the workings of earth or the universe. By the eighteenth century this idea reached the popular imagination in terms of God as the watchmaker who built the universe as a finely geared instrument, wound the mainspring, and thereafter let things follow their course without interfering (Leibnitz).

Francis Bacon published his *Novum Organum* in 1620 which marked a major break with Aristotle's deductive approach, but did little to modify the basic dualism which concerns us. Since Bacon's ideas opened the way for the advance of science, we are still stuck with that dualism on the part of most scientists and technologists. They see spirit as apart and different from matter. Matter has observable atomic structure, but not life or spirit because that is unobservable. These dualistic assumptions have subtly exalted physics and chemistry while they have debased biology and anthropology. Only in the past eighty years have scientific investigations forced researchers increasingly to abandon these assumptions because they conflicted with hard data (we see this, for example, in the increasing willingness among physicians to discuss psychosomatic causes of illnesses). The truth is that spirit and matter cannot be kept apart in neat compartments at all. But the Platonic lie—the spirit of antichrist—still has an enormously strong grasp on the thinking of us all.

Thus we falsely think that the Holy Spirit inhabits man as water fills a glass, whereas in truth the Holy Spirit permeates man much as hydrogen does water (H_2O). The incarnation of Jesus was not God poured into the can of flesh unchanged. The incarnation was a glorious marriage of body and Spirit as one, a union, not a visit. "The Word *was made flesh*" (John 1:14). Just so, the Holy Spirit does not slosh around in a container; He indwells a man. The body is not a canning jar out of which, at death, God removes the spirit for heavenly use. The body is itself a part of the new creation, the new order of God's sons in the universe. We are not destined to die and lose the body to decay and corruption. We are destined to be raised bodily just as Jesus was.

Paula and I have wept in the spirit upon hearing church members, especially in some Pentecostal churches, straining to be spiritual, as though that were not a birthright in the Holy Spirit. We ache when we hear men change their voices, adopt queer religious inflections, and in countless other ways reveal that they think that something other than what they are is what God wants. Their minds, schooled in dualistic thought, fracture life into Spirit "working upon" the matter of their bodies, rather than infusing, uniting, and acting naturally in and through. John the Baptist and Jesus were filled with the Holy Spirit, yet in every way and place acted as normal men, even when walking on water or rebuking the waves. To pray, in the most powerful way in the Holy Spirit, is as natural as eating bread.

We have already mentioned how Victorian prudery was a consequence of this spirit of antichrist. Day after day in marital counseling we deal with couples full of fears and inhibitions about sex. Even if they have overcome their fears and realize that God has made sex holy and clean and good, they all too often fail to find the glory. They think that the body is the body, and spirit has only to do with prayer and nothing to do with sex. To pray about and in the act of sex seems not only outrageous but blasphemous to them. We meet spirit to spirit in touch of hand to hand or hand to body or lips to lips or organ to organ.

Because of this confusion, men fail to realize why God gave the laws for sexual behavior. God wants mankind to enjoy sex. He created us for love, and sex is a part of love. But he designed us so that only the woman whose spirit has been tuned by Him in marriage shall be right to meet the husband and fulfill him in sex. "Do you not know that he who joins himself to a prostitute *becomes one body with her?*" (1 Cor. 6:16 RSV). Sexual union is spiritual union, but men foolishly think it is only a bodily thing. This is not a matter of attitude; it is so whether we are aware of it or not. Immorality thus confuses and shatters the inner being (Lev. 20:12). If a mate dies, God may consecrate another—but it is He who must attune the two to become one, or there can be no glory. Outside of God's law in sex there must and will be destruction of identity. What havoc our split mentality has created. If all men knew that only their own wives could present to them the true glory of sex, who would seek a cheap imitation?

Because of these same dualistic assumptions, some Christians have thought that miracles are the imposition of mind over matter. But that is a contradiction in terms. For a Christian, there can be no such thing as mind over matter. The Bible never anywhere uses any term remotely like that. Miracles happen by the cooperation, union, and interplay of spirit and matter together.

Confused by split-thinking, men have thought that they must take leave of common sense and the stability of principles, as though there had to be violation of principles for miracles to happen—and therefore rationality must be thrown out in favor of superstition, if we would grow in spirituality. What rot, bunk, and confusion! Miracles happen by releasing power within matter according to God's principles.

Men believe that matter has no will. Therefore they seek ways to push and pull, laying stress upon stress, never thinking that there is anything in matter which has any will or intention of its own, afraid to entertain such a thought for fear of being called superstitious or animistic. Therefore we make ourselves incapable of thinking of a miracle as anything but the imposition of an unknown power upon matter, *forcing* it to do something. Never. That is one of the consequences of the work of the spirit of antichrist—force and discourtesy. Nature, being filled with the Spirit of God, has immeasurable power, locked within its tiniest cells. All of nature *wants* to give to man. But when man fell, nature could no longer *yield* its increase to man (Gen. 4:12). The fellowship of man and earth was fractured by sin. Jesus, Lord of heaven and earth, overcame that disunion; nature *could* yield its increase to Him. Five loaves and two fish expanded to feed five thousand (Mark 6:38), and seven loaves to feed four thousand (Mark 8:3). We now know that the splitting of one atom releases enough energy to devastate a city. Miracles happen by the operation of the Holy Spirit within principles far beyond our ability to comprehend but nonetheless scientific and rational in every way.

Christian Scientists, rightly discovering that there are holy principles within which the Holy Spirit moves within us, were however formed by dualistic thought and are the modern inheritors of the docetic heresy. Because I have sometimes been called a Christian Scientist when lecturing on these subjects, we must distinguish what we say, which we regard as vital to creative prayer, from Christian Science.

Not knowing the healing miracles which resulted from their practice happened because they had stumbled onto the operation of some correct principles, they thought that the miracles vindicated their whole way of thinking. Not so. Miracles vindicate God's truth, not our views of it. A.A. Allen was mightily used of God for salvation and healing up to the night of his death as an alcoholic. The sinful priest, Eli, blessed Elkanah and Hannah, and she conceived and bore Samuel (1 Sam. 1:17). The miracles proved only God's righteousness, not that of A.A. Allen or Eli.

Jesus talked *to* the waves and the winds, and they obeyed Him (Luke 8:24). He spoke *to* the fig tree and it withered (Matt. 21:18-22). He rebuked the fever (Matt. 8:14,15). He said, "If ye have faith as a grain of mustard seed, ye shall say *unto this mountain*, Remove hence to yonder place, and it shall remove" (Matt. 17:20). The Western mind, captive to the Aristotelian viewpoint, thinks either that the Gospel writers were being poetic or that was the silly animism of a nonrational age. But Jesus spoke *to* the winds. No poetry. All of God's creation has the Spirit in and through it. Nothing is incapable of hearing the Son of man. The Bible is not speaking poetically when it says, "the pastures of the shepherds mourn" (Amos 1:2), "the hills sing for joy together" (Ps. 98:8), "The voice of thy brother's blood crieth unto me from the ground" (Gen. 4:10). That is not animism nor figurative speech. That is not a foolish imputing of personality to an "inanimate" creation. There is no such thing as an inanimate creation. Jesus said, "If these were silent, the very stones would cry out" (Luke 19:40). St. Paul told us, "For we know that the whole creation groaneth and travaileth in pain together until now" (Rom. 8:22), "waiting for the revealing of the sons of God" (Rom. 8:19 RSV). Every plant and bit of earth, all seas and winds, each animal and thing has intelligence, will, and desire within it. Therefore every part of the creation waits for man to be delivered from sin and to awake from his haunted sleep to deliver the creation from corruption. But we have learned to relate to things only as "its." We live in an arrogance of utter unconcern for the inner life of anything less than human.

Whoever would become a prophet of the Lord must recognize and renounce the lie of the spirit of antichrist. We are not Greek philosophers. "Greeks seek wisdom but we preach Christ crucified" (1 Cor. 1:22,23). God has revealed what is true. We are now on the verge of depleting fair earth, plundering and raping her treasures, because we can think in no other terms than the ridiculousness of human philosophy behind our science.

Cleve Backster has scientifically shown that plants react to human emotions (*National Wildlife*, February-March, 1969). The Bible has told us that all the way from Genesis 3 through Isaiah 11 to Revelation 22. We thought the Bible writers, poor fellows, were just not as informed as we. They lived in an "unscientific age." What blind pride we have lived in. We are the ones confused about the nature of reality, not God's Holy Spirit. Scientists have demonstrated that plants react to prayers and curses, and they have discovered that electrons move within a mysterious will of their own. We now see a mystery of space and energy behind what we used to think of as solid and inert. The success of technology demonstrates only the truth of the particular principles in operation, not the basic philosophy of hard and thoughtless atoms which came from Democritus and was incorporated into Aristotelian thought. The philsoophy is wrong. The technology is demonstrable. But the Bible is true.

George Washington Carver is the greatest agricultural scientist this country has ever produced. He revolutionized American economy by his discoveries. He talked *with* a peanut to discover three hundred uses for it. He held conversations with the flowers. (Glenn Clark, *The Man Who Talks with Flowers*, Minneapolis: Macalaster Park, 1946.)

We do not become inhuman by becoming spiritual. Indeed, only by becoming truly spiritual do we become truly human. Satan's work was to cut up and divide. The work of the Holy Spirit is to unite. We are one with all nature. Jesus Christ has lifted the curse (Gal. 3:13). All nature *will* yield its increase. We relate to and speak directly to the body and all creation in the creative power of prayer. Every thing and living being in creation is to be *met*, not *used*. God wants to speak His word of power through us to His creation.

God wants not only to bring all that is afoul to the cross. He wants to resurrect. He will not only destroy the old wineskin. He will provide the new. We are in resurrection business.

If we stop at the cross, we are merely dead—clean of sin, yes, but still dead—and so is whatever we pray for. Re-creation is the true end of prayer. God must speak His Son's resurrection life into all that breathes and every *thing* that does not. Let us pray life into all that is.

Creative prayer is the command of Life to life. Creative prayer imparts both energy and form to whatever is, to work it into new life and form. Prayer which moves man's spirit toward God—like thanksgiving, praise, or petition—is the work of every believer. But God's Spirit moving through man to His world is that intercessory creative prayer which is the prophet's peculiar task.

A prophet sees the vision of an orphanage, for example. He sees a new wing, a driveway, a new bus for their travel. When he affirms that thing, when he sees that vision and speaks it in prayer before God, God will pour energy through him and move His servants until that vision is fulfilled. It is not that the prophet is manipulating life, imposing his will. It is rather that he is presenting his body as a living sacrifice unto God that through him God may rule.

God both gives the vision and fulfills it. Religion is man's striving to do for God. But in true faith, not man but God is the initiator. Man is not passive. He is called upon to act creatively. But all his energies are bent to let the flow of God's life move through his to establish the Father's will. Whatever man builds amiss will crumble. Whatever God builds through man will stand so long as God intends.

The prophet may never see the fulfillment of many of his visions. He only sees the vision, the blueprint, and its power set in motion. God will bring the thing to pass in His own time and way. Maybe the prophet will know how the thing came to completion, and maybe he will not. The prophet may even forget in time what he prayed for; certainly he relinquishes it, that it may be for the glory of the Father. No Old Testament prophet saw in his own lifetime the birth, life, death and resurrection of the Lord Jesus Christ which he prophesied. The prophet merely spoke the word of authority. It is only God who brings to life through the prophet's word of power.

Can any believer sincerely maintain that history shall go any other way than that announced by St. John the Divine in the Book of Revelation? Could history have gone any other way than to the cross which Isaiah foresaw? Through His prophets God will set the mold for the future.

Nations shall eventually learn war no more because God has so spoken through Isaiah. So shall all the nations be healed.

God will raise up men and women to restore the ancient paths through the wilderness of life. To one He will give warning visions concerning politics, and visions of His re-creative purpose. To another the thunder of rebuke and positive visions of what movies and TV can do to create and educate rather than destroy. Another prophet may receive warnings and positive dreams for the restoration of economy. Even now the Father is moving to restore the family. The churches must learn to catch such visions, repent of sins which bring on dire predictions, and affirm the glorious promises of the Lord into physical reality. God the Father would move to restore *every* area—sports, newspapers, books, education, commerce, justice, police work, agriculture, energy sources, mining—to the life of His kingdom.

We are not forecasting an easy coming for Utopia. Destruction shall come first. Nevertheless, to whatever extent man will learn to repent and build anew, to that extent holocaust is lessened. The church cannot use the dire prophecies of the Bible to excuse itself from prayer and labor that the kingdom of God may come on earth as it is in heaven. Perhaps that destruction and the revealing of the new heaven and the new earth may be the very task of the church for this age. Let us cease to try to calculate when and how He shall return, or at what point in the process of destruction and re-creation He shall come. The Elijah task is to restore until that moment when the Lord says, "Rest, all is done."

An intercessor in creative prayer soon learns where true power originates. "Then said Jesus unto them, When ye have lifted up the Son of man, then shall ye know that I am he, and that I do nothing of myself; but as my Father hath taught me, I speak these things. And he that sent me is with me: the Father hath not left me alone; for I do always those things that please him" (John 8:28,29). The Lord Jesus conquers all in order to return all to the Father (1 Cor. 15:28). Whoever learns this will seek death and the consequent joy of obedience, for he knows that from every such fall emerges the spring of creation. We are not alone. Let us open our eyes and ears to the song of creation, and speak the vitality of healing order to a tired universe.

PROPHETIC LISTENING TO GOD

Throughout the remaining chapters I am writing primarily for those called to prophetic listening. All Christians, hopefully, should be able to glean something from these pages, but it would be presumption and a spiritual dead end for Christians not called to be prophets to start trying to listen beyond their calling. David said, "LORD, my heart is not haughty, nor mine eyes lofty: neither do I exercise myself in great matters, or in things too high for me. Surely I have behaved and quieted myself, as a child that is weaned of his mother: my soul is even as a weaned child. Let Israel hope in the LORD from henceforth and forever" (Ps. 131).

A prophet set over an area may hear for the entire area, as I was given warnings for the Silver Valley. David Wilkerson, having an international ministry, was given visions to match that scope. Normally, since God is eminently practical, a Christian's guidances will concern his own life and church. We all need to stand against presumption in ourselves.

This section, except for the last chapter, is also a working manual for prophets. These chapters may therefore seem rather prosaic after the three preceding. There I searched for new revelation, with all its consequent thrills and dangers. Now I must

149

turn to more down-to-earth matters.

Indeed, we need to guard carefully against super-spirituality, that excessively pietistic attitude by which we seek to elevate ourselves above others and to avoid looking at who we really are. As with most sins, it is not overcome by saying to one's self, "I'll never do that again," and trying very hard not to look super-spiritual ever again. The problem is in our hearts and needs to be confessed and cleansed as haughtiness and hypocrisy. Furthermore, when we see that super-spirituality cannot be distinguished from genuine mysticism except by the discernment of the Holy Spirit, we are in danger of trying to hide our super-spirituality. If we do that, we'll never be free to hear God invite us into mystical venturing because we'll be afraid that someone might accuse us of being super-spiritual.

A person is neither more nor less spiritual because he has mystical experiences. Spirituality is measured in terms of fruit. Rationalist, pragmatist, mystic nut—whatever our disposition—we are only spiritual to the extent that the fruit of the Spirit grows in our lives. To come to that life in Christ is the aim of us all, and it requires that each of us bear our cross and are "crossed-out" by our opposites, the rationalist by the mystic, the liturgist by the free-worshiper, the common sense fellow by the brilliant scholar, the plodder by the leaper, the artistic by the prosaic, the complex by the simple. Mystics need the counsel of the rationalists—and the rationalists need the challenge and the excitement of the experiences of the mystic. "Iron sharpens iron, and one man sharpens another" (Prov. 27:17).

Though I list in this section so many ways of listening, I don't expect that every prophet must walk in all of them. Some may have only one way, or some far more. Again, the degree of mysticism is not what is important, but whether the many ways a man may hear God are checked among the brothers. And is the listening brother being kept humble in the awareness that whatever gifts may be his, nothing short of bearing fruit is of profit to his own soul?

150

Chapter Eleven

PRELUDE TO LISTENING

Listening to God is fun. God has not one but trillions of ways to speak to us. Even when we hear wrongly He turns it to glory, for we learn anew His grace. If our listening does not bring us closer to Him, whatever else is accomplished through it, it is wide of the mark.

Listening to God is difficult, for the flesh so quickly interferes. To remain at rest to hear Him involves a constant struggle with the flesh. Listening is not passive; God does not write on us like chalk on a board. Listening is active work, although the key to it is restful abiding in trust. It is especially difficult to abide in His presence when we begin to hear what we do not want.

The most difficult to listen to are His words of love and affirmation to us, for our hearts leap up in joy, but our minds say, "You are only making this up." Or we simply flee out of His presence. We are afraid to come too close to God, knowing as we do that false demand that "we can't live up to it." Nothing slays us so effectively as being loved by God.

Often what He says will smash our preconceptions and send us reeling to the Bible. Fresh revelation is especially smashing, for what God tells us may seem at first to be contrary to the word. It

151

never is truly so if God speaks, but it may seem so, for what it actually destroys is not the true Word, but our opinions about what it means.

Imagine the plight of the disciples. All their lives they had been carefully taught, "Hear, O Israel, the LORD our God is one LORD" (Deut. 6:4). But, with Jesus' coming, they had to begin to see that there are three in that one. Scripture had always admitted the three, but no one had yet fully comprehended that fact. Imagine how the disciples' minds staggered. They could see that He was doing the true works of the Messiah, and yet He continually spoke strange words which could even be blasphemy. What they thought the Word said was being "blasted to smithereens."

Some years ago, a girl stood before me, arms akimbo, and said, "Oh, how I would love to separate your soul and spirit!" I fled in terror of that "most unbiblical thing," not knowing the scripture to which she was alluding (Heb. 4:12). Revelation comes again and again in the seeming garb of heresy. Jesus said you could spot a false prophet by his fruits (Matt. 7:20), but fruits are not always immediately evident. One must wait for maturity before plucking and tasting. Therefore listening demands patience and trust. Fear must be banished by the love of God in the surety of ones's salvation, which allows us to be wrong. Listening demands willingness to fall on one's face again and again, until we have learned through practice to distinguish what is true from what is false (Heb. 5:14).

An uptight striver will miss the sparkle of God's wit. Timmy jumps on his daddy's back and climbs him like a tree, knowing that if he knocks his glasses or tears his clothes, his dad will forgive. Andrea loves to jump on her dad's lap, knowing that if she knocks his wind out, his temper has only love in it. Children who know they are loved are free to fall, to make mistakes and to sin, thus free to try, to adventure, to have fun. Life is a game, however serious, and joy undergirds all. But the uptight, who fear they will be lost if they fail to perform rightly, will never discover the twinkle in the Father's eye. That is, until His love breaks the shackles of performance. His laughter bubbles behind the melodramas of human life, and His chuckle is suppressed by His hand, even as our parents put hand to mouth so as not to embarrass us.

Our minds often wander when we try to listen to God. Our flesh does not die easily. Our thoughts have a life of their own. Therefore the mind would plunge us into problem after problem rather than let simple truth floodlight its darkness. Therefore, listening becomes a contest between the Spirit and flesh. It is sometimes the very battleground of God's Spirit in union with our spirits against the entrenched lines of the antichrist. Let us cease to think of the antichrist only as something exterior to ourselves (Rom. 8:7). Listening is a smashing of independence. Therefore the mind wanders—purposely.

Since conversation with God is two-way, it involves, just as does our daily human conversation, much that is subtle and subconscious. A husband may say to his wife, "Gee, you look lovely tonight." And she may respond, "You make me furious!" To the outsider her answer seems rude, but there may be factors at work in the couple's relationship of which we are little aware, so that her answer may have been both appropriate and needed. Who can say what goes on subliminally in our conversations with God? Recently the Lord told me to do something I hated. But I responded with a simple, "Yes, Lord." Immediately came a feeling of lightness and mirth and the voice, "Okay, you don't have to," and I knew the Lord had only tested my willingness. Listening is not merely with our minds, but with our whole beings.

We are like radios, sometimes jangled by static and sometimes clear as a bell. We can be sure that clearness is a work of grace, not of ourselves.

One ordinary response by those who begin to try to listen to God is discouragement and outright unbelief. Truly it requires patience and persistence. Coolidge asserted that neither talent, genius, nor

153

education could replace persistence. The Lord warned about those who were so unsure of God's goodness that they buried their talent rather than risk His displeasure (Matt. 25:14-30, Luke 19:12-28). At the base of all listening is simple trust in the goodness of God, which enables a man to be a fool for God.

No one will graduate from the Lord's school of listening with his pride intact. In fact, no one will ever really become adept in the art of listening. There are simply those who know that God can speak to them and who plead that His mercy may continually override their stubborn hearts and minds. We remain fumbling children, starting from ground zero, to hear God anew every day. Otherwise we are on a ladder with broken rungs, or living in a leaning tower which shall someday topple.

Finally, listening is embrace. It is the hug of God's welcome to His kids. It is what makes of prayer a two-way street, a visit rather than a pass-by in the night. Through it God becomes more real than by almost any other way. Listening is not proof of faith. One must believe that God is, or listening will never begin. But listening strengthens the faith which exists. It makes all of life a personal walk with God in the cool of the garden rather than a wistful hiding behind the leaves of shame (Gen. 3:10).

Listening comes by whatever door God finds open, or by His wisdom of choice for His purposes in raising His children. God speaks by whatever mode He knows is available within the opportunities we have allowed Him, and by the best possible way to communicate or teach the most. God loves us.

Numbers 12:1-8 lists five ways God speaks to men. These are in a continuum, from the most indirect to the most direct. The most indirect way, which involves the least interference from the conscious mind, is through a dream. The second is by vision. There are three types of visions: a trance, in which the mind is nearly totally arrested; or a picture flashed upon our inner screen while we are vividly alert; or a direct seeing into the world of the spirit. Whatever the type, our minds are active and participating

154

but the Holy Spirit is in charge and shows us the picture. Both dreams and visions are basically nonverbal, though we may hear words as well. Thus dreams and visions transcend language. The third way is called dark speech. In dark speech God uses language figuratively. Language comes into the mind; the mind is involved, but the message itself is something beyond present comprehension. The mind is used but still by-passed.

The further He goes up the scale of mental involvement, the more the Lord runs the risk that our own understanding in the flesh will distort the meaning. God speaks in the spiritual mind but the flesh is also involved. God communicates in dark speech which is by puns and parables, most of the time. We shall discuss why later.

The fourth step up the ladder is direct speech. We still hear this within our spirits, but God is speaking clearly to our minds. There are no puns, no parables. "Get up and go to church" means that you should get up and go to church.

It is difficult to separate the ways of God's speaking, and sometimes something He meant sharply and directly we symbolize into confusion, and vice versa.

Finally, the fifth way is the most clear; He speaks audibly, as Aaron, Miriam and Moses all heard Him (Num. 12), as Jesus, Peter, James and John heard on the mount (Matt. 17:5), as those at His baptism heard (Matt. 3:17), or as the disciples and the crowd heard in the streets of Jerusalem (John 12:28).

We must test our listening repeatedly. God will never speak falsely, but because of who we are we may hear wrongly. As soon as we begin to converse truly with God, both our own flesh and Satan become upset. The mind and soul cannot let this kind of thing go on unchecked, or God will have His way with us, and they will be off the throne of our being. That inner battle in turn gives Satan a field to play in. Satan seldom bothers to attack the nonbeliever. He already has him; why bother him? But both flesh and Satan attack one who draws near to God. Few of us enjoy the honeymoon of God's love long before the flesh and the enemy

155

begin to jam our wavelengths.

And what sorts of devices do they use to do this jamming? Occultism is a very prominent device. Both the flesh and Satan copy every gift God has given man.

Whoever would learn to hear God must stay absolutely away from all occult things—fortune telling, astrology, card reading, crystal balls, seances, palm reading, magic, witchcraft, alchemy, Rosicrucianism, enchantments, oaths and curses, hypnotism of self and others, etc. (see also Deut. 18:9-14; Lev. 20:6,27; Isa. 47:12-14.)

Whoever has become involved in occult things will have a far more difficult time after his conversion than one who has not. One whose family has a history of occult involvement may have great difficulty, though the involvement be two or three generations removed (Deut. 5:9). "Many times clairvoyance and other psychic powers appear as a consequence of occult involvement, usually in the second and third generation. Edgar Cayce, for example, whose grandfather was a water dowser, gave evidence of occult subjection at an early age, relating various psychic and clairvoyant experiences. Strong mediums usually develop in this manner, as a result of what might be termed "psychic heredity." Personality and character defects, as a consequence of occult sins by one's parents or grandparents, are often seen in their descendants in the form of morbid depression, violent temper, irresponsibility, immorality, chronic fear, hysteria, agnosticism and atheism, hate, persistent illness, unpredictable behavior, and many other abnormalities" (Hobart Freeman, *Angels of Light?* p 28).

Paula and I can testify to the truth of what Hobart Freeman said. On the Sandford side there are thirteen "Praying Ezekiel" Sandfords, traceable to a "Praying Ezekiel" Sandford who was with Ethan Allen at the taking of Ticonderoga. On my maternal side is a longer line of Osage Indians, very devout and mystical, among whom were those who could charm snakes and who had other mystical powers. My parents became involved in going to fortune tellers and then in Rosicrucianism. I also went to see "Aunt Fanny" for a reading, and became personally interested in Rosicrucianism. Paula and I both out of curiosity read some mediumistic books (Edgar Cayce, et. al.) and were observers at a seance held by the renowned Dr. Arthur Ford in Chicago.

Soon after we were converted, the devil struck back. I began to be really troubled by a spirit which had inhabited me since my earlier associations. As soon as the baptism of the Holy Spirit came the battle was on. The demon rose to the surface and was cast out. During the exorcism, which took place in our home, even the cat went berserk, dashing madly throughout the house, three separate times striking the same note as it jumped on the piano. The exorcism set me free, but the battle was only begun. For several years thereafter we were subject to attacks by dark forces. Many times we were jumped on in our half sleep, paralyzed and unable to make a sound. Repetition of the name of Jesus silently would begin to loose the hold of the demons until we could speak aloud to command the evil spirits away. Sometimes I would be carried away into what seemed mystical but was not in the Holy Spirit. It was only after we learned to claim that everything in the ancestry stops on the cross (see Jer. 31:29,30) that the door was ultimately closed.

When I realized that the occultism in my ancestry had interfered with my relationship with God for years after my baptism in the Spirit, I got really angry. It happened in an Assembly of God church. All of us were holding our hands high, praising the Lord, and the glory of the Lord was there. Suddenly, in the midst of rejoicing in the Lord, I thought, "Why, I was blocked before my birth. I never had a chance! It isn't fair." Down came my hands, and "Umph" went my emotions! Many, many deep lessons were to be learned before I was free again to praise God with a full and willing heart. I had to learn that we are rebels from our birth (Isa. 48:8). I had to see that I wanted to blame God for my problems. We really do hold it against God that we have been subjected to this earth's fallen conditions. We think it unfair that "in Adam's fall we sinned all." "When a man's folly brings his way to ruin, his heart rages against the Lord" (Prov. 19:3 RSV). It may seem inconceivable that we could hold God at fault, yet the Holy Spirit will help us see that we do.

Nothing can ever be gained by any dabbling in occult things. It is a long, long way back from the deceits of Satan.

Divination, which is a forbidden seeing of the future, or clairvoyance generally, are accomplished principally by our own soulish powers, with or without satanic aid. They copy God's gracious gifts of revelation, knowledge, and insight. Samuel told Saul what had happened to the lost asses, though Samuel was not the mere seer Saul thought he was (1 Sam. 9:18-20). That Jesus knew things afar off and that the apostles also did is common throughout the New Testament. Satan and the Holy Spirit both disclose wisdom and information not normally available to people. Satan does it to trap and kill. The Holy Spirit does it to bring life. Divination is a counterfeit, a second eating of the tree of the knowledge of good and evil. Fear and untrust prompt it, for if we trust God we are willing to wait in faith, not seeing.

Spiritualism, and all contacting of spirits of the departed (necromancy), is Satan's copy of the fellowship of heaven and earth. Angels and saints are appointed by God to watch over us: "Seeing we also are compassed about with so great a cloud of witnesses. . ." (Heb. 12:1). We are not to turn to angels or to saints, as Hebrews 1 makes clear. God may send angels or saints to visit men, as He did throughout the Bible, or as He sent Elijah and Moses to visit with Jesus on the mount (Elijah had never died, but Moses had); but all such visits are initiated by God, not men. And His messengers say only what God directs. Throughout the Bible we are told that God's angels watch over us to do us good (Ps. 91:11; Isa. 63:9; Dan. 3:28; 6:22; Mark 1:13; Luke 16:22; Acts

5:19; 12:7; 27:23; Heb. 1:14). The communion of heaven and earth is important. But God's order is that He and He alone shall watch over us through His servants only. Any attempt to worship the saints and angels, or to pray to them plunges us into immediate trouble. The issue is, who will be God to us, and in what way. God guides us for our own good, in courtesy and freedom. Satan comes but to kill and to destroy (John 10:10), to blind (2 Cor. 4:4), to deceive (Rev. 20:3), and to climb in by whatever way to steal and rob (John 10:1).

Magic is Satan's copy of miracles and healing. Magic is any operation of the principles of the universe by psychic energy to bring about something marvelous with wrong motivations. There is consequently a thin line between magic and prayer. Samuel told Saul when Saul wrongly conducted the rites of offering unto the Lord, "Behold, to obey is better than sacrifice, and to hearken than the fat of rams. For rebellion is as the sin of witchcraft" (1 Sam. 15:22b-23a). Rebellion is *as* witchcraft because if we operate right principles from unholy desires—even in prayer—that is akin to witchcraft, for by soulish powers we activate principles to bring about results contrary to God's will. Many of our prayers, when we have not tarried before God to hear His will, are an attempt to "manage" God to obtain our own selfish wills. Our soulish prayers then come dangerously close to witchcraft.

True prayer is humble. It petitions God and leaves both man and God free. It controls nothing. It pumps no spiritual levers. Many times we have heard preachers list things men can do, and then proclaim, "and God *must* answer these prayers," or, "You can get a handle on God!" Or, "Let me teach you how to get God to do what you want." That borders on magic. We must be very careful what we teach about prayer. Since magic is the operation of principles by psychic force to bring about a desired result, we need always to die with Christ in prayer, lest we operate magic in the name of prayer. Prayer is a two-way personal visit. Magic is the operation of impersonal principle. Prayer retains the primacy of personal courtesy. Magic invades, disregards the primacy of free will, and forces its desired result.

Some years ago a teaching went through the church about "broadcasting prayers" into people's psyches at night when they were asleep. This, which seemed good to some, was magic. It operated on the psychic plane, had nothing of courtesy in it, and often became suggestion or telepathic hypnosis. We once received a gift in the mail from a well-known evangelist. He was operating the principle of seed faith, giving in order to be given to. God would have us give alms in secret (Matt. 6:1-4), or as He otherwise directs. God will then give back to us from His many sources. But this evangelist wanted men to give him gifts and was pumping a principle. That perverts true principle into magic.

True power is union of free wills and energies in courtesy and cooperation. That produces miracles, healings, signs and wonders. Magic attempts the same apart from love. There is no white magic. It is all black. Whatever operates or manipulates life apart from free will has departed from love into use, manipulation and exploitation, and its true name is hate. Samantha on TV seems innocuous. But such is the deception of evil. Whatever power is "operated" has behind it satanic delusion and control, however unaware of Satan the operator may be.

One for the Dark Lord on his dark throne
In the land of Mordor where the shadows lie.
One ring to rule them all, One ring to find them,
One ring to bring them all and in the darkness bind them,
In the Land of Mordor where the shadows lie.

> Tolkien, *The Lord of the Rings*, vol. I, p. 81

Whoever prays discovers that he does so because God's Spirit moved upon him and freely urged him to it. Whoever uses magic will someday discover that the one ring of deceit lured him into it and by it bound him and brought him to the land where the shadows lie.

Charming, enchanting, spells, curses and hypnotism are all

copies in the flesh of the power of God to subdue all things into cooperation through love. The first command was to subdue (Gen. 1:28). But we are subject to Christ out of reverence for Him, and subject to one another likewise (Eph. 5:21 RSV). Nature must freely yield its increase to us. All spells, incantations, charms, and hypnotic powers are an overcoming of beasts, nature and men not by increase of free will in love but by seductively lulling the will to sleep in order to control. Hypnotism can achieve powerful effects, but increase of power does not make right. Our wills must not be surrendered to any person less than the Holy Spirit of God. There is nothing hypnotic in all of God's dealings with man. No spell is innocent, whether for fertility in farmland, or for Mammy Yokum to find out what Li'l Abner is a doin' off in the hills. Like magic, it has the same dark lord as its ultimate wielder.

We could discuss many other aberrations—telekinesis, telepathy, teleportation, psychometry, materializations, astral projection, etc. They all bear the same root fallacy, in that they operate by the psychic power of man, usually aided, whether the person is aware of it or not, by Satan. They are all copies of true gifts of God. One way or another they depart from love and freedom and the power of the Holy Spirit, in order to enter into hate, delusion, binding, blinding, coercion, and the power of darkness. An evil tree cannot produce good fruit, nor can a good tree produce evil (Luke 6:43).

Whoever has had any involvement with anything occult (and who has not in these days), or knows of it in his heritage, will do well to make a project of ferreting out every memory of every incident in order to repent of it, renouncing the occult and the ways of the devil. Each contract must be broken. Only the cross and the blood break the bonds and wash the filth.

The prophet of the Lord must renounce all aids other than the

161

Family Ties

Holy Spirit. Even friendships may trap and blind his hearing. Loyalties to relatives may influence his hearing. Patriotism and civic loyalty may stand in his way. Consider how Jeremiah must have felt under the lash of both leather and tongue, as men called him traitor.

> And unto this people thou shalt say, Thus saith the LORD; Behold, I set before you the way of life, and the way of death. He that abideth in this city shall die by the sword, and by the famine, and by the pestilence: but he that goeth out, and falleth to the Chaldeans that besiege you, he shall live, and his life shall be unto him for a prey. For I have set my face against this city for evil, and not for good, saith the LORD: it shall be given into the hand of the king of Babylon, and he shall burn it with fire.
>
> Jeremiah 21:8-10

Elisha destroyed his oxen, yokes and plow, that he might not return from the Lord's calling. Jesus calls to an even deeper severing.

> And he said unto another, Follow me. But he said, Lord, suffer me first to go and bury my father. Jesus said unto him, Let the dead bury their dead: but go thou and preach the kingdom of God.
>
> Luke 9:59,60

The young man wanted to stay at home until his father died, in order that he might perform the filial duty of burying him. Then he would be free to leave home to follow the Lord. But the call of the Lord supercedes family ties. "If any one comes to me and does not hate his own father and mother and wife and children and brothers and sisters, yes, and even his own life, he cannot be my disciple" (Luke 14:26 RSV). The word "hate" is used in as many ways as is its cousin, "love." The Lord of love does not command us to hate in the usual sense. The word means in this context, a cutting free, a hating of continuing carnal influence. Our character, personality, and soul are formed amidst our father and mother, brothers and sisters, other relatives and friends, heritage and nationality, race and culture. All of them are sick with sin, however wholesome in appearance. When we accept Jesus Christ as Lord and Savior, that is a dying to that womb and a new birth into a new life of joy in Him. If we fail to cut the umbilical cord, all the ways, motivations, loyalties, belongings, jealousies, fears, carnal loves—all the inner urges—come nearly unchecked into our new life in Christ, masked under seeming goodness. When we die in Christ, we are dead to everything in us, good or bad. We are dead to everything we are and have been. Therefore we need to renounce the past—all our relatives, teachers, race and culture. Christ is still in the love-thy-mother-and-father-business, still in the business of loving the wife and children and husband. The issue now is who will do the loving, through what nature? Will it be the Lord in us through His nature, or still our undead self in all its ways?

I have always had a loving relationship with my mother and father. Nevertheless, I renounced them in faith. This does not mean that I hated them or reviled them (Luke 14:26). It meant that I cut my soul's umbilical cord. It meant that I renounced the ways in which I still gave rule and place to my carnal nature in my relationship with my parents. And I set myself to deny all approaches from their carnal nature to mine. Before I did this, if either of my parents came to visit, unconscious forces were at work so that I subtly became a young son, regressing into attitudes and ways of relating which belonged to the former childish patterns. How many wives have seen this same thing happen when her mother-in-law walks in the door? After the renunciation, my parents came to visit. The same psychological things were operating, but now I no longer had to be drawn into them. I was free and Paula still had her husband. No blame nor hurt is intended by these candid words. I now can love my mother and father far more freely and fully, for it is the Lord who is now free to love through me. It was the untoward hidden things of carnal human love which died that a purer love, God's love, might live.

Paula and I have had twenty-six years of an exceptionally

163

affectionate marriage. The candle of romance never did splutter out. Nevertheless, when the time came, I renounced Paula (and she me, later). To our surprise, love increased, and became far more delightsome. God was still in the marriage business; He only wanted to break us apart from our old ways in order to set us free for each other in Him.

I was also called upon to lay down my own life. By then my life was pastoring, preaching, teaching, and most importantly praying and counseling for the healing of the inner man. God gave Isaac to Abraham to make of Abraham's seed a mighty nation which would bless all the families of the earth (Gen. 12:1-3). Nevertheless Abraham was called upon to sacrifice Isaac. Abraham needed to be willing to lay down his ministry, his gift, his life and blessing. Had he not, Isaac would have remained Abraham's handle on God. Arlington Cemetery, an old soldier once said, is full of indispensable people. It's true in the world and doubly true in the kingdom of God. No one can be needed. No one is necessary to God. All our Isaacs—those ministries we have developed for God—must be brought to the sacrificial altar (Luke 14:26). All our ambitions, all our own work must cease (Heb. 4:10). It is God who will bless all the families of the earth by Abraham, not Abraham.

When I laid down the ministry of the healing of the inner man, I meant it. I was resolved never to counsel or pray for another person regarding any inner problem. Twelve years' experience died on that altar. I even announced publicly that I would take no more counselees. Quickly God brought more people than ever, and moved with far more alacrity to heal. God had merely wanted Abraham to be *willing* to sacrifice his son. God had wanted me dead to my ministry that He might minister through me. It must not be John ministering with God's help, but God ministering with as little help from John as possible. Listening is hard when our ''sons'' of ministry have not yet been sacrificed on the altar—we hear only God's support of *our* ministry, not His pure Word. We want God to support and serve what we are doing, rather than give our unquestioning obedience to Him.

Another obstacle to clear hearing is our desire to be special. And it becomes more difficult to die to specialness when God has told us that He has chosen us for high service. How could a Jeremiah, consecrated from before his birth and appointed a prophet to the nations, not regard himself as something special? Or Abraham? Or John the Baptist? The servant must learn that the fact that God has chosen him in no way makes him special; only God is special. If he does not learn this, he will become "puffed up by his own sensuous mind, taking his stand on visions, not holding fast to the Head who is Christ" (Col. 2:18,19). He will continually stray into his own peculiar revelations (strange fire), and think that he has a mandate to lead others. In short, he will not hear as he should, for his own "specialness" will warp and twist his hearing God.

In C.S. Lewis's *The Horse and His Boy,* an aged hermit tells the great talking war-horse, Bree, who had just undergone a humiliating experience, "My good Horse, you've lost nothing but your self-conceit. . . . You're not quite the great horse you had come to think, from living among poor *dumb* horses. Of course you were braver and cleverer than *them.* You could hardly help being that. It doesn't follow that you'll be anyone very special in Narnia. *But as long as you know you're nobody very special, you'll be a very decent sort of Horse,* on the whole, and taking one thing with another" (pp. 127, 128). Because God has called us, we need continual humbling to remember that we are nothing special.

The most important positive prerequisite for listening is a voracious devouring of God's Word. The Word must become our breath and thought, the exercise track of all our training, the structure of our mind's temple, the memory bank, the constant checkpoint, the perennial reference, the center of all associations and connections of thought to thought, the germinating ground of ideas, the quarry of every notion, the guardhouse and prison of every motive, the corral of every steed of fancy, the diamond bed of wit and wisdom. Nothing must be thought outside of it. It is the pantry of the Spirit's speech to us. Every thought and whim, intuition and notion, speech and revelation, dream and vision of Spirit to man must come garbed in its statutes and censored by its limits. Nothing must be allowed to settle into the mind which cannot pass naked and clean past the x-ray of His Word. Does it follow that no one ought approach the speech of God without sure girding in the Bible (2 Tim. 2:15)?

There is no methodology for listening. Bob Mumford warns wisely against learning methods rather than principles (in the preface to *Take Another Look at Guidance*). We hear God because he chooses to speak to us. No system of meditation or other learned practice can conjure up a word from God. Whether the word floats up into the mind, or one ''hears'' an inner voice, or one has simply an inner knowing—however it happens—it is because God speaks. But there are many who have learned a method and practice it to try to hear God. Imagination obeys the impulse, and soon overworks. Delusion results. Therefore whoever would hear must pray until the presence of God fills, infills, permeates and rests the being. Then we are ready to hear God. Let us beware of those voices that rush in upon us.

It is not that God cannot or will not speak if we are not in prayer. He may speak at any time by any means. But Jesus was at the height of walking in the Spirit, after forty days of fasting and praying, when He heard the voice of Satan tempting Him. There are no guarantees. It is merely safest and wisest to try to listen when most in the Spirit of God.

Another guideline by which we can test what we hear is God's love. He speaks in love. One must know the shape of love. Every effective river has banks. God will never speak in hate, bitter condemnation, or malice—but His stern discipline may come with the same words which, if said by us, would be hate. It follows then that we must *know* God. This knowing is not merely mental. I do not always know specifically what Paula may say, but I so thoroughly know her heart that seldom do I miss what she means, whatever she says. The effect of prayer, of walking in the Spirit, should be that the man learns "to know His voice" (John 10:4), not so much by recognition of a sound as John would know Paula's tones, but as one friend knows another's mind. We test what we think we hear because we have the mind of Christ (1 Cor. 2:16).

We can often distinguish between God's voice and our imagination or the voice of Satan by the measure of courtesy in what we hear. Satan invades. God respects. Aslan, the great lion, who is our Lord in *The Horse and His Boy,* tells Aravis when her curiosity pries too far concerning another, "Child . . . I am telling you your story, not hers. *No one is told any story but their own"* (p. 171). Ken Hagin points out that many who thought they received the gift of perception or knowledge received in fact only the gift of suspicion (*Ministering to the Oppressed,* p. 4). Satan and the flesh are only too willing to reveal juicy tidbits about others. God is not. The Lord has alerted me many times when one of our older children, Loren or Ami, was in danger, but He seldom warned when they set their hearts to sin. Our sins are our private business. God does not invade. If He does reveal the sins of one to another, it is with discretion. We must know not only the mind of God but the heart of God. He speaks by His nature. Whatever is not His nature, He did not say.

The Spirit will never speak contrary to sound doctrine. Doctrine is vouchsafed in the Word, but it is not the Bible; it is the church's historically tested deposit of understanding about the Bible. Doctrine is the compacted and treasured learning of the church throughout the ages. The Lord reshapes it by revelation. Fresh light breaks forth, upsetting the old. The wise move slowly, for the Lord will begin early and confirm with long sure signs before upsetting long held doctrines. Nor will He ever change the core doctrines of the Trinity and Christology. So it is that God will speak to us also through man, both in his long history as recorded in doctrine, and presently. A friend wisely said to me, 'But John, can't the Lord be speaking to you through me as well as by your own private revelations?'' God inhabited our forefathers and indwells our brothers. We must balance our private hearing with our brother's word. We will learn by listening to God to know our brother, and we hear God through our brother.

The more we know Him, the more purely we shall hear, and the more we hear, the more we shall learn to know Him. This is the sweet joy and delight of listening. Confirmation upon confirmation deciphers what is and what is not our Lord. Love increases by revelation. For we see daily how much more He loves us than the mind and heart could first grasp.

How do we learn to hear God? We learn to love Him and serve Him. He will manage to get through to us when we need His word for that life and service. How do we learn? We learn to swim by swimming. We flounder, but we learn.

Chapter Twelve

DREAMS, THE SLEEP LANGUAGE OF GOD

Dreams are one of the primary consequences of the outpouring of the Holy Spirit (Joel 2:28). A prophet is known as a "dreamer of dreams" (Deut. 13:1). God had guided His children at nearly every major turning point in biblical history through the language of dreams. In a dream God warned King Abimelech that Sarah was Abraham's wife and caused him to send Abraham away a wealthy man (Gen. 20). The Lord appeared to Jacob in a dream as he fled from Esau (Gen. 28). It was in a dream He later told Jacob how to wrest cattle from Laban, and again when to flee from Laban to return to Canaan (Gen. 31). Joseph was given two dreams which foretold his dominion over his brothers (Gen. 37). When his jealous brothers sold Joseph into slavery, he rose to power in Egypt as an interpreter of dreams (Gen. 40-41). Daniel rose to power in Babylon interpreting the dreams of Nebuchadnezzar, and in both the king's and Daniel's dreams, the coming of the Lord Jesus was foretold. So we could trace much of the saving action of God in the Old Testament through the language of dreams.

In the New Testament, Joseph was commanded in a dream to keep Mary as his wife (Matt. 1:20), and to flee with the child Jesus to Egypt (Matt. 2:13). The wise men were warned by God in a dream not to return to Herod (Matt. 2:12). And Joseph knew when to return to Nazareth, by means of a dream (Matt. 2:19). If every instance involving dreams was removed from the Bible, one third of its contents would be missing, and most of its important revelations and events.

The virtue of a dream is that in one fast-moving reel God may speak with minimum conscious interference. And He can often teach us more profoundly by dreams because they will stimulate us to think about a subject and make discoveries. This is much better for us than if God told us outright what He wanted us to learn. The eastern courtesy of speaking indirectly is founded upon this same principle, that each man retains best what he has discovered for himself. So God often prefers to speak indirectly. We may prefer to be like Thomas, who directly put his fingers in Jesus' side, but Jesus pronounced us more blessed who have believed not seeing directly (John 20:29). When God speaks in dreams, we usually need to counsel to gain understanding.

Dreams can be external or internal, or both. An external dream reveals something which has little to do with our personality or character. An internal dream reveals something about our own inner being. Nebuchadnezzar dreamt of an image of a man whose head was made of gold, his breast and arms of silver, his belly and thighs of brass, his legs of iron, and his feet and toes of iron and clay (Dan. 2). Daniel was wise enough to see both the interior and exterior meanings of Nebuchadnezzar's dream. This, however, was Daniel's first instance of dream interpretation for the king. The king might not trust Daniel enough to receive a message concerning his own inner soul's condition. Daniel elected therefore to explain only the exterior meaning, the familiar prophecy of four kingdoms and the coming of the Messiah who would smash all other kingdoms and establish His own.

But here is a possible interior meaning. His head is of gold; he has been given much wisdom and somewhat of God's nature. His breast and arms of silver indicate that he thinks, decides, and acts

170

with knowledge in the Lord's redeeming grace. The belly of brass indicates a burdened heart. (The belly in the east is the place of storage of thoughts, or the unconscious.) The legs of iron mean that he acts with strength and forthrightness. But the telltale warning is in his feet of iron and clay. Nebuchadnezzar has a hardening heart and "feet of clay." If he does not humble himself, overcome his pride and delusions of grandeur, the stone hewn without hands (the Lord) will grind him to bits.

Daniel offered no such interpretation because the king was not yet ready for it. But God did give the king a second warning, (God almost invariably gives men more than one warning) in the form of the dream of the great tree which is cut down (Dan. 4). In dream language, the image being chopped to bits by a stone and the tree being cut down are identical. Nebuchadnezzar was to be brought low from his haughtiness.

Daniel told the king what he sensed the king could receive. He did not feel compelled to tell him all that he knew. Modern-day prophets need the Lord's help to decide which of the many meanings ought to be told to the dreamer. What virtue was it for the Lord to give a man a dream in order to make him think for himself if some interpreter explains what God also could have told him directly if He had chosen to? Perhaps God will want a thing revealed and perhaps not. The Holy Spirit may prompt the prophet to ask the man such leading questions that he himself can discover its meanings.

At one time, I was puzzling how God could know before hand everything I thought or would do, as Psalm 139 and Ephesians 2:10 say, and yet leave me with free will to decide things for myself. Accordingly, the Lord gave me a dream. In it, I walked onto a green lawn and then into a cluster of evil men who dispersed. Changing directions on the lawn, I walked into another cluster, who dispersed. Changing directions again, I walked across the lawn onto a porch, and since one can do anything in a dream, stepped through a bay window. Then I had a warm heart-to-heart

171

talk with a lady (about the age of my mother) whom I recognized. At the end of the talk, she said, "Reverend Sandford, you have helped me so much, could I give you a kiss?" I, being very straight-laced, was embarrassed, and said, "Well, I suppose if you give me a kiss on the cheek, it wouldn't hurt anything," whereupon I bent down, she kissed me on the cheek, and the dream ended. In the morning I could remember the entire dream, except who the lady was.

During the day I forgot all about the dream and went about making calls. In the evening I visited the hospital. While talking to one lady, the conversation became lively, a good exchange of meaning and understanding (the green lawn, green being the symbol of growing life). The conversation then became counseling, and a group of problems were discussed and settled (green lawn again), with the same result (second group of men). The conversation changed the second time, again becoming counseling, in which the lady opened her heart wide (the bay window). A most beneficial heart to heart talk followed, at the end of which the lady said, "Reverend Sandford, you have helped me so much, could I give you a kiss?" I was embarrassed (not at all remembering the dream) and said, "Well, I suppose if you give me a kiss on the cheek, it wouldn't hurt anything." I bent down, the lady kissed me on the cheek—and the Lord popped the dream back into my mind. I had freely decided where and on whom I would call; we had freely decided what we would discuss and how. I asked the lady, "Did you plan all along to give me that kiss, or was it something spontaneous?" She assured me it was altogether spontaneous. I saw that God knows beforehand exactly what one will do, down to the least detail.

Some time later I was teaching about dreams at a School of Pastoral Care, in which the other John Sanford, Agnes Sanford's son, was also one of the teachers. When I told this dream, he interrupted the lecture to say, "But you missed the point of the dream altogether, John." He then explained that the dream also

172

had an interior meaning. (I had seen only the exterior.) My life was out of balance. I was expressing far too much only the logical, structural side of my being. John Sanford explained that the dream called me to recognize and embrace the suppressed half of my being, which is emotion, spontaneity, sensitivity, and feeling. I was afraid of this half of my nature, would not let it live, and when invited by the dream, would only let that half of my being "kiss me on the cheek." I took it to heart. My emotions had been so suppressed—"Osage Indian boys don't cry"—that when hurt I would only smile, or, when all others in a tear-jerker movie were sobbing, I would laugh. I prayed that the Lord would set that half of my being free. Now I *can* cry, and not feel awkward or embarrassed.

One night I dreamed I was standing by a hospital bed, asking a lady (whom in the dream I knew), "What has happened that you are in here?" In answer she took her left hand and threw back the coverlet to show her right arm, which was broken and in a cast. Her nightgown happened to be askew, and the right breast was exposed; I was embarrassed, end of dream. The next morning I could remember the dream but not who the lady was. So I prayed about it, and went on about my work. That afternoon when calling in the hospital, I found a parishioner who had not been there the day before. I asked, "What has happened that you are in here?" For answer she took her left arm and threw back the coverlet. The right arm was broken and in a cast. The nightgown was askew; the breast was exposed; I was embarrassed, and the Lord popped the dream back into my mind. This time preparatory prayer had done its work; I asked a few leading questions, and saw that the greater fracture was in the lady's relation to her mother (symbolized by the breast). But the dream was for me as well. The Lord showed me that I needed to examine prayerfully certain aspects of my childhood relationship with my mother. This dream followed shortly after the other I described and also confirmed the message that God does know exactly what we are going to do, detail by

173

detail, and yet leaves us utterly free to be our own person.

Some dreams are a "state of the union" message, a report by the Holy Spirit on the condition of our heart and soul. A man who is striving mightily to be righteous in all his conduct toward women may have extraordinarily lascivious dreams. A mild-mannered man may be a horribly violent, bloody warrior in his dreams. A man so determined to be honest that he swears to his own hurt on income tax reports may be a first-class fraud in his dreams. Such men have forced their natures out of balance by striving under the law. Repressed, subconscious urges are demanding expression. But these men do not want to face who they really are and how greatly they need to be saved. "No one is righteous, no not one" (Rom. 3:10). Apart from me you can do nothing" (John 15:5). Whenever we strive to live up to the law in our own strength, the Lord who loves us will show us that we are not at all that holy, that only by abiding in Jesus Christ can we keep the law. Whoever does not heed the warnings of God—dreams, friends' words, the Bible, etc.—may suddenly snap beyond healing. "He who is often reproved, yet stiffens his neck will suddenly be broken beyond healing" (Prov. 29:1 RSV). This is one reason why righteous ministers and deacons suddenly have wild affairs. Such warnings call us away from self-righteousness to rest more in our Lord. We need not sin that grace may abound, but we should thank God for letting us see the truth, confess the wickedness of our hearts and plead for heart-changing mercy as those who have no power in ourselves. Thus dreams are one of the kindest and most private ways our loving Father can warn us. We should cease to shudder at such dreams, laugh at ourselves, and relinquish our striving to the Lord. Such dreams are meant for our comfort.

By dreams we are often told of the death of a loved one, or an illness, or something of that sort. Nearly every Christian can recount some instance of being told something in a dream. Strangely, as common as informative dreams are, ignorance of what to do about them is almost as common. Dreams that foretell death or disaster are not to be received as something inevitable. There is nothing fatalistic about Christian faith. God will hear us. He calls us to prayer that He might have opportunity to save, rescue, or turn whatever happens to blessing. He sent the Son not to condemn the world but to save it (John 3:17).

To understand dreams and call the church to intercessory prayer when dreams have given warning is a primary function of the Lord's Elijah prophets. As times worsen, our merciful Lord will raise up thousands of prophets, hopefully at least one in each cell of His body, to interpret dreams and call the church to prayer.

On March 27, 1974, I was in prayer and sensed that God was speaking to me, "The time for intercession is past; it is now the time for discipline . . . it will be utterly destructive, for boilers will explode and wreak havoc." A few nights later I dreamt that the eastern sky was ablaze with violent boiling flames—as though the Van Allen belt and all the clouds were writhing in flames. In thinking about these ominous warnings I remembered that, though the Lord said He would destroy Sodom and Gomorrah, Abraham still pled with Him until He agreed to spare Sodom and Gomorrah if ten righteous men could be found there (Gen. 18:22-33). The words "the time for intercession is past. . ." did not deter me; I prayed for mercy. Each morning in prayer I felt that if I could only throw myself on the floor and weep uncontrollably, I might begin to express some of the massive grief welling up in my spirit. All day for days and days I walked about under a cloud of vast dread. (The last time such dread had hung over me was before the Sunshine Mine disaster, before that during the prayers for California, and before that for two weeks before President Kennedy was shot.) Then came the tornadoes which destroyed so many lives, from Georgia up to the Great Lakes (April, 1974), perhaps the most destructive of the century. The weather man on Channel 4, Spokane, spoke of the skies as "great *boilers* of pressure which seemed to explode in violence upon the ground." This side of heaven we may never know how many Elijah prophets had been called into intercessory prayer beforehand, how many had indeed responded, nor how much effect their prayers had, if any. Obviously, too few responded for tragedy to be completely averted.

Our people have so departed from God's word that at present God's Elijah prophets seldom find a national hearing. David Wilkerson prophesied great natural disasters, like tornadoes, in his book, *The Vision*. David, having national status and recognition, had used all the media available to him—TV, radio, publicity, the book, etc.—to pronounce the warning to the largest audience possible. What did it get him? Accusations that he was doing it all for greed.

> To whom shall I speak and give warning, that they may hear? behold, their ear is uncircumcised, and they cannot hearken: behold, the word of the LORD is unto them a reproach; they have no delight in it. Therefore I am full of the fury of the LORD; I am weary with holding in: I will pour it out upon the children abroad, and upon the assembly of young men together: for even the husband with the wife shall be taken, the aged with him that is full of days. And their houses shall be turned unto others, with their fields and wives together: for I will stretch out my hand upon the inhabitants of the land, saith, the LORD. For from the least of them even unto the greatest of them everyone is given to covetousness; and from the prophet even unto the priest everyone dealeth falsely.
>
> Jeremiah 6:10-13

We are not much different from Israel. We respond to our prophets about as they did. But our judgment will be greater, for we have the life of the risen Lord Jesus, the power of the Holy Spirit, and two thousand years of Christianity as witnesses—we ought to respond differently than did they (Matt. 11:20-24).

Informative dreams do not always mean that we should ask God to stay His hand. The Lord frequently told me before He called one of my parishioners home in death. Two years before Kennedy's death, I saw the entire assassination scene in a vivid dream. Except the shots did not come from the Book Depository, but from a house, set where the Book Depository actually is. If I ever see that house in real life, I will know it as the place where the plot was conceived. I also saw a car, full of malicious men, pull away in haste afterwards. I know beyond doubt that the assassination was the work of many men, not merely Oswald. Concerning Kennedy and the other deaths, the Lord did not call me to pray that it not happen, but for blessing in the situation. A prophet must not naively assume that he knows the will of God. He must listen carefully for His instructions in every instance.

Not all informative dreams warn of evil. God also speaks to us in dreams that we might pray for the blessing the dream foretells. Bertha Coffin of Council Grove, Kansas, dreamed (in 1968) that Paula and I were no longer in the pastorate. Instead we were writing and counseling, blessed of the Lord and happy, and living in a beautiful house given to us by the Lord. In March, 1974, Bertha and her husband Don came to visit us—she recognized our home as the very house of her dream. That was an encouraging confirmation to us.

In 1961 we were preparing to leave the First Congregational Church of Streator, Illinois. We believed that God wanted us to do this, but we weren't at all certain where we were to go next. I had resigned effective June 1. It was in late spring that we fell asleep praying that the Lord guide us.

That night I dreamt. An angel said to me, "Come with me, I will show you where you are to go" (cf. Acts 16:9). The next second, the angel and I were floating along above rolling green pasture land through which a dirt road wound to a great white house with many parapets and awnings. The house sat on the brow of a hill, from which a forest of oak trees descended to a valley filled with trees. The spirit pointed to the house and said, "This is where you are called; you are to minister to this man." Then, while I pondered why I should be called to a man rather than a church, we floated on

177

over a wide valley filled with trees and farmlands until we were looking down at the roof of a church. Beside the church was a great maple tree. Up the hill behind the church was a sidewalk and then a bare foundation, with building materials and tools lying all around. The spirit said, "There is a highway and a river. People turn in here to rest. You are called here to minister." Over the foundation he said, "They are building here."

Within a week, a long distance call came from Council Grove, Kansas, inviting me to come as a candidate to visit among the congregation; I would also preach and if the congregation voted for it and I agreed to it, I would become their pastor. When I arrived, as soon as I walked up the sidewalk and saw the roofline of the church and the great tree, I knew God had called us there. The people also chose to call. The foundation I had seen in my dream was also there, and when I asked about it, I was told, "Harry White's house stands right where the new dam will go. He has to move it. He is moving it here, and they are preparing this old foundation, to set his house on it. The old church used to stand on that foundation before it burned down and they built the new one."

Six weeks later we moved into the parsonage, standing between the church building and Harry White's house, which had by then been set in place. At first I didn't realize it as the house I had seen in my dream, but, as soon as the porches and awnings were reattached, it was clearly the one. I asked where it had sat. Parishioners gave me directions. As I drove in on the dirt road from the highway, I recognized it as the same road and pasture land of my dream two months before. Sure enough, the foundation stood exactly where I had seen the house in my dream. Why, I mused, did the Holy Spirit send an angel to call me to minister to Harry White?

A few months later, when I felt that Harry knew me well enough, I called on him and told him about my dream. "Why do you suppose that happened, Harry? What does it mean?" He had no idea.

A year afterwards, when I attended a state conference, I happened to overhear "Tiny" Meador talking in the hallway to another delegate about a proposed camp for the Kansas Conference of the United Church of Christ. A committee had been formed to find a site for it. I immediately thought of Council Grove with its lake and the new reservoir being built. Certainly that ought to provide a great spot for a church camp. The next day, when I returned home (Sunday evening), Paula and I prayed about the possibility of a church camp near Council Grove. It was as though the Lord emptied the lake of heaven all over us. As light poured all about us, we knew that God was about to do something wonderful.

Monday morning I told Warren Gilman, secretary of the city chamber of commerce, about what I had overheard. Warren carried the idea that noon to the city council; they formed a committee to inquire concerning properties. The committee approached Harry White and his nephews, Hale and Henry. They gave to the Conference 117 acres of prime land, surrounded on three sides by water. Council Grove Reservoir is formed by a dam immediately south of the confluence of Neosho River and Monkers Creek. That spearhead of land rising out of the lake between its two arms was the land given by the Whites (Harry gave the major portion), easily worth hundreds of thousands of dollars.

Amazing as was the gift, so were the hundreds of "coincidences" connected with it. An access road had been built and used in the 1880s. Trees and bushes had filled it from end to end, but there it was, still fenced off and waiting to be reclaimed. No major legal hassles would bar access to the camp. The architect belonged to one of our Topeka churches. The state head of water resources was in one of our churches. Stone for the buildings was procured, free for the taking, from abandoned houses and barns in the lake bed before the dam was completed. Volunteer teen-age work camps, using local tractors and wagons, brought the stone up to the camp. So it went. The Lord had planned His camp from the beginning. Now, Holy Spirit retreats are held there every year, and

179

countless young people and adults are blessed every year through the camp program. When God wanted to bless His children, He began by calling one of His prophets into position through a dream.

This was the Lord's method of operation throughout the Old Testament. He did no major work of blessing, unless He informed and procured invitation first. We saw this in Jacob's dream, in Joseph's saving of many from starvation in the seven lean years, in the prophetic dreams of the Messiah in Daniel, and in so many of the other prophets foretelling Jesus' coming.

Just as the prophet who receives a warning dream is amiss if he does nothing, so if a servant fails to affirm and invite and take subsequent appropriate actions concerning a blessing dream, he frustrates the Lord's purpose in giving the dream. As times grow more and more difficult, God's servants will need to be increasingly alert to hear His promises of blessing and to call the church into position to receive them.

Some informative dreams I call "medicine" dreams. Jacob's dreams of blessing and Joseph's dreams of his brothers' bowing before him were of this type—a dream in which the Lord lays out our path and gives us some instruction or warning or blessing with it. In Genesis 28:13-15 the Lord first identified himself to Jacob, gave the promise of blessing, and encouraged him that He would be with him where he was going and would bring him home again. Throughout the fourteen years of his servitude for his wives, and beyond, that promise of his returning would remain as a hidden seed in the back of Jacob's mind.

The Lord's prophet must hold to his course. The Lord may redirect our aim somewhat, but that will never amount to more than an amendment. In parliamentary rules, an amendment may not kill the original intent of the bill. A medicine dream locks a man onto course until whatever is intended is fully accomplished.

The word "medicine" is borrowed from my Osage Indian heritage. Each brave, coming to maturity, fasted and prayed that Wahkontah, the great spirit, would give him signs or dreams to indicate his purpose in life. Such dreams and signs were then brought to "The Lodge of Mystery," where the "little old men" (who were neither little nor old, but named themselves so for humility) interpreted their meaning with the young brave. Whatever was concluded from that meeting (which included prayer) became the young brave's "medicine" for life. He would live out that purpose. It would be said of a man "He has good medicine" or "His medicine is weak."

Thus we use this term to describe a dream that significantly affects our purpose within the kingdom of God. We see St. Paul's calling to come over to Macedonia (Acts 16:9) and Peter's trance-dream to minister to the Gentiles (Acts 10:9-20) as such medicine dreams. I prefer to use the word "medicine" rather than a "calling dream" because it implies more of what God is doing. The dream works deep within our memory banks as a medicine or healing upon our intents, and the servant is himself a medicine for others.

Some dreams may be no more than the flotsam and jetsam of a sick mind or body. No one should become addicted to dreams. It is not dreams we follow, but the guidance of the Lord Jesus Christ. Not all dreams are spiritual. Not all spiritual dreams are from the Holy Spirit. Zechariah 10:2 and Jeremiah 23:32 speak of false dreams. Isaiah 29:8 reports of instances when bodily needs prompt dreams which prove unreal upon awakening. Solomon warns us, "For a dream cometh through the multitude of business; and a fool's voice is known by multitude of words" (Eccl. 5:3). "For in the multitude of dreams and many words there are also divers vanities; but fear thou God" (Eccl. 5:7). If the Lord gives a peculiar or startling dream, especially a calling or medicine dream, He will confirm by signs, and the dream will meet all the tests of Scripture and sound doctrine. It is always only Jesus Christ whom we follow. We do not know the voice of strangers (John 10:5).

Each person must learn by experience what his own dream language is, what its symbols mean to him. For me, for example,

181

dreams of flying forecast great spiritual happenings soon to come. They also tell me that I will rise in the Spirit to have wondrous revelations and graces of the Lord. And they warn me to keep myself grounded in common sense and biblical testing, lest I fly off into my own fleshly mysticism, and become like Icarus who flew too high with his wax and feather wings so that the sun melted the wax and he fell to his death in the sea. A different Son has melted my wings in the past and plunged me into the sea of embarrassment and consequent hard lessons.

I remember, in particular, a dream in which I flew through lines of high tension wires, while men were shooting guns with tracer bullets at me. By then I knew to pray about it before the upcoming teaching series. Sure enough, the mission was blessed by the Lord greatly, but at the end I spoke about things filled with high tension, in which lines had to be drawn precisely, and men shot hard questions at me, but the Lord blessed and protected.

Symbols are the peculiar language of dreams. Some symbols have universal meanings, some have tribal or social meanings, some are distinctive to nations, localities, and cultures. Each individual has his own set of meanings. To better understand symbols a study of comparative religion, art, Bulfinch's mythology, or some other anthology of myths will help, as well as a general knowledge of nursery and fairy stories, such as Mother Goose and Grimm's or Andersen's fairy tales.

Many symbols have double meanings. For example, the lion stands both for royalty and courage, and for destructive carnal violence. If a man is walking with the Lord Jesus, then the lion of Judah (Rev. 5:5) is his strength, authority, dignity and courage. If he walks apart from God, the devil comes like a roaring lion seeking a prey (1 Pet. 5:8). A serpent on a pole symbolizes healing (Num. 21:8,9) and bears a striking resemblance to the caduceus, a pagan symbol that is an emblem of the medical profession. But that ancient serpent and dragon who is the devil also appears from Genesis 3 to Revelation 20. Chains stand either for those negative things that bind us, or for the bonds of love which make us prisoners that we may be free indeed. The axe or the knife either cut to the root in friendly fashion, or wield death. The sword is two-edged to separate for God, or brings wounding. The cross itself was the instrument and sign of torturous death and disgrace, turned by the Father to mean redemption and victory.

That symbols so often mean more than one thing keeps us from assuming too easily that we understand what we see in our dreams. We are forced to seek the Holy Spirit to clarify.

Colors are double symbols. If we walk with God, red is the color of the blood of forgiveness and of the fire of love, but if we walk apart, then red is the color of anger—"I saw red!" Blue is the color of hope, of healing, of eternity, and of our Lord's mother, or we are depressed and sad, without hope—"I feel blue today." Yellow or gold is for wisdom and the nature and light of God, or for cowardice—"He has a yellow streak down his back." Green stands for life, eternity, and new growth, or for sickness and jealousy—"Green with envy." Purple is for royalty or rage, for we either rule with Christ, or we are frustrated and angry—"He turned purple with rage." Black is the primordial color of creation, the symbol both of life and of death, of wholeness and hope arising out of the ground of all life, and it is the symbol of death and despair, darkness and evil—"It all looked black to me." White is purity and innocence or its opposite, fear—"I turned white as a sheet." And so it goes.

By far the most important symbols in dreams, however, are people. Most often dreams of parents, relatives and friends are more internal than external. Dreams of mothers, grandmothers, aunts or sisters—any woman—often tell us about the feminine side of our nature. Dreams of fathers, grandfathers, uncles or brothers—any man—often tell us about our male side. To dream of giving birth often means that the Holy Spirit is telling us of some new aspect coming from our lives. To dream of the death of a person may represent the dying of some aspect of our nature. A dream of someone being ill can inform us of interior illness in our character. But, in dreams, birth, death, and even illness are not in themselves good or bad. Therefore, though it is helpful to know about symbols, we can never make our knowledge into something pat, so that we don't need the Holy Spirit any more.

The man who discovered organic chemistry saw it in a dream. Some people wrongly think that that was revelation. Gardner Murphy has written (*Personality: A Biosocial Approach to Origin and Structure*, New York: Harper Bros., 1947) of "co-conscious creativity." It is a common human process in which we think hard about something (like where we left the house keys we can't find) and then, for one reason or another, turn our attention elsewhere or go to sleep. During this time of quiescence, our minds frequently pop up with the answer or solution. Even if the Holy Spirit has a direct hand in this commonly observed process, it is not revelation.

We must be most especially careful about revelation. It can build on no other framework than that which is laid (1 Cor. 3:11). Any revelation which counters what the Word of God says is not revelation but delusion. David Wilkerson's visions seemed to us to further detail that which is already prophesied in God's Word. Revelation of God's nature surely still occurs. To many of us, our sainted grandmother, or some other person, stands in memory like a rock of revelation in a sea of turmoil. But any dream which purports to reveal some new doctrine ought to be checked very carefully. Herein the Mormons and Christian Scientists and others went astray—no revelation can be given other than that within the Bible. Whatever revelation occurs of doctrine ought only to be a fresh light upon that which is.

Paula and I have seen many many things we thought were from God. Nevertheless whatever was not solidly biblical had to be thrown away—and we have been the better for the discarding. There may be many present ideas we regard as revelation which tomorrow we will count as heresy. Let every man hold loosely what he thinks he has been shown. If it is of God, God will prosper it (Acts 5:34-39).

It is God we serve. The Trinity is Father, Son, and the Holy Spirit, not Father, Son, and revelation, or Father, Son, and dreams. Especially the Trinity is not Father, Son, and knowledge. We are not saved by knowledge but by the person of Jesus Christ. Now that we've shared what we know about dreams, remember, none of it is crucial. It is the Holy Spirit who guides us. He leads us in the paths of righteousness for *His name's sake*.

Chapter Thirteen

VISIONS, THE PICTURE LANGUAGE OF GOD
Acts 2:14; Proverbs 29:18; Habakkuk 2:1-3

Much of what we have said about dreams applies also to visions. The important difference between dreams and visions is that when we receive a vision we are awake.

Visions are thus more subject to our control. In a dream, the Holy Spirit has a freer hand in what we experience. But in a vision our minds can embellish and interfere. That means that we have to die to ourselves more thoroughly in order to receive a vision safely. As in dreams, so in visions the Lord speaks to us indirectly, that He might enlist us more in the enterprise, and that we might grow in knowledge and wisdom and stature.

Visions come in many degrees. Sometimes the Holy Spirit flashes pictures across the inner screen of our minds with or without interruption of conscious thoughts. Some think such visions are less ''in the Spirit,'' since they happen less dramatically than visions in trance. Not so. God simply chooses how He will communicate to us according to His wisdom. Such visions are not less valuable, forceful, imperative, or truthful. We must apply the same disciplines of testing and obedience to them as to the most vivid visions in trances.

Sometimes the things we see in our minds are products of our

187

imaginations. But we must not discount them, because the Holy Spirit operates through our imaginations. Sometimes such visions are symbolic, in which the Holy Spirit uses a cartoon or representation to convey a message figuratively to us. Or we may literally see what is actually transpiring, at some distance. Paula once came out from a prayer meeting to discover that her glasses were missing from her pocket. Without them, headaches would soon disable her. I prayed that God would help us. Immediately the Holy Spirit showed me a sidewalk, tufts of tall grass, and the glasses tucked in a pocket between patches near the sidewalk. We walked right to the glasses. Such simple visions are so common nearly every Christian can relate something similar. Countless saints of God have seen relatives or friends in their mind's eye, and prayed accordingly. We ought not to let the simpleness or quickness of such pictures make us think they are not visions or not of God. How dramatic a vision is measures neither its truth nor its importance.

God wants to walk in simple, quiet daily ways with us. That is preferable to dramatic visions. Thomas was not more blessed for having put his fingers in the Lord's side, but less. Sometimes the Lord must hit us over the head with a big one precisely because we disregarded the continual little daily pictures.

We most often fail to think of those pictures which commonly come to our minds as visions because (1) our own minds seemed to be doing it, (2) it was so quick and easy, (3) we may not have been in prayer at all. Where do our thoughts and imaginations come from? There are only three sources: the devil, our flesh, or the Holy Spirit. We who belong to the Lord should at least not exclude the possibility that God would speak to us by a vision. We need only ask by what source our imaginations are being stirred. We should be careful not to give ourselves credit too quickly for a good idea that might just be a gift of the Holy Spirit.

Let us not say hastily then that we have never received visions from God. We may be frequently receiving visions and yet never have given them that name nor God the credit He deserves.

The next degree of vision is that which we commonly regard as a vision, when in prayer the Holy Spirit pops a picture before us vividly, without the aid and usually to the surprise of our minds. Such a vision is not a seeing with our physical eyes but is within us. We mark it as a vision because we recognize that we had no part in setting it up. We may even catch our minds trying to embellish or transform the picture some way, and have to exercise self-discipline to keep out of it. Sometimes we have asked for the vision and sometimes not. In each case the distinguishing mark is the fact of rest. We had no discernibly active part in the formation of what we were seeing. It is like sitting in a movie house, watching what goes on, sometimes whether we want to or not.

The next degree of vision contains a sense of actual seeing, outside ourselves, though we realize we are seeing with something else or more than our physical eyes. We are awake, alert and in full control. St. Paul had such a vision of Jesus on the road to Damascus before he fell slain in the spirit, into a semiconscious state (Acts 9). Ananias and Stephen likewise saw outside themselves while not in trance (Acts 9 and 7). To what degree our physical eyes are involved matters little.

In the Old Testament, and in the New prior to the coming of the Holy Spirit, most of the vital turning points of man's history with God were marked by dreams. After the coming of the Holy Spirit, those turning points commonly came by visions rather than by dreams—Paul's conversion (Acts 9), Peter's commission to eat with and minister among Gentiles (Acts 10 and 11), John's apocalypse, and Paul's call to Macedonia by "vision in the night" (Acts 16). We can infer from this that God can risk more direct conscious involvement with His servants when the Holy Spirit dwells in them.

The final degree of vision occurs by trance. As in a dream, the conscious mind is taken out of it. A Christian trance is in no way akin to hypnotic trance. Hypnotic trance is a deliberately induced state, both by the hypnotist and the hypnotized. And in hypnotism the subject's will is controlled by the hypnotist. One cannot, however, deliberately enter a Christian trance. It happens *to* him, perhaps by overpowering of his circuits, but without over-powering his will. An entranced person can haul himself out of the trance, whereas normally a hypnotized person cannot.

Whether God puts us into a trance or we fall into it, we do not know, but the Scripture says that Peter "fell into a trance" (Acts 10:10), that John was in the spirit on the Lord's day, saw the glorified and risen Lord, and then *"fell* at his feet as dead" (Rev. 1:17). Daniel was given great and grievous visions of the Lord and the future, and though "the visions of my head troubled me" (7:15) he did not fall into a trance. However, in chapter 8 Daniel saw great and glorious visions and was stable in heart and mind *until "He came near where I stood*: and when he came, I was afraid, and *fell* upon my face" and "as he was speaking with me I was in a deep sleep on my face toward the ground" (vv. 17,18). In each case the recipient is simply overcome by the power of the Lord's presence, and falls into a trance. God apparently does not prefer that, for as in Daniel, "but he touched me, and set me upright" (v. 18), and in Revelation when John fell, ". . . he laid his right hand upon me, saying unto me, Fear not . . ." (Rev. 1:17). The Lord, knowing that the awe of His resurrected presence overcomes us and throws us into a trance, touches us that, if possible, we might commune with Him in full faculty, rather than by trance. Wouldn't any of us prefer to visit with our own children when they are fully awake rather than comatose?

Visions which are beyond us, or which show us the world of the spirit, and which may induce a trance, are not beyond suspicion or testing. Nor should we value them above other kinds of visions. When Gabriel appeared to Mary in a vision, he gave her sure signs to confirm that he was from God. It doesn't please the Lord if we too glibly accept whatever is obviously spiritual. We must test our visions and what they portray. And the more heavenly they seem to us, the more carefully we ought to test them (2 Cor. 11:14). Even if a vision promises a sign which comes to pass, that does not authenticate the vision. Wonders and signs can be given by one who leads astray from God (Deut. 13:1-3). Devils can work miracles (Rev. 16:4). Satan promised miracles to Jesus. Jesus didn't dispute his ability to perform them. We must test *every* vision by the Word, by the nature of God, and by sound doctrine. Whoever wants to become spiritual should keep his guard, otherwise he will be like a city without walls (Prov. 25:28).

We have an even greater responsibility to obey visions. Dreams can be forgotten. Our minds and wills are not fully engaged during dreams and thus not fully responsible. But in visions, since we are awake, we are fully responsible not to forget. That may be why the Holy Spirit has chosen to present His imperative by vision rather than by dream.

But how shall we obey either dream or vision, if the meaning is unclear? It behooves us to pray, think, ask questions of our brothers, and wait for the Lord's revelation. We should not strive to interpret, for that opens doors to the flesh and Satan to interfere. Rather, we should state our desire to understand, restfully meditate, and perhaps do a little research. Sometimes the Lord will quickly answer. But most often that would cut off the process of discovery that began with the dream or vision. We are referring to visions which are allegorical or figurative. Occasionally the Lord appears to us in a vision and tells us directly, without figures or parables, what we are to do. Ananias had no cogitating to do about the command, "Arise, and go into the street which is called Straight . . . for one called Saul . . . that he might receive his sight" (Acts 9:11,12). But, apart from that, if the Lord gives us a vision to provoke us to thought and learning, He will reveal its meaning at the right time.

We know a mother who once had a series of dreams and visions of a pond, around which were green lawns and trees here and there. In the shallow pond, face down, was a small boy. For several days that picture returned again and again. She puzzled and prayed. One evening, as she was doing the dishes, she suddenly threw her dish and towel on the counter and ran full tilt across several lawns to a neighbor's fish pond, where she reached in and plucked up her son just in time to save him from drowning. Because she was waiting quietly upon God, at the right moment He showed her what to do.

Sometimes God will show us something by visions and dreams which will remain with us for future use. Scientists can position instruments in a rocket which remain inactive for months while the rocket flies through space. At the right moment, those instruments will activate to swing cameras, take pictures and flash messages to earth.

People have come to us to ask the meaning of some particularly cogent, recurring childhood dream. Usually we find that that dream or vision has already been effective; the Holy Spirit has prompted our discussion because the crucial moment is imminent. Recently, Betty, a mature Christian, brought Ann, a troubled friend of hers, to see me. Ann was convinced that her soul had died the previous Friday (this being Tuesday). Betty had already begun to discern that a lying spirit inhabited Ann. That demon told Betty that Ann belonged body, mind, heart, and soul to Satan, that Ann was choosing death and was at peace in Satan's peace. God had told me—that same previous Friday—that He was bringing three people to see me, one of whom was insincere. I was to tell him so. That had puzzled me, but I had prayed about it and put it out of my mind. Then the two women came. Ann kept saying, "I'm a phony, you're a phony, everyone is a phony, everyone is a liar." And, "I am at peace, death is peace, and I just want to be left alone." I suddenly remembered what the Lord had told me on Friday. I then understood. The third person was the demon inside Ann; it was not she, but he who was doing all this talking. The devil had convinced Ann that death was peace. (Psychologically she was fleeing from the tensions of life with her son and husband.) But the Holy Spirit had given me the key to her deliverance. "You say that all men are liars. So you, too, are insincere. Doesn't it then stand to reason that you are also lying when you say that death outside of Christ is peace and rest? That is a lie. You are insincere. Satan has no peace. He is a liar." That word began to crack Satan's delusions by which he held Ann's mind captive. A major exorcism followed. Afterward Betty asked me, "Perhaps you can tell me why, twenty-seven years ago, when I first became Ann's friend, the Lord kept giving me a dream about her which I could never forget. I prayed and prayed about it." She had dreamed that Ann bore a baby and then killed it. The dream had variations, but that was the continuing motif. The Holy Spirit then showed me the meaning. Ann had always coped with life by running away. It finally ended in delusion and demonic bondage. God knew her and foresaw that bondage and had taken steps to deliver her. In dreams, killing a baby often signifies our own hatred of life and flight from it. That Friday she had, she said, "actually felt a death blow to my soul. I felt it die and go from me." God had waited until then to effect His salvation, but He had all along prepared His servants for just that moment.

Many many times people have come to us with problems—divorce, parental conflicts, sexual guilt or incapability, depression, etc.—and we discover that in childhood they had a recurring daydream, which we could see as something God had sent for a warning and guidance. Such dreams, visions, and daydreams are often important clues to healing and deliverance. In this sense, perhaps, we ought to classify these daydreams as visions—a vision being a picture implanted by the Holy Spirit upon our minds and hearts. Not all daydreams are visions, but *recurring* dreams or daydreams ought to be examined, if only for psychological value, not to mention the possibility of God's guidance.

I continually had a daydream as a child in which I was in a room with bookshelves where people came to visit me. And it was in my home which was filled with love. Was it only a daydream? That very situation is now fact. Or was it the Holy Spirit implanting guidance into a child's deep mind?

Frequently the Lord will give a vision or dream years in advance to prepare one of His servants to do a work for Him. Joseph dreamt of elevation, in which his father and brothers would bow before him. Then he underwent years of hardship and humiliation without which he could never have been safely elevated. Perhaps Jonathan (1 Sam. 14) saw a vision, at least he had some hunch that God would do something through him. So he and his armorbearer set out to do battle for God alone against thousands. Did God give them an escalator so that they could arrive fresh and strong? No, they had to climb arduously up a cliff—then enter battle. Between every vision and its fulfillment is usually an arduous path. So, if it seems that all hell has broken loose and nothing is going right, rejoice and praise God under your sufferings. These afflictions may confirm your vision more than anything else. God is breaking you in order that the fulfillment of the vision may be of Him.

Nevertheless, when opposition comes, it is difficult to know whether God is saying, "I am not in this," or "Take heart, this is the sign that this is of me." This is one reason that we are placed within the body of Christ. "In the mouth of two or three witnesses shall every word be established" (2 Cor. 13:1b). But seldom are a man's closest friends his best confirmers. Often their own interests block their judgment. So the Lord frequently will give His servant confirmations from nearly total strangers or people who otherwise could have no conscious awareness of what their words might mean to us. This is especially true when the word or vision God has given runs counter to what the local body is doing or thinking. It is a truly remarkable church that can confirm God's servant when he speaks things they don't want to hear. God prefers to confirm our visions through our brothers closest to us in the body. Unfortunately, often we are not dead enough to self to let that happen.

If confirmation comes and you are convinced of your vision,

obey it no matter what (Acts 26:19; Deut. 23:21). You may be wrong, but the Lord will honor your intention to obey, forgive you and haul you out of trouble. Psalm 91:51b says, "I will be *with him in trouble*; I will deliver him, and *honor* him." Not that God will keep us out of trouble; He will be with us in it. He will get us out of it. And He will honor us. One time a vision led me in a way my heart spoke against. But brothers confirmed. I seemed undeniably led into it. Therefore I said, "Lord, I take this to be of you. If it is not, you know that my intentions were sincere, and I trust you to get me out." Sure enough, time revealed error; I found myself oppressed, confused, sick. But what a comfort it was to know that the Lord was there with me in it all the way; He did deliver me, and I was honored by God, not shamed for my error.

If we're afraid to be wrong and we're still trying to live the Christian life, then we have gotten ourselves into a trap (1 John 1:8). We think we have to possess some righteousness in ourselves, and are afraid we might lose it. But we remain sinners redeemed by Christ. We wear His righteousness (1 Cor. 1:30). So, when we are "right," it means only that we heard correctly and did what God told us, not that we were somehow intrinsically right. Intrinsic rightness is only self-righteousness.

Another problem with visions arises from our sinful propensities. Whenever a person is convinced that God is speaking to him, he is likely to get a big head about it—to use it as a means to elevate himself above his fellows. Paul warned, "Let no one disqualify you, insisting on self-abasement and worship of angels, taking his stand on visions, puffed up without reason by his sensuous mind, and not holding fast to the Head, from whom the whole body, nourished and knit together through its joints and ligaments, grows with a growth that is from God" (Col. 2:18,19 RSV). Any of us at any time may become puffed up, taking our stand on visions, not holding fast to the Head. God gives no guarantees. None of us will run the race flawlessly. Let us restore one another in kindness (Gal. 6:1; James 5:13-15). Prophets must have freedom to fail, or they

195

cannot receive with boldness whatever fresh revelations God would bring to the body.

When God shows a prophet some hidden or forgotten sin, it is to save him from the effects of that sin. We, however, usually object violently and try to suppress the sight. We hate to look at our sin because we think it disqualifies us (which only shows how much we are still relying on ourselves and not on Christ). "All things that are reproved are made manifest by the light: for whatsoever doth make manifest is light" (Eph. 5:13). We should be glad to see our sin, for that will mean healing, but "men loved darkness rather than light because their deeds were evil" (John 3:19).

So the Lord shows His prophet how things really are and what, consequently, is going to happen in order to set the machinery of salvation in operation. Many times a prophet, when he sees the future, humbles himself and asks God to show him his sin. Such prayers are frequently answered by a vision that replays some segment of the prophet's life in such a way as to sharply reveal the sin in question. This may momentarily bring agony to God's servant, but only enough to bring him to heartfelt repentance and the joy of restoration.

Sometimes, however, we see not our own, but other people's sin. In such cases, the Lord is trusting us to act as He would: to counsel, forgive, and heal the other. Satan accuses. The Lord reveals in light. We have never found the Lord's visions which reveal ours or another's sins accompanied by anything other than compassion. Satan pries unbidden. The Holy Spirit only reveals another's sins if the sinner has given his will to the Lord so that He has that invitation. That's why God showed David's murder and adultery to Nathan (2 Sam. 12:1-14). Ahab was rebellious, but he was still anointed by God to be king. And so his sin in the case of Naboth's vineyard was revealed to Elijah (1 Kings 21:19-29).

Visions frequently help Paula and me in our counseling. The Holy Spirit will characteristically describe the appearance of a house, the description of a room, and then an incident in a given year of a person's life. On hearing us recite these things, the person will exclaim, ''Why, yes, that is exactly how my house looked and that was my room, and that thing did happen just as you describe it.'' Such a vision usually unlocks confession, healing, or self-understanding.

All of us who counsel need this gift of knowledge. Countless times women have complained to us that they are incapable of really enjoying sex with their husbands. Many times, the Holy Spirit would show me a picture of the woman being molested by a brother or father or uncle or grandfather. These women have often repressed the memory of it quite deeply, but it cannot be healed unless it first comes to the light. Until then, these repressed bitternesses act as a root to spring up to cause trouble in the present (Heb. 12:15).

Often persons come to counselors with planned speeches, incapable of full honesty or outright confession. Truth is a gift of the Holy Spirit, for the heart is deceitful (Jer. 17:9). Thus a secondary effect of these words of knowledge is to prod the counselee into uncustomary honesty.

Limits must be carefully drawn, however. There is a fine line between the Holy Spirit's gift of knowledge and the human gift of suspicion. They look alike, but the former is used to extend the kingdom of God, the latter to extend the kingdom of self. We should daily, momentarily surrender every gift of vision, knowledge and perception to death on the cross, so that only the resurrected life of our Lord Jesus Christ may be in operation. But, just as we do not cease to drive cars because some drive dangerously, or to swim because some drown, we must not cease to prophesy because of the pitfalls.

Everyone who receives a vision should learn to follow the Lord, not the vision. If the vision is true, the Lord will bring it about. If the recipient tries to make the vision happen, he is inevitably indulging selfish desires under a cloak of religious earnestness.

Sometimes visions are given to encourage and guide. Paula and

I were praying for a Christian who was being called to stand while his wife floundered in rebellion against his authority, his fledgling business was in upheaval, and the cell groups around him were in turmoil. I saw a great ship sailing in a storm, while a voice called out, "Steady as she goes." Strangely, great winds and waves were pounding against the bow, while the sails were puffed toward the wind, not away from it. Then I saw that behind the ship was a wake of peace. I told my friend my vision and said, "Your sails are filled by the wind of the Holy Spirit, not by the winds of the storm, and you are sailing by His strength *into* the storm that He might settle it for you. Take heart, the Lord is blessing you and telling you not to fear, your sails are filled by Him, not the confusion around you."

Beginners may rashly think their gift entitles them to behave arrogantly. But God will take them and us through the discipline of trial and error. His goal is always as much to develop character as it is to accomplish the task at hand. Paula often receives humorous visions while praying for others. But the Lord uses her embarrassment and the humor to relax the counselee and help him to laugh at himself, a sure sign of healing.

God wants to send forth His word to rebuild His earth. It is an earth given into our care, returned there from Satan's supposed dominion by the resurrection of our Lord. Therefore the Lord wants our invitation and affirmation. God therefore wants to give us pictures of how He would bless the earth, and then join with us to bring those things to pass. And He wants to show us harm coming that it might be derailed by repentance. Let us plead like Abraham for the deliverance of our modern Sodoms and Gomorrahs, while remembering that we are called to far more than defense. We are called to be transformers of the earth and its tragedies into glory. Let us stand to catch the vision of God, that fair earth may be transformed into more than Eden, and mankind may be free at last to live in love.

Chapter Fourteen

DARK SPEECH, GOD'S STRANGE AND JOYOUS WAY OF SPEAKING TO MAN

Numbers 12:6-8; Psalm 78:1-3; Matthew 13:34-35

Often the Lord will speak to His children in dark speech—a pun, a conundrum, a figure, or a parable—when He could more easily have spoken directly. Why? We have hinted at many answers: the politeness of indirectness, His desire for us to mature, and so on. Perhaps the simplest reason is that He must remain hidden to us.

I have declared the former things from the beginning; and they went forth out of my mouth, and I showed them; I did them suddenly, and they came to pass. Because I knew that thou art obstinate, and thy neck is an iron sinew, and thy brow brass; I have even from the beginning declared it to thee; before it came to pass I showed it thee: lest thou shouldest say, Mine idol hath done them, and my graven image, and my molten image, hath commanded them. Thou hast heard, see all this; and will not ye declare it? I have showed thee new things from this time, even hidden things, and thou didst not know them. They are created now, and not from the beginning; even before the day when thou heardest them not; lest thou shouldest say, Behold, I knew them. Yea, thou heardest not: yea, thou knewest not; yea, from that time that thine ear was not opened: for I knew that thou wouldest deal very treacherously, and wast called a transgressor from the womb.

Isaiah 48:3-8

God knows what He is doing. If we become peeved or impatient that we cannot understand what He has told us, the flaw, if there be any, is with us, not God. When the disciples urged Jesus to interpret dark sayings of His death, they failed to retain them anyway, and only remembered their significance long after the event (Luke 9:28-45; 18:31,34; Mark 9:30-32).

If we are thinking about a given subject, God may speak to us in a pun or a parable, letting us suppose He is speaking about what we are thinking about, when in reality He is speaking of something else. He knows we will get the point sooner or later. Sometimes the Old Testament prophets were not aware of the fullness of what they were prophesying, but thought they were speaking only of imminent events like the return of Israel from the Babylonian exile (Isa. 40). The Holy Spirit was speaking in dark speech of greater events than they knew. Jesus used this method of dark speech with Nicodemus in John 3 and with the woman at the well in John 4. Each thought He was speaking of one thing, being born of a woman or getting a drink of water respectively, whereas in each case the Lord used the conversation to draw them into deeper meanings in the Spirit.

Often the Holy Spirit communicates to His prophets by awakening them to perceive meanings in common things. Jeremiah watched the potter's wheel (Jer. 18 and 19) and saw God forming His creatures. Saul in his anxiety caught hold of Samuel's mantle; the cloth tore in his grasp, "And Samuel said unto him, The Lord hath rent the kingdom of Israel from thee this day . . ." (1 Sam. 15:28).

One time the Lord told me to pray for Turkey. I remembered that

Turkey had experienced several earthquakes; therefore earthquakes were on my mind. The Lord then warned me that a great quake and shaking was coming upon Turkey, and that over 50,000 would be killed, unless men prayed. Three weeks later, the dispute between Turkey and Greece over Cypress broke out (July 22, 1974). I had been told specifically to pray for Ankara where the epicenter of the quake would be. As the capital, Ankara was naturally the center of political and military shaking that could have drawn Greece and Turkey into war. I didn't make any of this public. Had I done so, I would have felt foolish. God's dark speech didn't mislead me, but it kept me from pride.

One day the Lord said I should call on Mrs. Barth, an elderly lady, because "death was hanging over her." I found her in good health. But she soon told me that she had wanted me to come by because she wanted to talk to me concerning her fears of death. Death was indeed "hanging over her."

I knew another woman who was caught in her own mental prison. She could not face her problems because the child within her was desperately fearful. I prayed for the child to be filled with love and set free to come out and live life. Before her next visit the Lord told me that she had come out, was vibrantly alive, and would tell me so. Sure enough, she came wreathed in smiles, but proceeded to tell me a story about someone else. The Holy Spirit helped me to see that this was nevertheless her own story. Her new base in life was too precious for her to look at and talk about openly. I entered into the game and enjoyed the story; we talked back and forth in doubles. A stranger hearing us would have thought us both crazy. Had the Holy Spirit not let me see the dark speech and understand it, I might have failed completely to help her that day. At the end, she beamed more widely and said, "I'm well, am I not?" Had I blown her cover and "handed truth down to her," she would have been put down. She had subconsciously chosen the game as a way of saying, "Here I am, I'm out; can you

201

see me and recognize me? Will you accept me?" Finding acceptance, she could choose to stay out. Thus dark speech was a part of the Lord's way of allowing her to grow so that I could say, "Go in peace, *thy faith* hath made thee whole."

Farmers understand the value of cover crops. They sometimes plant oats and alfalfa together. The oats act as a cover for the more tender alfalfa. When the oats are cut down, the alfalfa is ready to stand exposure. Our loving and wise Father often lets us try something in which we have confidence, knowing that it will prepare us to do things for which we have no confidence as yet.

Dark speech often brings with it a note of humor. A friend of mine named Margaret and I were once praying with a woman whose lungs and intestines were filled with cancer. As we continued to pray for her, she became nauseous and deathly pallid, and, convinced she was dying, began to throw up. Margaret and I were prompted by the Holy Spirit to tell each other jokes between prayers. At times our laughter was downright embarrassing, considering the seriousness of the situation. Later she confessed that the laughter and joking was just what she needed. That lightheartedness was God's dark speech to her. He was telling her not to be afraid; He had it all in His hands. Solemnity would have been out of order, especially since she was a fearful person who took herself entirely too seriously.

Soon after I began to lecture in Schools of Pastoral Care, I became caught up in over-serious mysticity, confusing that with true faith. At one of the schools in Whitinsville, Massachusetts, I became overburdened, overtired, carried away with visions and insights, and finally fully deluded. Satan's delight is to come to someone who is enjoying a true spiritual experience and then help him to go too far. His hope is that we will throw the baby out with the bath water or become so humiliated, sickened, or frightened that we will simply never try again. With his help I soon became altogether sure that the Lord had revealed to me the exact moment of imminent rapture. It was going to happen at four o'clock that afternoon! The people with me at Whitinsville in the school, and selected others in various retreats and prayer places, would be the only ones to "go up." I came full of tears into a group at prayer, who soon perceived where I was. Paul Malicote said, "John, why don't we all go for an ice cream cone?" which was probably the best antidote at the time. But I thought, "Oh, these poor people; the world is going to end; we'll never see our families again, and all they can think of is an ice cream cone!" I broke down sobbing. They called for Agnes Sanford, who said, "John, you're overtired. Go up to bed." I thought, "Well, I can take off from there as well as anywhere, so why not?" I went upstairs and lay down on my bed. Little did I know that in that town was a volunteer fire department, which was called by a great bull horn. Of course, wouldn't you know it, there was a fire alarm, and the horn sounded out full blast just at four o'clock. From about four feet up in midair I cried out, "My God, it's Gabriel!" . . . How good those sheets felt at 4:05. Shortly after entertaining a few misgivings that maybe the Lord had come and gone, I settled back to earth with a sigh—and then burst out laughing.

Often the Lord will give His children half-on, half-off guidance. For example, the Lord may say, "There is a man coming to see you wearing a black suit; watch for him." The man may come wearing a black suit and he may not; the Lord may have meant that the man would be clothed mentally in despair, pain, or fear of death. If we think God would never speak like that, we should remember that most of the prophecies of the first coming of Christ were never clear until after they were fulfilled. Most of our mistakes in Scripture interpretation have come from trying to pin down prophetic Scriptures to certain precise historic situations and only to those. More than one proud scholar has been humbled by a four o'clock horn blast. If God were to give us too precise guidance beforehand, we would almost surely say, "Okay, Lord, I've got it now. I don't need you. I know what to do." Even in the important matter of selecting the king of Israel, Samuel was only told that one of the sons of Jesse would be the one. Not until the moment of reviewing the eight sons, did the Holy Spirit guide him to David (1 Sam. 16:12). Dark speech gives us general guidelines, but perhaps its greatest value is that it keeps us constantly dependent upon the Holy Spirit.

His word is a lamp unto our feet (Ps. 119:105), but we want a searchlight 300 feet down the road, because we don't like to walk by faith but by sight. We try to turn listening into divination. Dark speech is one of the ways God protects us from that. If we press too far, saying, "But Lord, show me clearly," He may let us have the spirit of divination we have asked for, until, sick of its misleadings, we are willing to settle for daily manna again rather than quail's flesh (Num. 11).

Dark speech keeps us humble. It is the third up the scale. Dreams come when the mind is asleep. Visions come when the mind is awake, but their pictures bypass understanding and control. Dark speech is given in direct listening to the voice of God, but again the mind has been bypassed by the fact that the words cannot be overtly and surely understood. Unlike most of us, Moses, who had become "very meek, above all the men which were upon the face of the earth" (Num. 12:3), could be spoken to "mouth to mouth, even apparently, and not in dark speeches" (Num. 12:8). The Lord had so broken Moses that He could trust Moses to stay by Him if He spoke to him plainly. Dark speech, and consequent unclarity, is thus our protection by the wisdom of God.

We often attend a nearby, Friday-night Catholic charismatic meeting of about two hundred people. Just before one meeting I heard the Lord speak to me darkly, "There will be an explosion in the meeting tonight." Later it happened that the Holy Spirit fell on the meeting in a remarkable way. Interpretation and teaching came out of the assembled group that exceeded anything the leaders had been expecting. When I saw this "explosion," I was reassured that it was of the Holy Spirit because of the dark speech I had heard earlier. Otherwise I might have feared some disrespect for the leaders. Before the explosion actually happened, I had no way of knowing the precise meaning of what God had told me.

Once the Lord told me, "I will bless you today with a gift of love." That sounded good to me. And I began to have a pretty clear idea of what it would mean. I spent much of the day expecting something nice to happen to me. But I was disappointed. In fact, about the only notable thing that happened that day was that one person gave me a particularly memorable bawling out for something I had done. At first I couldn't understand what the Lord had meant by those words, until my eyes rested on Psalm 141:5. God had wanted me to see that it was really He who had prompted the rebuke, that it meant He does love me, and that I needed the humbling of misunderstanding while listening.

Jesus told Peter, "Simon, Simon, behold, Satan demanded to have you, that he might sift you like wheat, but I have prayed for you that your faith may not fail; and when you have turned again, strengthen your brethren" (Luke 22:31 RSV). Whatever Peter may have thought Jesus meant by that when He said it, he discovered His true intent soon enough, and it's quite clear to all of us today. But I would like to suggest that it might still qualify as dark speech prophecy for us in the twentieth century. The paschal blood on the lintels not only signified that the angel of death would pass over the homes of the Israelites (Exod. 12:7), but also foreshadowed Christ's sacrifice (1 Cor. 5:7). When Moses lifted up the serpent in the wilderness, it promised protection from the biting serpents (Num. 21:8,9) and typified Christ's elevation on the cross (John 3:14). So, it is not inconceivable to look back from today's perspective and see something more in Jesus' words to Peter. I suggest that Peter typifies the Roman Catholic church which Satan has sifted like wheat. But, because of Jesus' intercession, the tribulation and humiliation are being turned to glory in our day. As God pours out His Spirit on all flesh, we see the Catholic communion "turning again" and becoming a source of strength to its brethren in all the communions of Christendom.

Not everyone will thrill to this idea, but that's all right. If it is the truth, the Holy Spirit will make it plain at the right time. If it is false, then I am wrong, which should surprise no one. But the main point is that the Holy Spirit may want to speak fresh truths to us from the Bible by dark speech.

We are subject to conflicting opinions and error. God keeps it that way by dark speech. It prevents Babel towers. God keeps us from agreeing too completely, lest we think we "have it." When we "have it" we think we can do it without Him; consequently we take over the vineyard, banish His messengers, and run things our own way. But, if He leaves us in a measure of uncertainty, we must continually repair to Him. Unity means Christ at the center, not uniformity or agreement in particulars. Such carnal uniformity inevitably becomes a means by which we put ourselves in the center.

Sometimes the Holy Spirit will bring Scripture references to mind and prod us to look them up. We usually do not know what those verses are until we open the Bible. Then the Holy Spirit quickens a personal meaning. This is not to be confused with opening the Bible at random and plunging a finger. That is superstition. When the Lord causes us to hear Bible references, it is so that we can hear what we might otherwise block out.

One time I asked the Lord to reveal my sins that I might confess them. He gave me a long list of Scriptures to look up. Each described a particular sin, which the Lord helped me to see I was committing. Amazement, shock, and shame followed in painful succession. The last Scriptures were all about the surety of forgiveness and restoration. I did not know whether to be more stunned by my sinfulness or the pinpoint accuracy of the Lord's method of showing it to me. There was no way I could have stood it if God had chosen to tell me those things directly. Dark speech gave me time to receive grace to still my protesting heart and listen.

We have said a lot about the lighthearted nature of God, and the consequent fact that life is not as serious as we make it out to be. That's in Jesus, but outside of Him, life is deadly serious and sometimes desperately grim.

One time Paula and I felt the Lord was leading us, day after day, to Scriptures which spoke of false accusations and persecutions—even unto death. At first, we thought that the Lord was telling us He understood the persecution we were then enduring. But day after day, He kept up the theme. Finally, we understood that He had been calling us to pray for all manner of men who are being falsely accused. We began to pray for men in government, for Christians behind the iron and bamboo curtains, and for pastors persecuted by their congregations. Still we sensed there was more; and the Lord kept up the theme, each morning giving us more Scriptures of man's accusations against man, and his brutality.

We finally got the idea that there was much more accusation of men against men than we knew, especially against Christians and, ultimately, against the Lord. We had been sheltered and only vaguely aware of the extremity of man's sinfulness and inhumanity to man.

The next day after that realization, Paula and I went to the grocery store. I walked to the magazine rack and picked up a *Saga* magazine. Normally I never read magazines like that, but I bought it. At home my eye fell on a startling article, "Torture, over half the countries of the world use torture, and it's on the increase!" (Nivo Lo Bello, *Saga*, August 1974, Vol. 48, No. 5). The article chronicled case after case of horrible torture, inflicted lawlessly upon innocent victims in Europe and North America, in third world countries, and behind the iron curtain. It revealed a massive epidemic of callous, inhuman, bestial treatment of men and women all over the globe. The Lord was calling Paula and me, and doubtless countless others, to intercession. We knew, at last, why we had been weeping before Him in prayer.

In the Lord Jesus Christ, life is joy, and sparkles with humor, but outside of Him life is ultimately solemn, even dreadful. Without the joy and the security we have in Christ, we cannot long stand to sally forth into the rottennesses of mankind; we will soon wind up angry at God, and perhaps lose our faith altogether. On the other hand some Christians have been seduced by the joys of the faith until they do not want and will not hear of any of the tragedies of the world that might call them to intercession and service. They want to flee into the sanctuary to celebrate. Those who have lost the joy tend to scoff at those who celebrate calling them "cop-outs," whereas the celebrators rightly retort, "But you have lost the faith that Jesus *is* Lord of all." Celebration and service must be bound together in every Christian's life. We can groan and weep with God for His children, and rejoice at the same moment. We are not called to be consistent; we are called to be Christians.

Dark speech teaches us that human knowledge cannot encompass reality, and therefore we do not live by the mind but by the Spirit. We learn to rest in inconsistencies. The world and Satan cannot stand illogicalities and inconsistencies. The guilty seek to cover every loophole and insure that everything looks sane and logical. But the redeemed of the Lord know they are sinful and inconsistent; they no longer have to make everything conform to a consistent standard.

But when Satan gets hold of a people, there is a desperate urgency to make everything conform to some pattern. That is the case in every totalitarian regime. We can see it easily in Nazism and communism. But wherever men walk with the Lord, carnal logic is fractured. We are set free from the guilty mind's demand for uniformity and consistency. Our consistency is in the Spirit,

208

where the personality and character of our Lord sparkles through brokenness. We have sometimes built our pat systems of thought and behavior over years, and it may take many years of hearing God's dark speech and being fractured by it before we are willing to rest with a God whose thoughts transcend ours. But the day will come when we can rest with the jagged edges of the unknown, and trust that God has us in them.

Chapter Fifteen

MOUTH TO MOUTH, CLEARLY, AND AUDIBLE SPEECH

Deuteronomy 4:25-40; Psalm 95:6, 7

For a long time Paula and I wanted to hear God speak directly more often, rather than in dreams, visions, and dark speech. But that was before we learned that much brokenness must precede its coming. People who often hear God speak directly are subject to enormous temptation. Humble dependence is easily lost by those who think they know. Those who are truly broken can hear directly and remain meek, as did Moses. But most of us shift too easily from following Jesus and begin to make an idol of *what* He has said to us. The "thing"—the art of listening, the concreteness of what is said, the confidence gained—soon becomes an object in itself, and the relationship between God and His servant is lost.

When I was a child, I used to love to listen to my uncles tell stories. They were great storytellers, and the family would gather 'round to hear stories we had all heard since we were "knee high to a grasshopper," all of us laughing at the right places as though every joke were new to us. What was important was the fellowship. The teller's personality embellished the story, and each part recalled some cherished common memory, so that all of us could relive our feelings. One came away from those gatherings feeling refreshed and strengthened.

211

God wants in the end to visit with His children. He wants to meet with us heart to heart, and share old familiar stories. He wants to laugh and love with us. "We'll walk and talk as good friends should and do. We clasp our hands, our voices ring with laughter; my God and I walk through the meadow's hue" (Latvian Hymn, "My God and I"). Perhaps we have no greater purpose than that through our passage here, God might give birth to sons with whom He can have simple fellowship (1 John 1:1-4).

But how easy it is to make a work of listening, to reduce the fellowship to an "it." Since fellowship gives the grace to keep what is said, the more we practice to listen rather than to seek His face, the dryer and more impossible becomes the walk. We cannot keep even the first thing He said, much less the more. But the more we worship, the more the listening resides within, aiding worship and service, never becoming a thing in itself. In short, we should not seek first to listen, but to worship Him, and the listening will follow (Matt. 6:33).

At first, Job wanted to talk things out, to understand, to be shown what were his sins (Job 9 and 10). Job would use what he heard to regain the fellowship. But it doesn't happen that way. Just as we want our own children to trust us before we explain our acts, so God never answered his questions. Rather, by chapter 38 He had so confounded Job's mind that Job cried out, "Behold, I am vile; what shall I answer thee? I will lay mine hand upon my mouth. Once I have spoken; but I will not answer: yea, twice; but I will proceed no further" (Job 40:4,5). But God was not through. He added mystery unto mystery until Job cried out:

I know that thou canst do everything, and that no thought can be withholden from thee. Who is he that hideth counsel without knowledge? Therefore have I uttered that I understood not; things too wonderful for me, which I knew not. Hear, I beseech thee, and I will speak: I will demand of thee, and declare thou unto me. *I have heard of thee by the hearing of the ear: but now mine eye seeth thee. Wherefore I abhor myself, and repent in dust and ashes.*

Job 42:2-6

When we truly see or experience God, He breaks beyond all that even the mind of the spirit can endure, and both mouth and ear are stopped. This is the end of listening. Our words only interfere and our thoughts become doggerel when He is fully there. In the fullness of His presence, listening breaks free of all it has been and becomes a new dimension of attentiveness, appreciation, awe, and worship of His majesty.

Much of the time, however, God chooses not to awe us in His embrace, but to instruct us practically in the midst of the workaday world. A father at work with his sons in the field gives orders quickly, but there comes a time when he chooses to sit and visit. We need to be able to tell the difference between these two kinds of visitations from God. And we need to leave the choice between the two in God's hands. To insist on rapture and bliss is idolatry. But so is our dogged refusal to leave our work and visit with Him. The mature son detects his father's will and meets Him on His terms, dead to his own demand.

One wonders, did God always speak to Moses clearly, or only sometimes? Did Moses always want God to speak directly, or was he also content with dreams and visions and dark speech if God so chose? St. Paul said, "I have learned, in whatsoever state I am, therewith to be content" (Phil. 4:11). But in the same letter he also said, "I press toward the mark for the prize of the high calling of God in Christ Jesus" (Phil. 3:14). So, we must be contented and discontented, full and yet hungry. Moses, filled with God's presence, still sought to see Him more clearly (Exod. 33:18).

How does God speak to us? Does He whisper in our ears from without? Does He send an angel? Or does He speak from within? It probably matters little which way God has chosen to speak to us. Our failure to answer these questions with certainty humbles us, and dispels our tendency to put things into tight boxes. God may cause a voice to rise within us, or He may speak to us through a heavenly messenger. Whatever way, we want always to be sure it is He, and through the listening, to seek more and more to love Him.

Sometimes we want more certainty and think that if only God would speak audibly, we would know. But even audible speech is often heard differently by different people. When Jesus was baptized, Matthew 3:17 tells us that the voice from heaven said, *"This* is my beloved Son, *in whom* I am well pleased." But Mark 1:11 and Luke 3:22 say, *"Thou* art my beloved Son; *in thee* I am well pleased" (Luke 3:22, Mark being identical except for saying "in whom"). The Lord causes His children to hear the same words differently, usually according to His purposes and their needs. God's truth is not lessened by the differences, but heightened. When Saul saw and heard the Lord, those standing by "stood speechless, hearing a voice, but seeing no man" (Acts 9:7). Saul's reception of the event was qualitatively and quantitatively different from those who were there with him. When Jesus cried, "Father, glorify thy name. Then came there a voice from heaven saying, I have both glorified it, and will glorify it again. The people therefore, that stood by, and heard it, said that it thundered: others said, An angel spoke to him" (John 12:28,29). Sometimes we wish, "If God would only speak aloud and just tell us (more often, them) exactly what He wants!" But the problem is not with God, but with us. Even if He did spell it out, some would think it had thundered and others would think an angel had spoken. Not one of the people with Jesus that day thought that God had openly spoken. So long as free will exists, and men remain hearing and perceiving individuals, God may send a vision to a group, or speak aloud, or speak a message through a preacher or prophet, and men will hear it differently.

How often have we heard men say, "There is only one truth" and then proceed to reveal that they think only they have that truth? Whatever the truth may be, our listening (perceiving, comprehending, receiving, retaining) is always subjective. How I perceive a given event must not be taken, however incisive it may be to me, as all encompassing and exclusive. My perceptions will always need my brother's correction (Prov. 11:14; 20:18; 24:6).

To see more clearly why we need to subject what we hear to our brethren, let's look more closely at the pitfalls attendant upon listening to God. The first are of the flesh. Each of us naturally wants to become special, distinct from our brothers, unique, and dominant. How often have we heard of brothers who thought listening to God brought them some special revelation that they, and all they thought, were above their brothers? Nearly every denomination at one time or another has thought its own revelations were the only right ones, and its members the only ones qualified for heaven. Pride has a way of deceiving all of us (Obad. 3).

The second danger, of course, is Satan. It was through pride that he fell (Ezek. 28:14). And he leads anyone who will let him down the same path. He comes to sicken those who pose the greatest danger to the fading shrouds of his kingdom. Let no one enter the battle alone. It is no longer the Don Quixote saints who charge into battle. It is now the body, knit together, which will "not break their ranks: Neither shall one thrust another; they shall walk everyone in his path; and when they fall upon the sword, they shall not be wounded" (Joel 2:7,8).

Satan's work is to cut up and divide. He wants to elevate men one above another. God does not. God humbles and makes us interdependent. He makes the chiefest as the least, the saint as the chiefest sinner (1 Tim. 1:15).

Satan comes upon the wings of prayer, at the height of listening, as to Jesus after forty days of fasting and prayer. We would like to think that if we could only become most filled with the Spirit, most enraptured in prayer, most sure of His word, we would thereby be safe from Satan's onslaughts. It does not work that way. When was Jesus more filled with the Spirit than after His baptism? At that height came Satan. Unsuccessful, Satan departed "for a season"

(Luke 4:13). When would he come again? When Jesus would be low in energy, dispirited, hurt and broken? Rather, when Jesus had just been transfigured in glory. And he came in the mouth of a beloved disciple, Peter. "Get thee behind me, Satan: thou art an offense unto me: for thou savorest not the things that be of God, but those that be of men" (Matt. 16:23). When would he come next? At the very institution of communion, at the highest moment of unity and worship in the life of Jesus and the apostles. "Then entered Satan into Judas surnamed Iscariot, being of the number of the twelve" (Luke 22:3). Satan comes then not when he has us already down, but when the heights of glory provide opportunity.

Listening therefore provides no safety. In a multitude of counselors there is safety. Spirituality provides no safety, rather exposure. Being knit together with our brothers in Christ is safety. Experience, vast and rich, is only a treasure to be plundered when the strong man is bound in pride (Mark 3:27). Bible knowledge shall not protect us; Satan quotes Scripture very well. Only humility in the body shall be the access of God to protect us. Once that protection is there, all these things may help—spirituality, Bible knowledge, and listening to God.

Spiritual growth in listening is not from weakness to strength, from error to unfailing, from exposure to safety, from uncertainty to certainty, from dependence to independence. It is the very opposite. It happens when a man becomes aware that he needs his brothers about him. If he is sure of his own strength, he is weak and easily deceived. If his knowledges are absolutely sure, he has already fallen. If he is sure he can take on the forces of darkness alone and win, he will not need to—they already have him. If he praises God for his independence, his praise is hollow and he needs God to show him his need. Listening directly to God is blessing, but that blessing shall humble the hearer to ever greater dependence on his brother's wisdom. Why did Moses strike the rock rather than speak to it in kindness (Num. 20:10,11), if it was not that he had begun to feel special, different from and scornful of his brothers' weakness? "Hear now, ye rebels; must we fetch you water out of this rock?" How did Moses become so apart from his brothers that when they sinned he no longer fell on his face as he had done in Numbers 12 and 16? He had reached the heights of direct listening; his face shone with splendor—did he become proud?

So much for warning. It is God who keeps us. He shall be with us in trouble, deliver us, and honor us (Ps. 91:15). We need not fear the heights. He is worth it. He will always catch us and set us upright one more time than we can fall.

217

Chapter Sixteen

BALAAM'S ASS, AND OTHER SURPRISING THINGS

Psalms 29; 19:1-5

And when the ass saw the angel of the LORD, she fell down under Balaam: and Balaam's anger was kindled, and he smote the ass with a staff. And the LORD opened the mouth of the ass, and she said unto Balaam, What have I done unto thee, that thou hast smitten me these three times?

Numbers 22:27,28

God may use anything to speak to His sons. In 1 Samuel 7:10 He thundered from the heavens and discomfited the Philistines. In 2 Samuel 22 David celebrated that God had spoken through the thunder (v. 14), lightnings (v. 15), and the channels of the sea (v. 16) until the foundations of the sea were discovered. In Exodus 14 the Lord parted the seas for the Israelites and closed them upon the Egyptians—to say nothing of what He had already said through nine plagues of frogs and boils and the angel of death (Exod. 1-14). He spoke out of the midst of a burning bush (Exod. 3:2), through the earth which opened to swallow up Korah and all his company (Num. 16:32), in a rod that budded, bloomed and produced almonds overnight (Num. 17:8), through fire that burned up flesh and cakes (Judges 6:21), and through an ass that fell on its knees and spoke (Num. 22:27,28).

219

However, it is God who speaks, not the ass or the thunder. Many mystics have turned aside to commune with flowers, more enamored of the flower than of God. We need to beware of this because God is quickening heaven and earth by His outpouring and His approach. Who knows how many "asses' mouths" shall be opened?

Who has not known that "coincidences" are often God speaking? A friend of ours lost her husband to debauchery and finally to divorce and remarriage to a woman far beneath him. Yet he would continually come to visit her, seeking her friendship and counsel—wrenching her heart in commingled hurt and pity each time. Her friends counseled, "Throw him away. He's no good. Forget him. Find another." Their counsel was of the flesh, but it weighed upon her nevertheless. Just before their separation, her husband had given her a beautiful ring set with twelve diamonds. Soon after he left, one diamond fell out and was gone. A lost diamond is seldom ever found again. But one day there that diamond was, stuck in the drainer in the sink. She had it reset by a jeweler, only to lose it again less than a week later. Again, some time later, she found the diamond, and again had it reset. For the third time it fell out and was lost. Later, in the restroom, it was as though the Lord turned her eyes, and there, twinkling in the pile of the carpet, was that same diamond. The Holy Spirit came over her as she thought, "This is too much; this is more than coincidence. God must be telling me something." Then came the voice of the Lord, "Your husband is a diamond whom I have not cast away. He will yet be saved." One week before he was killed in an accident he finally turned to the Lord.

A group of people bought a ranch near Yellowstone Park. They thought God had told them it would be a center for the dissemination of their particular brand of the faith, which was more off center than they knew. Then came the disastrous earthquake which created Earthquake Lake below Hegben Lake. The epicenter was directly under their ranch, and all of their buildings were wrecked. That twentieth century repetition of Numbers 16 shook their thoughts free from delusion in a hurry.

When God speaks through our brothers, our brother is sometimes aware that he is God's vessel. More often he is not.

Frequently the words of our brethren contain double entendres by which God speaks to us. And psychologists speak of latent language. If we understand that the body is the temple of the Lord, and that the soul is the vessel of character through which our inner spirit speaks, then we can understand double entendres and latent language readily enough.

Latent language is the way our unconscious speaks through telling movements of the body or through symbolic words or actions. It is not the same as body language. Body language refers more narrowly to the way our unconscious reveals itself through what our body does. The way we stand, or fold our arms, or drum our fingers, or turn the corner of the mouth may say far more accurately what we really think than we are consciously admitting at that moment. Latent language is more inclusive, embracing not only body language, but also inflections of the voice, key phrases, and symbolic meanings of choices we make. A woman came to me for counsel, and upon arriving at a crucial point of decision as to whether she really wanted to come out of her mental traps to life abundant, said, "I don't know whether I really want to or not." But I had watched the way she walked into the house: how she was sitting straight up, alert, and her eyes were twinkling. Therefore I was able to assure her that she did know, that she had chosen life. Time proved that the Holy Spirit had helped me see the truth.

In *The Hustler* George C. Scott was called in by Minnesota Fats (Jackie Gleason) to watch "the kid" (Paul Newman). George played the part of a man skilled in reading latent language ("watching the 'tells' "). At the height of the kid's success against Minnesota Fats, George told him, "Stick with him, Fats, this kid's a loser." His prediction proved true.

Both body language and latent language express only the

221

messages which the inner psyche can send through the heart and mind and body. There are deeper levels. We are tripartite creatures. The soul sometimes imprisons the spirit. Consequently our spirit sometimes needs to send out coded signals to those who have ears to hear. "The purpose in a man's mind is like deep water, but a man of understanding will draw it out" (Prov. 20:5). But to hear such coded signals is not a skill one can possess apart from the Holy Spirit. He alone bestows on us ears to hear this language.

Elisha lay sick upon his deathbed. Joash, king of Israel, came to visit. Elisha commanded him to string the bow and shoot an arrow, whereupon he cried out, "The arrow of the Lord's deliverance," and told Joash he would smite the Syrians in Aphek until he had consumed them. Then Elisha commanded him to "Smite upon the ground. And he smote thrice, and stayed. And the man of God was wroth with him, and said, Thou shouldest have smitten five or six times; then hadst thou smitten Syria till thou hadst consumed it; whereas now thou shalt smite Syria but thrice" (2 Kings 13:14-9). Elisha had invited Joash into a drama. He could then watch Joash in his part and "read" him. Not only the meager three taps on the ground but also the way Joash administered them told Elisha that Joash's spirit was too faint. He would not pursue his enemy relentlessly until the full victory was won.

Perhaps the Holy Spirit in Joash told Elisha through Joash's human spirit; perhaps it was entirely Joash's own spirit which was speaking. We do not always know. Was it the spirit of the ass which spoke to Balaam, or God's Holy Spirit? (Num. 22:27,28). We do not know. We prefer to believe the latter. Israel often heard God speak through the Urim and Thummim and the ephod (whatever these were). Surely no spirit was resident in the articles which spoke, but God's Holy Spirit spoke through them, just as when the lot discovered Saul for anointing (1 Sam. 10:17-21) or Achan for destruction (Joshua 7). But among God's animate creatures there is the possibility of cooperation between God's Holy Spirit and the creature's own resident spirit. In man, the

latent language

question whether it is man's or God's Spirit speaking is so
unanswerable that we must carefully test every double entendre.
Nothing is beyond reproach or testing.

Elijah was taken up, but Elisha, who had a double portion of
Elijah's spirit, nevertheless died. Did Elisha's great spiritual
keenness become a trap to him? When I first became aware of
latent language and God's double entendres, I let it carry me off
balance. I saw double meanings in everything. Every event carried
mystic meanings. Like Wordsworth I had to catch hold of a tree
and remind myself it was only a tree. And, as I saw my idolatry
more clearly, I had to die to all such seeing, and be careful not to
cherish insight more than the Lord. A friend said, "John, you had
better consider all such experiences and powers your enemy rather
than a blessing." Is it possible Elisha was too caught up in
experiences to turn from them and stand naked, blind and
unhearing before the Lord? St. Paul tells us the Lord gave him a
thorn in the flesh "lest I should be exalted above measure through
the abundance of the revelations" (2 Cor. 12:7). Paula and I have
learned to let the Holy Spirit hold us open to hear and see—but only
when He would have it so.

Jesus said, "Take heed therefore *how you hear* . . . (Luke 8:18).
The longer we are with Jesus, the more our minds are prepared to
hear according to His true nature. The more our hearts are cleansed
of rebellion, the more our hearing clarifies (Ps. 18:26).

One spring we put in a garden, yard and fruit trees, which took
considerable time. The work was so tonic to me, I kept at it
continually when I should have been following the Lord's Spirit
into other works. The Lord warned me several times. In effect I
was asking Him to bless the garden, while I neglected some of the
works to which He was calling me. The Lord blessed the garden
abundantly. It produced wildly. But He shut down finances to a
trickle. Until the disciplining was finished, there would be no healing. God gave me what I asked for, but it was not what He wanted
or I needed. "With the crooked thou dost show thyself perverse"

(Ps. 18:26). God abundantly provided food on the table all during the disciplining (see Deut. 8), but He was scoring the lesson of obedience into my heart as I complained about the shortage of money. But I finally saw my crookedness. He seemed to me quite perverse by not providing according to His promise. He gave more in one area and took away in another.

Incidentally, this was at least my second go around for this lesson. One time I kept giving more counseling appointments than the Holy Spirit wanted me to. He warned and reproved; I kept on. So the Holy Spirit swamped Paula and me for six weeks without a letup with counseling, exorcisms, and visits from people all hours of the night and day until we cried out, "Lord, we've had enough!" God was willing to appear rude and inconsiderate, swamping us with work, until we learned. It is not always blessing when God gives us what our hearts yearn for or our minds ask.

The Lord may use any event in our lives to speak to us. Countless times people tell stories from their lives and add, "And all of my life has gone like that." This kind of thing sometimes signals a discerning listener to see something about a person. And, if that discerning person is a Christian prophet, the Holy Spirit might quicken him to say "That pattern is now ended," or "That disciplining is accomplished," or "Mercy through the cross now ends that," or on the other hand, "Let's affirm that good thing and praise God for it." Whatever type of vision or prophecy is given to us, nothing is unchangeable in our Lord. We need to affirm the positive and repent of the negative. That is our calling as prophets.

Scientific tests are now measuring effects of prayer and cursing upon plants. Many people now speak to their plants as they would to any other friend or animal. One might ask, "And can animals, plants, and things speak back?" Allen Boone has written a most provocative book on the subject, entitled, *Kinship with All Life*.

It is not our place here to discuss whether such communications between man and God's other creatures can happen, or should. We suspect God has many new doors to open. Job 12:7,8 has these intriguing words to say: "But ask now the beasts, and they shall teach thee; and the fowls of the air, and they shall tell thee: Or speak to the earth, and it shall teach thee: and the fishes of the sea shall declare unto thee." Saint Francis of Assisi preached to the creation, even to the fishes. The psalmists sometimes addressed the plants, animals, winds, skies, seas, rivers, earth and stars (Ps. 103:22; 145:10; 148; and 150:6).

We are speaking primarily of how God may speak through any part of His creation, not of how we may communicate with the creation. There are pitfalls, both in hearing God through the creation and in attempting to commune with nature. False spirits, especially elemental spirits (Col. 2:8 RSV), find such inquiry a fertile field for strong deception upon the children of God. We must be inordinately circumspect—it was while Eve was talking with a beast that she was deluded.

But it is primarily through our brothers that God chooses to speak to us. So *how* does He do it? We all are cognizant of conscious ways—prophecy, interpretations, dreams and visions given to our brother about us, as well as sermons, teachings, rebukes, etc. Let us discuss here then the unaware speakings.

The most common way the Lord speaks to us through our brothers when they are not aware of it is in the trivia of conversation. He causes a phrase to leap out at us, or a thought to lodge in our minds like a cocklebur. That thought keeps irritating until we have to do something about it. A brother may mention something about pruning trees and it lodges and works until the Holy Spirit discovers the meaning—the Lord has been pruning us and wants us to understand. We read a book, magazine, or newspaper, or watch TV, or glance at the children playing, and the Lord quickens a word to us. Or our golf partner shanks one into the rough and chips out to a beautiful recovery and the Lord awakens

225

hope for our own situation.

A man attended a School of Pastoral Care, where both Agnes Sanford and I ministered to him. Afterwards I visited Agnes in her home at Westboro. The man made a special trip there to give me a gift of cuff links. On them were images of a Buddha. I puzzled why the gift, why the special trip, and why my spirit leaped when the gift was given. After the man left, the Holy Spirit guided me to put those cuff links into the fire then crackling merrily in the fireplace. Agnes and I were lead to understand that the man was symbolically relinquishing his idolatries and that was why my spirit had leaped for joy. Not all gifts have such meaning or should be destroyed. But some do. The prophet needs to be alert.

Sometimes gifts are given as signs. Each time I have been called into a new dimension of ministry, the Lord has prompted someone to give me a pendant cross. When the Lord was calling Paula and me to be a team, four people, praying together, saw us in a temple in heaven where we knelt before a great altar. Before we knelt, a golden cord was wound about my left and Paula's right wrists, binding us together. (Ever since then, whenever the Holy Spirit comes upon me, I can feel the pleasant burning of that cord on my wrist.) Also in the vision a great sword was placed in our hands. Neither of us could wield it separately. But together we went out and swung that sword again and again, releasing each time the latches on prison doors, from each of which emerged man and wife couples. Shortly after that we spoke in Peoria, Illinois. Our host pastor gave us each identical pendant crosses simultaneously. He knew nothing of the Lord's custom with me to give such a gift as a sign. I had not worn any crosses while there. Never before had Paula been given the same cross at the same time as I. The Lord was confirming the vision and our new joint mission.

Upon returning home, a woman counselee brought a gift. It was a plaster of paris bas-relief figure fastened to a board background. The figure was of an eagle with two heads behind one shield, with a separate helmeted head between the eagle's two heads. She explained that the figure was a marriage symbol, whereby two eagle Christians become one, behind one shield (faith), under Christ's headship (helmet of salvation, Eph. 6:17). It was a second confirmation.

Then Andrea, our six-year-old daughter, drew a picture and gave it to us. It was a man and woman, from whom descended expanding lines, under whom were smiling people standing in a great circle. Inside that circle were two tables. Happy people were eating at one and playing a game at the other.

The Father had used three separate people and their gifts, a Protestant minister, a Catholic laywoman, and our own child, to confirm our ministry. Andrea's gift was the most significant because our team ministry could conceivably cost her a considerable amount of time with her parents. Each of the three was ignorant of the deeper purpose behind his gift. The Holy Spirit was the speaker through the gifts, not those who gave them.

Not everything in life is frought with such meaning, nor is every gift. We need to be alert whenever the Holy Spirit quickens us, but not on tiptoe every moment, lest we go off balance.

Often the least welcome but the best communication for us is unintentional rebuke (intentional too, but we speak here of God's word given through those unaware of it). Never will we forget how a young girl visited our prayer group, proclaiming her inability to pray. But as she unaffectedly confessed her sinfulness before the Lord, each succeeding phrase opened up new vistas of our own hidden sins. None of us could deny that the Holy Spirit had brought her for that very purpose. Has not every one of us found the vitality of a sharing session to be that fact that the testimonies and sharings in the meeting seem fashioned precisely by the Lord to cut at our tenderest knots? Do we not sometimes find ourselves hating another's joy and power in the Lord because that very blessedness rebukes and exposes our sense of failure?

One day I was walking through the church worrying about people I knew who were opposing the gospel. A member walked up and teasingly pulled off a long string which had clung to my jacket, saying, "I see someone has strings on you today, John." The person meant nothing by it. (I later asked). But it was no coincidence. God was calling me to stop feeling sorry for myself, to praise Him and cast all my cares on Him (1 Pet. 5:7).

Another time I called on a man at the request of his wife. She hoped, as did I, that the talk might help in resolving their marital problems. This man and I had a thing going about whose favorite baseball team would win each day. As I entered, the man said, jokingly, "You're not going to win today." It was a not-too-subtle challenge to my authority in Christ, though, of course, he would have denied it by saying he referred only to our baseball competition. Each person needs to learn when and how the Holy Spirit would have him hear a double entendre. Usually the Holy Spirit alerts me so that I feel a lively expectancy as the other speaks. In this case, just before the man opened his mouth, the Holy Spirit flashed through me and I was alert. Immediately as we went through banal chitchat, I began to intercede and repent silently for the man, feeling that the Holy Spirit was alerting me to opposition. Today, I cannot remember whether the Lord broke through that day or not. If He didn't, it was probably because I stumbled by believing my friend's negative suggestion.

In 1963 I remember watching on TV a man presenting cowboy boots to President Kennedy before he went to Dallas, Texas, saying, ". . . to protect you from snakes in Johnson's backyard." Was that only irony, or was the Holy Spirit trying to alert both Kennedy and those with ears to hear? We don't know, but we do know that God is raising up men and women everywhere who will hear and heed His voice. Our tragedies, national and personal, only underline how great is the need for God's prophets to arise. Roman soldiers learned to read the signs in their own lives. If they continually dropped things on a given day, for example, they would not go to war that day if they could help it. How often have we heard, "I *knew* something was going to happen today. Oh, why didn't I listen!" "For wisdom is a defense, and money is a defense: but the excellency of knowledge is, that wisdom giveth life to them that have it" (Eccl. 7:12).

God also speaks through those over us in the Lord, both by their conscious knowledge and unconsciously. We need to be obedient. If the one in authority has spoken, our own listening is preempted. We are not to prefer our own listening to what our pastor commands in the Lord. Many pastors teach falsely. To that we are to prefer our own listening. But a command to serve is different. St. Paul carefully distinguished what he suggested from what he commanded, and what he knew was the Lord's command from what he only hoped was His word (1 Cor. 7:6,10,12,25,26 etc.). When the word of anyone over us in the Lord is a distinct command, debate and discussion are out of order. We are rebellious, even if we are "right" when we disobey. God will honor our obedience even if what we do is wrong; and He will deal with the person in authority, not us. We are to disobey only if the person in authority distinctly commands against God's word—for example, to steal or lie or commit adultery (Deut. 13:1-5), for that would be to go after false gods. But where no clear mandate of God's word is broken and the elder or ruler commands our obedience, we are to obey even if the command seems unwise or wrong.

Aaron and Miriam spoke against Moses because of the Cushite woman whom he had married, and they said, "Has not God spoken by us also?" (Num. 12:2). But God never let on whether Moses was wise or foolish about the Cushite woman. That was now irrelevant. "Why then were ye not afraid to speak against my servant Moses?" (Num. 12:8). Miriam was struck with leprosy; only Moses' quick intercession saved her, and then she had to remain outside the camp for seven days.

Recently a friend of mine was asked to speak to a college class about the Holy Spirit. He showed the invitation to the Northwest Christian Fellowship in Spokane, where I also was submitted. The group felt that he should not go alone, and elected me to accompany him. That morning as I drove to the college, I was aware of a trap, and heard the Holy Spirit saying to me, "John, don't go, this is a trap. Turn around. Go home." To this day I still believe that the Holy Spirit was really saying that to me, testing me to know whether I would obey the Lord as I ought. As I thought and prayed, I remembered that the brethren to whom I was then submitted had anointed us both in prayer to go, and I recalled the lesson of Numbers 12. I said, "I may be wrong, Lord, but I put the principle of obedience to those over me above and beyond my own listening. I know if I am wrong, you will forgive me. I must go on. I must not obey my own listening to you in this issue." The Lord turned the session, which *was* a trap, into a grand witnessing session. We must do what we say we will do for those in authority over us. God speaks preeminently to us through those in authority over us.

We can always humbly ask our superiors to reconsider, check their guidance, or pray for protection, but we are out of order if we say, "My own listening says do this or do that." My own listening cannot be anything but rebellion or testing when the command has been given.

The Lord is building an army. Every soldier must learn that when an order is given, he must employ all his resources and ingenuity to fulfill that order. And, when he thinks or hears something that goes beyond the authority delegated to him, or directly countermands it, he must not obey that personal listening. God is not a God of chaos that He should give conflicting orders.

But God is still not confined to this principle in any sense by which we can control Him. Some people use unquestioning obedience as an excuse to escape the responsibility of living one's life. When that happens, God will probably give us guidance that will put us between a rock and a hard place, and thus compel us to work out our own salvation with fear and trembling.

One time my parents got very upset about something I said in a sermon. A brother to whom I was submitted at that time urged me

to go and rebuke them on the basis of Matthew 18 and Luke 17:3. I
set out to obey, but I felt badly about it. I kept remembering Paul's
admonition to Timothy, "Do not rebuke an older man but exhort
him as you would a father . . ." (1 Tim. 5:1 RSV). I also realized
that my parents simply weren't ready to understand what I had
said. I finally concluded not to rebuke them. Instead, as I entered
the room the Holy Spirit melted my heart and I knelt to ask
forgiveness. My parents were gracious and our time together was
warm and happy. But, of course, the question of what I had said
was not entirely resolved. A year later my folks heard another
person preach the same thing that had so offended them. This time,
however, they understood it and were not offended, and I was
vindicated.

The Lord sometimes humbles us by putting us under conflicting
loyalties. He is ever aiming to open our hearts to reveal hidden
motives and intentions. Thus the things that bother us the most or
seem of the utmost importance are often secondary to God's
purposes (as with the content of what I taught that upset my
parents). Thus our hearts should be set to obey God through His
designated authorities, but free enough to be wrong either way,
either in terms of what we personally think the Holy Spirit is saying
to us or of what authorities tell us in the name of the Lord. An
unwillingness to be wrong is often a prominent symptom of
self-righteousness.

We must learn when to prefer our brother's listening above our
own, and when not to. Humility among brothers is essential to
growth in listening. Only pride prevents our willingness to submit
to the counsel and authority of brothers in the Lord.

All the various and strange ways God can speak to us are part of
the gift of wisdom. The man of God is to be fully equipped (Eph.
4:12, 6:15, and Heb. 13:21 RSV) "in *every good* work to do his
will working in you that which is pleasing in His sight" (Heb.
13:21). Wisdom is a gift, but like so many gifts, the Giver must
prepare the receiver to hold it. We learn wisdom by trial and error

231

and by being discipled within the body. Rich experience is the crown of the aged (see Eccles. 1:16). Wisdom is the crown of the church's life, the glory of God for this age, foreshadowed by Solomon in the temple (1 Kings 10). But let us hear the warning of Ezekiel 28:17, "thou hast corrupted thy wisdom by reason of thy brightness." The greater the store of wisdom He gives us, the more we must humble ourselves before God and our brethren. If we do not, He will humble us, for God will not allow another to have us.

Chapter Seventeen

THE SUMMUM BONUM

1 Kings 18:30-39; Ephesians 3:8-11; Isaiah 66:5-18

The *summum bonum* (highest good) is the Lord at work through His church. The church was brought into being to reveal God's mighty purpose and wisdom, not only to the earth, but also to the principalities and powers in the heavenly places (Eph. 3:10). The church will be that wisdom, "a crown of glory in the hand of God" (Isa. 62:3), because "as the bridegroom rejoiceth over the bride, so shall thy God rejoice over thee" (Isa. 62:5). The church will be magnificent not because of itself, but by the grace and power of God (Isa. 42:4; 62:11,12).

The Lord is now building His church into a spiritual house of lively stones (1 Pet. 2:5), fitly framed together with each part working properly, upbuilding itself in love (Eph. 4:16). In this generation, unbeknownst to many, He has been raising up those who *will* care for His flock (Jer. 23:4). Through them He has been preparing those who will respond. The harness has been laid upon the few who are being humbled and prepared.

The Lord is not yet ready to reveal His army of sons (Rom. 8:19 and 1 Pet. 1:5). One prerequisite, I believe, is that He must discipline, train, and reveal His two witnesses (Rev. 11:3). We think the two witnesses are His latter day apostles and prophets.

They are the foundation for His church (Eph. 2:20). They speak with such power that their breath slays their enemies (Rev. 11:5).

No one can know for certain who the two witnesses are. Some say they are Enoch and Elijah, the only two historical people who never tasted death. But it is possible that the two may stand for two classes of people, as we have suggested.

As on that memorable day on Mount Carmel (1 Kings 18), so today it is the Elijah task to call out the body of Christ to the mount of glory, to build the trench of protection about the apostles and prophets, to cut to the heart and expose the bull of man's mentality to the sword of truth. And to lay all before God as an offering—when? At three o'clock in the afternoon, the time of the evening sacrifice, and the hour at which Jesus died. We believe that hour of Elijah's offering is almost upon us.

It was also Elijah's task to destroy the 850 false prophets. Psalm 149 says, "Let the high praises of God be in their mouth, and a two-edged sword in their hand; To execute vengeance upon the heathen, and punishments upon the people; To bind their kings with chains, and their nobles with fetters of iron; To execute upon them the judgment written: *this honor have all his saints*. Praise ye the LORD" (Ps. 149:6-9).

The Lord has gathered His prayer army into small fellowship and prayer groups under pastors and elders across Christendom. These are those saints of Psalm 149 who will spend themselves for Him no matter what the cost. They are presently at work, and He is gathering more. Only they need cohesive direction. Therefore He is raising up His Elijah prophets.

In every community, hopefully in each church, and, at best, in every small cell in His body, the Lord will have raised up His prophets to hear Him call and forward each message to His army of intercessors. Here and there, both for their own local, and for regional, national, and worldwide concerns, prayer warriors respond like lights springing up in the darkness, until across the map of the world a blaze of light responds to, or even arises before,

234

each onslaught of darkness.

The Lord should be like a great general surveying His armies as He enters battle. Here and there He should see reserve troops ready for the warfare of prayer. Other troops may already be engaged on other fronts. Others may be just back from the front in rest camps. The Lord should have the firepower of prayer at His command, a people awake, alert, and prepared.

A beehive is protected by several kinds of troops. Warrior bees attack enemies. Scout bees find resources. Fanner bees ventilate the hive by their wings. Every cell of the church must know how to intercede. When the Holy Spirit moves, His prophets should listen, and call to action. Prayer warriors then arise to ward off danger by covering prayer, or use insight and perception to discover and secure the blessings the church needs, or fan hurt and sorrows to the cross.

Prayer is our first and most powerful weapon. Faith comes through hearing and hearing through preaching (Rom. 10:17). But the sword of God's Word can flash only where prayer has prepared the way.

In a magnificent tape, "Remember Them That Are in Bonds," Ray Barnett reports that in 1975 Mozambique fell to communist control, and Christians there were characteristically imprisoned for their faith. And he reported how the Brazilians arose in prayer and saved their country. He cries for America to awaken and respond. He gives a ringing call to American Christians to arise as a prayer army before it's too late. He calls (in his literature) for 100,000 prayer warriors to arise to save America and roll back the tide of darkness.

Will he be heard? It's hard to say. Mankind is traditionally deaf both to the lessons of history and to the summonses of the Holy Spirit. Jesus asked, "Will there be faith on earth when the son of man returns?" (Luke 18:8). We would like to be optimistic, but much depends on how seriously we are willing to take God, and to what extent we will give ourselves to Him. Saul was promised the kingdom through his line forever (1 Sam. 13:13) but it had to be given to David. Even David's dynasty had apparently failed to receive the promise until Jesus came. How shall God's promises to us be fulfilled unless and until we respond?

God unwillingly sends the woes (Amos 4 and Rev. 4ff.) because mankind will not let the Son of man rule until its own rule has disgusted and frightened it enough. The few, those chastened and prepared, cannot force His rule upon the many. Mankind must reap the harvest of its waywardness until despair has done its work. And even the willing in mind must become willing in heart from the pit of brokenness.

I remember a time when I had commanded an evil spirit to come out of a woman. I did it by the authority (Greek *exousia*) of Christ. But the demon did not leave her in that moment. The Lord did not choose to expel him immediately by His power (greek *dunamis*). A week later that woman was praying with a friend when that demon surfaced. Shaking all over, filled with nausea, the woman looked in the mirror and saw strange and horrible eyes looking out at her. Then the spirit left her. I was reminded of the boy who was convulsed and lay motionless after the devil left him (Mark 9:14-29). That expulsion had not been immediate either. I remembered then that Jesus said, "*Now* shall the prince of this world be cast out" (John 12:31). But the devil is still here.

When our Lord died and rose again, the devil was defeated and told to leave, just as I had commanded the evil spirit to leave this woman—by Christ's *exousia*. But the final act of Christ's *dunamis*, by which Satan is cast into the lake of fire, has yet to happen. But the Lord has been raising His army so that the devil will have to surface and be completely cast out.

The deeper the sword of God plunges into the hearts of mankind, the more will be the shuddering and convulsing of the demon-ridden world.

The devil wanted to remain hidden in the spirit and soul of man, subtly controlling him by his mesmeric spirit. The Lord could have ripped him by force (*dunamis*) from the psyche and spirit of man. But that would not change man's heart. Rather, the Lord effected his *exousia* by His passion, death, resurrection, and ascension. Then he sent the Holy Spirit into His people. Since then the contest, already won, has been on. The Holy Spirit more and more exorcises mankind and earth, and Satan must surface and be revealed.

This means that the coming increase of darkness is not by the power of Satan but by his defeat. Before I was converted, the devil had inhabited me through my curiosity about occultism. Until the coming of the Holy Spirit, I could playact righteousness by dint of fleshly determination, and congratulate myself that I was a pretty nice guy. Satan did not want to disturb that phony front. He had a secure hiding place in me. So when the Holy Spirit came, I could not be as "nice" a guy as I had been. The Holy Spirit was causing the enemy to surface and be revealed. That is the last step before complete healing. The increase of evil all about us may well be the result of the Holy Spirit at work in the deep mind of mankind, bringing to the surface what is really there. Satan wants mankind to put on the front of goodness. That way, he remains hidden, controlling mankind through unconscious levers which plunge men into hatreds and enmities, which they rationalize behind "good" motivations. Therefore it is God, not Satan, who sends leanness and hardships, that what s in man may be revealed (see Amos 4).

When the real me surfaces and I must look at it, it's humiliating. And it's heart-changing. Some Christians, however, mistakenly believe that this surfacing is evil and should be avoided at all costs. Not so. It is the mercy of God to reveal sin. It is the work of Satan to conceal it.

Whoever understands this looks through the tribulation praising God. The victory has already been won. Satan's delusions have honeycombed the mind and heart of all mankind and painted whitewash over all. God knows our hearts are wicked (Matt. 15:19). He knew it all along. He only wants us to see it, admit it, and be made whole. Therefore tribulation comes (Rev. 16), for though woes are not God's first will, He must send them if men would be made whole.

The Elijah task is consequently to expose evil directly or cause it to surface that it might be repented of. The axe is still cutting to the root. The sword of truth still divides soul and spirit. God's psychiatry is at work. His prophets must hear and obey because light uncovers what the darkness hides. It rends and struggles and dies. And he who is forgiven much, loves much.

It's all right for God's servants to be humiliated and seemingly of little account before men. For men will still honor their own, who scale the highest mountains, smash the longest homers, triumph in war, and win in politics. And men will still flock to hear great preachers, heap accolades upon miracle workers, and troop off to massive crusades, only to miss His quiet tap on the door of humble submission. It serves God's purposes for men to be that way, for whether they attack or applaud His servants, it is humiliating for those servants and thus, in turn, works His glory deep into their hearts. And when His work is deep enough in them, they will turn the world upside down once again.

Whether by miracle or by humiliation and suffering, whether by victory through prayer or by brokenness in action, the Elijah task is a preparation. We all want to reap the white harvests (John 4:35), but before that many of us will have to heap manure (Luke 13:8). Obedience is the watchword of preparation. As Jesus learned obedience through what He suffered (Heb. 5:8), so the church learns by humiliation true obedience of the heart. But the moment an individual or church lets success fill it with presumption, that moment the Holy Spirit goes to work to bring that evil to the surface. God is not afraid to embarrass His own before the world

God is not defeated if men fail. He may send a prophet to men knowing not only that those men may fail (as in Isa 6) but that they might stone the prophet. Throughout biblical history God sent some to shine that the darkness of others might be revealed (1 Cor. 11:19). He did it to bring repentance. Often it is not until we are exposed, until we revile God's messengers, that we discover the evil in us. God is not afraid of the darkness. Neither must his witnesses be. "The light shines in the darkness, and the darkness has not overcome it" (John 1:5).

The world demands peace and harmony, the fulfillment of its own guilt-ridden dreams. But the Lord uses the trials of life to perfect Christian souls. Therefore, the prophet is not dismayed if evil persists. "I form the light, and create darkness: I make peace, and create evil: I the Lord do all these things" (Isa. 45:7). He serves a God who turns all to good for those who are called (Rom. 8:28). The world insists that everything be all straightened out, or else God isn't on His throne or doesn't care. The prophet's loyalty is not to dream of restored earth, but to a Lord who may not restore at all in the way we would hope—though, in the end, all shall be restored. A prophet must learn to live contentedly in the middle of the mess, trusting the hand of God in all things.

Troubles persist in the world so that what is true may be perfected. "For first of all, when ye come together in the church, I hear that there be divisions among you; and I partly believe it. For there must be also heresies among you, that they which are approved may be made manifest among you" (1 Cor. 11:18,19). God allows the imperfect, that the true gems may be uncovered and polished, while His protection overarches the process.

The *summum bonum* is therefore the work of God, the Lord Jesus Christ. He is the Father's testimony to men. He is the wisdom that sits by the throne of God. He is the expression and vindication of God among men. His life will more and more express itself through the sons of God among men. But the church must learn to trust as He shows us that we are not yet as He is. It is that work, whether by wonders or woes, of revealing sin, which is the Elijah task. Without it there can be no resurrection to glory. Therefore

Elijah comes as a refiner's fire to fulfill Malachi 3 among us. May the church rise to receive its Elijahs.

In the meantime, rivers must be damned and a child must be kept from being hit by a car. Visions and dreams, dark and direct speech will call men and women to play their parts. Bit and major parts will fill scenes and acts before the eventual denouement. Each scene adds detail to detail until the villain of the drama appears.

The church is crossing the Jordan to enter the promised land. The priests who now bear the ark before the people are the apostles and prophets of the Lord. We must learn to recognize, receive, and support them. Long we have received His pastors and healers, evangelists and teachers. Even exorcists are gaining a measure of recognition. But prophets and apostles are the last because they are the first. They go before to roll back the waters of Jordan. As with Barnabas and Paul (Acts 13:2), God will show us who they are that they may be set apart. The Lord calls. Who can but respond.

Will we receive them?

Products that help overcome life's challenges...

Healing Hearts Healing Nations

What Elijah House has to offer...

- ### Counseling
  ... Helping people around the world.
- ### Seminars
  ... Held in many cross-denominational churches.
- ### Schools
  ... Teaching and equipping the Body of Christ.
- ### Internships
  ... Training committed Christians and clergy to be counselors.
- ### Resources
  ... Biblical truths to heal your life in books, videos and audios.

For more information, or to schedule an appointment, 208-773-1645.

INNER HEALING CLASSIC

This sequel continues in the footsteps of **The Transformation of the Inner Man** by providing new insight and healing salve to such problems as rejection, child abuse, occult involvement and generational sin and depression.

Healing the Wounded Spirit is for everyone who suffers from hidden hurts — past or present. Through this book, God can help you to discern a wounded spirit in yourself and others and, best of all, He will show you how to receive His healing power in your life.

PROPHETIC INSIGHT

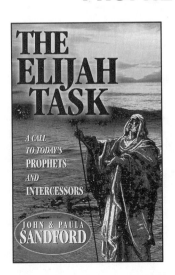

In the **Elijah Task,** John and Paula Sandford give a clear message, a balanced and practical in-depth study of the office of a prophet in the church and world today, the power and ways of intercession, and prophetic listening to God.

AVAILABLE AT CHRISTIAN BOOKSTORES EVERYWHERE.

RESTORATION FOR THE ABUSED

With profound empathy and clear understanding, Paula Sandford ministers healing to all who have been victimized by sexual abuse — the abused child, parents, relatives and friends, as well as the abuser. She has dealt with this problem through many years of counseling and teaching, and this book shows how the victims of sexual abuse can find new life and freedom.

TRANSFORMED BY THE RENEWING OF YOUR MIND!

THE RENEWAL OF THE MIND glows with fresh insights and anointing. Its revolutionary approach will still the battleground where carnal thoughts and feelings rage. There is a solution — a process of spiritual transformation by the renewing of your mind. As you read, new peace and life will fill your innermost being.

AVAILABLE AT CHRISTIAN BOOKSTORES EVERYWHERE.

A HANDBOOK FOR FAMILIES

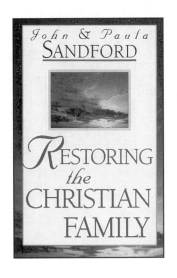

"And He shall turn the heart of the fathers to the children, and the heart of the children to their fathers" (Mal. 4:6). God is restoring families to His original purpose — to be the foundation of society, the seedbed for Christian values. Those who have discovered this treasure chest of teaching report that it has transformed their families. Fresh insights from the Sandfords' teaching and counseling ministry will enable your family to grow and develop according to God's plan.

WHY ADULTERY?

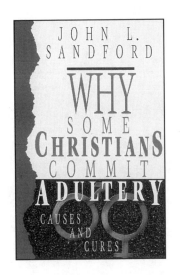

John L. Sandford founder of Elijah House, and author of several books on inner healing, provides answers for all who are concerned about this issue. He explores the personal causes that may lead a Christian into adultery and reveals biblical cures.

The book's main purpose, the author states, "is to provide informed bases for compassion and healing, and keys of knowledge for protection from falling."

BOOK ORDER FORM

To order additional books by John and Paula Sandford or John and Loren Sandford direct from the publisher, please use this order form. Also note that your local bookstore can order titles for you.

Book Title	Price	Quantity	Amount
The Renewal of the Mind	$ 10.99	_____	$ _____
Transformation of the Inner Man	$ 13.99	_____	$ _____
Healing the Wounded Spirit	$ 13.99	_____	$ _____
The Elijah Task	$ 10.99	_____	$ _____
Restoring the Christian Family	$ 12.99	_____	$ _____
Why Some Christians Commit Adultery	$ 10.99	_____	$ _____
Healing Victims of Sexual Abuse	$ 9.99	_____	$ _____
Healing Women's Emotions	$ 11.99	_____	$ _____

Total Book Amount $ _____

*Shipping & Handling — Add $3.00 for the **first** book, **plus** $0.50 for **each** additional book.* $ _____

***TOTAL ORDER AMOUNT** — Enclose check or money order. (No cash or C.O.D.'s.)* $ _____

Make check or money order payable to: **VICTORY HOUSE, INC.**
Mail order to: **Victory House, Inc.**
                   P.O Box 700238
                   Tulsa, OK 74170

Please print your name and address **clearly:**

Name _____
Address _____
City _____
State or Province _____
Zip or Postal Code _____
Telephone Number (___) _____

Foreign orders must be submitted in U.S. dollars. Foreign orders are shipped by uninsured surface mail. We ship all orders within **48** hours of receipt of order.

MasterCard or VISA — For credit card orders you may use your MasterCard or VISA by completing the following information, or for **faster service,** call toll-free **1-800-262-2631**.

Card Name _____
Card Number _____
Expiration Date _____
Signature _____
(authorized signature)

BOOK ORDER FORM

To order additional books by John and Paula Sandford or John and Loren Sandford direct from the publisher, please use this order form. Also note that your local bookstore can order titles for you.

Book Title	Price	Quantity	Amount
The Renewal of the Mind	$ 10.99	_____	$ _____
Transformation of the Inner Man	$ 13.99	_____	$ _____
Healing the Wounded Spirit	$ 13.99	_____	$ _____
The Elijah Task	$ 10.99	_____	$ _____
Restoring the Christian Family	$ 12.99	_____	$ _____
Why Some Christians Commit Adultery	$ 10.99	_____	$ _____
Healing Victims of Sexual Abuse	$ 9.99	_____	$ _____
Healing Women's Emotions	$ 11.99	_____	$ _____

Total Book Amount $ _____

*Shipping & Handling — Add $3.00 for the **first** book, **plus** $0.50 for **each** additional book.* $ _____

TOTAL ORDER AMOUNT — *Enclose check or money order. (No cash or C.O.D.'s.)* $ _____

Make check or money order payable to: **VICTORY HOUSE, INC.**
Mail order to: **Victory House, Inc.**
                 P.O Box 700238
                 Tulsa, OK 74170

Please print your name and address **clearly:**

         Name _____

         Address _____

         City _____

         State or Province _____

         Zip or Postal Code _____

         Telephone Number (___) _____

Foreign orders must be submitted in U.S. dollars. Foreign orders are shipped by uninsured surface mail. We ship all orders within 48 hours of receipt of order.

MasterCard or VISA — For credit card orders you may use your MasterCard or VISA by completing the following information, or for **faster service,** call toll-free **1-800-262-2631**.

         Card Name _____

         Card Number _____

         Expiration Date _____

         Signature _____

                     (authorized signature)